The Complete Guide to the

English Setter

Candace Darnforth

Publication Data

Author name Candace Darnfort

The Complete Guide to the English Setter – First edition.

Summary: "Successfully raising an English Setter dog from puppy to old age" Provided by publisher.

ISBN: 978-1-954288-73-7

[1. The Complete Guide to the English Setter – Non-Fiction] I. Title.

Design by Sorin Rădulescu

First paperback edition, 2023

Table of Contents

Chapter 3

Chapter 4

Chapter 7

Chapter 8

Chapter 9

Chapter 10

Chapter 13

Chapter 14

Chapter 15

Introduction

Did you just bring home your new English Setter? Welcome! You have joined the legion of those whose lives will be forever enriched by the unconditional love and selfish devotion shared with their English Setters.

English Setters have a reputation for being the perfect family dogs, and for good reason. English Setters are friendly, loyal, and patient, and their intelligence makes them highly capable working dogs. It is hard to find another breed that tries harder to please its owner.

The breed is considered to be one of the most beautiful of all dogs. With its silky coat, velvety ears, and regal carriage, the English Setter always demands attention wherever he appears. Blessed with typical English charm and joviality, this breed captures the hearts of everyone.

English Setters make excellent therapy dogs and lifelong companions. They quickly adapt to new situations and can be trained to do just about anything. The only thing your English Setter cannot learn is something you did not teach him.

The Complete Guide to the English Setter covers not only basic obedience training, but fundamental field-training lessons. English Setters are considered to be one of the most versatile of bird dogs. The dog's medium-length coat is long enough to protect it from thorns without getting stuck in bushes and hedgerows. Besides having an excellent sniffing nose, these dogs can flush out and retrieve on land and water and have more than enough energy to go all day.

Whether you are a veteran English Setter owner or are new to the breed, this book will provide you with everything you need to help you care for, train, and bond with your new lovable friend. You will learn what your English Setter needs to be a healthy and happy dog long into his senior years.

CHAPTER 1

Meet the English Setter

The English Setter is an athletic, agile, and medium-sized dog who loves spending time with you in the Great Outdoors. English Setters, like other hunting dogs, have an ample supply of energy to burn daily. English Setters have a great enthusiasm for life, and their joie de vivre is contagious!

What is an English Setter?

> 66
>
> *Setters respond best to a home with positive energy. They bring their good-natured disposition into the family relationship whole-heartedly. They want to be part of the family and stay involved in every aspect of the family's activities. They are a working breed and want to have a role in the 'pack.' Give them a place in the social hierarchy and a role to play—hunting dog, defender of the castle, copilot on car rides. It won't matter to them what they do—it matters to them to matter to you. They will seek lavish praise for their efforts and return it with loyalty tenfold.*
>
> MARK D. DENEKA
> *Twilight Setter Kennels*
> 99

Photo Courtesy of
Stuart Casey

The English Setter is one of the world's most beloved hunting breeds. They also excel in agility, obedience, flyball, rally, and as therapy and service dogs. The breed adapts to all types of climates and absolutely adores water.

English Setters have a long history of fieldwork alongside their human companions. There has always been a strong bond between man and dog when it comes to the English Setter. In fact, the solid relationship is so formidable that it has become one of the defining characteristics of this breed.

They are one of several dog breeds that fall under a sporting group. Sporting and field breeds are renowned for being alert and energetic. Your Setter is no exception to the rules, as he is full of energy and does not tolerate a couch potato lifestyle. Your pooch requires mental stimulation, exercise, and plenty of attention.

English Setters are medium-sized sport dogs with a gentle temper, often called the gentleman of the canine world.

Due to their good manners, they are especially good around small children. This breed is known to be alert and protective of their family and territories but are quick to calm down when told to do so.

The American Kennel Club (AKC) recognizes four types of British Setters: the English, Irish, Scottish, and Gordon Setter. The English Setter, smaller in stature than the Irish and Gordon, is praised for its pleasant demeanor and freckled coat. The English Setter has a white base coat with black, brown, or orange markings, referred to as "Belton."

This breed excels in setting and retrieving game birds.

English Setters are known to enjoy roaming, sniffing, digging, and jumping. They are very active as puppies but often mellow out considerably when they are fully mature. As a rule of thumb, English Setters require at least an hour of exuberant exercise each day, making them

Photo Courtesy of
James Justus

unsuitable pets for most apartment dwellers. Hikers or joggers will find this breed will blend into their active lifestyle.

English Setters are highly sociable dogs and do not adapt to being banished to the backyard or doghouse. Even more than similar breeds, English Setters need to be included in their people's daily lives. This is breed is not suited to live outside, as it suffers from separation anxiety. English Setters love the outdoors only when accompanied by their human companions.

As mentioned before, English Setters have very gentle personalities. Generally, a stern look or a sharp word is enough to get the point across to your dog when he is acting up. Be gentle yet firm when training, avoiding all types of harsh punishments. The English Setter breed does not cope well in a tense, stressful home environment filled with loud voices or noises.

Whether you have a puppy or an adult dog, your new best friend will enrich your life for at least a decade or more. Your Setter will not only provide you with hours of amusement, but he will protect your family, home, and your possessions.

Grooming a Setter is relatively easy as they have a short coat with longer feathering on the legs and belly. A weekly brushing session will keep your dog's coat looking healthy and prevent loose hair from piling up on your floor or furniture.

English Setters crave companionship, so they are susceptible to separation anxiety when left alone for long periods of time, expressing their anxiety by chewing and barking. As with all breeds, English Setters need to be properly trained and socialized.

HELPFUL TIP

English Setter Association of America (ESAA)

The English Setter Association of America (ESAA) is the parent club for the English Setter breed in America. The ESAA promotes responsible breeding, invests in health and genetic testing, and maintains the breed standard for English Setters. Members of the ESAA enjoy perks like a monthly newsletter and permission to show puppies at the club's annual National Futurity. For more information about this club and its research and events, visit www.esaa.com.

History of the English Setter

English Setters are regarded as one of the oldest gundog breeds. As far back as the fifteenth century, there is artwork portraying dogs with a close resemblance to the modern-day English Setter.

These dogs were called "setting spaniels" because of how this breed would help their hunter-masters by crouching down on their front legs to signal the presence of birds. As this breed "set" or lay down silently,

Photo Courtesy of Tracy Wiles

© Holloway

they were given the name "Setters." The dog's posture would prompt the hunter-master to throw his net over a large area, often including the dog; then he would make a loud noise to flush out the birds. The hunter-master would then, reap the fowl caught in the net. A standing dog on point, such as the Pointer, would have gotten tangled in the netting; therefore, the low-lying Setters were preferred for this form of bird hunting.

Hunters slowly replaced the nets with guns during the late eighteenth century, and English Setters gained popularity with nobility throughout the English countryside.

Dr. John Caius wrote the first book dedicated to British dogs, De Canibus Britannicis (1570; translated into English in 1576 as The Dogs of Britain). In the book, the doctor describes the English Setter at work in the field, silently stepping forward scenting the fowl, creeping forward and freezing to mark the point with his paw lifted to mark the spot or crouching down to set the spot.

In the early 1930s, one English Setter gained fame in the United States. There remains a sculpture of "Jim the Wonderdog" in a park in Missouri. It is believed the dog could predict the future and understand several different languages. However, skeptics claim the dog was just extremely intelligent and well-trained by its owner.

The Breed's Early Development

Edward Laverack began breeding English Setters by crossing them with dogs that belonged to R. Purcell Llewellin. In the beginning the breed was referred to as Laverack or Llewellin Setters to indicate their lineage. The breeders focused on the breed's athletic physique, a glossy coat with prominent feathering, and unique marking and coloring.

The Laverack line was regarded as being a show line, and the Llewellin line was developed for its excellent fieldwork qualities.

In the 1830s, the first English Setter was imported to the United States and was one of the first charter breeds to be recognized by the AKC in 1878.

English Setters are still one of the most popular dog choices for hunters, but they are also desirable companion dogs due to their gentle countenance.

Difference Between Working and Show Lines

The Llewellin lineage is often regarded as one of the most prestigious pedigrees in the world of gundogs. They are considered to be driven, close-working dogs that will happily chase game all day long.

Working English Setters tend to have a leaner, athletic build, whereas show line Setters may be slightly taller, longer, and broader.

Working dogs tend to have smaller ears, compared to show dogs, and can typically handle the heat better. Their smaller stature makes them ideal for running through dense marshes, and tackling prey.

Working Setters are not recommended for the average pet owner unless they intend to put the dog to work by hunting or performing sports. An English Setter from working bloodlines will never win in the show ring because he was bred for working, not showing.

English Setters used as show dogs often come from the Laverack lineage and are slightly larger. Show line Setters are very energetic, like their working-line counterpart, but turn into couch potatoes by the age of three.

Photo Courtesy of Karen Lishinski

The average cost for a working English Setter can be anywhere from $1,500 and up, depending on the amount of work the breeder has put into producing the litter. On the other hand, an English Setter with top breed lines and a superior pedigree for shows may cost anywhere from $1,500 to $6,500.

Physical Appearance

The English Setter is a medium-sized dog, though on the larger side, and has a long neck that complements a slender body. The leggy build gives the Setter the ability to run fast and cover large amounts of ground quickly. It is known for its well-feathered underbelly, tail, legs, and ears. The English Setter coat color has a standard white base with Belton markings or flecks or an intermingled roan. The most common Belton markings are orange, brown, and black (referred to as blue or tricolored).

A full-grown male English Setter stands between 24 to 27 inches and weighs approximately 50 to 80 pounds. A full-grown female English Setter stands between 23 to 26 inches and weighs approximately 45 to 70 pounds.

An English Setter's coat is not prone to tangles, but to maintain coat health, it is recommended you brush your pup daily. Extra care will be required if you are planning to exhibit your dog at shows. A Setter's coat is quite fine and easily snags leaves, grass, or small twigs while on walks through the woods, so you need to brush his coat out afterward. You may wish to trim some areas around your English Setter's feathered areas or around his ears.

The floppy, triangle-shaped ears are encased in short yet wavy, dense hair.

The dog's medium-length muzzle has a brown or black button nose. Your English Setter has a keen sense of smell that may get him into trouble at times, so only let him off the leash when you know you can trust him to come and stay by your side. Often, the English Setter is referred to as an inquisitive sniffing machine who will follow his nose right out of your sight.

Behavioral Characteristics

> 66
>
> *English Setters were originally bred to go out ahead of the hunter to find birds and wait for the hunter to catch up. This independent drive to hunt still carries through the breed today. In the absence of birds to hunt, English Setters will 'hunt' for items in your home. Their independence is often translated as stubbornness or an unwilling-ness to be trained. They aren't as biddable as retriever breeds like Labradors or Golden Retrievers, but they are very intelligent and can be trained—they just require a different approach to training.*
>
> JULIA CRAWFORD
> *Crown Setters*
>
> 99

The English Setter has an acute sense of hearing and is sensitive to loud noises. Your dog will alert you to any unusual happenings. This breed is protective of its family but generally is not aggressive unless taught to be. It is a well-known fact that the bark of an English Setter is worse than its bite. They have a built-in alarm system that is activated when a stranger approaches but will quickly quiet down when told to do so.

If you have a family with smaller children, the English setter is a great pet to have. English Setters can be great watchdogs, and since they are extremely patient, they will endure the constant ear yanking or hair and tail pulling by younger children.

The Setter is a very social dog who needs constant human interac-tion. This energetic dog requires regular mental stimulation, exercise, and attention; otherwise, it will quickly become bored and may display destructive behaviors. Like most breeds, the English Setter needs to be properly trained and well-socialized in order to grow up into a gentle, peaceful dog who gets along with everyone and other animals. They usu-ally enjoy the company of other dogs, and with the right introductions, they can live peaceably with cats.

Younger Setters often are excessively submissive and may acciden-tally urinate or dribble urine when they become overly excited or feel

Photo Courtesy of David Weaver

frightened. This is not a housebreaking issue and will go away as your dog matures. If your English Setter is left alone for long periods of time, he may start to whine, bark, or chew on your furniture.

Your English Setter will make it his mission in life to befriend any other furry friends who live in the same household. However, your pooch will also not hesitate to chase off any cats he may believe are trespassing on his property.

This breed ranks thirty-seventh in Stanley Coren's Intelligence of Dogs and is considered to have above-average working and obedience intelligence. However, they are not always easy to train because their high prey drive for wild fowl tends to distract them in outdoor environments.

One of the downsides to the English Setter's intelligence is that he will learn bad habits just as fast as good habits. This means that your dog will need to receive consistent obedience training as early as possible in life. The English Setter responds favorably to all types of positive-reinforcement training methods, especially when there is a delicious treat involved. Later on in this book, we will discuss how to successfully use these methods to train your Setter.

The English Setter has a tendency to wander, so a good fence is necessary. Your English Setter, like other breeds, will test his boundaries and limits throughout his life. This is why training needs to be consistent and fair.

Exercise Requirements

> Setters have a very strong prey drive and love to chase. They are also very active dogs. They need a fenced yard and an active family. These dogs also need a job. If they are not going to be used for hunting, they need another activity, like fly ball, shed hunting, or lure coursing. If you don't keep your Setter's mind stimulated, you will have a destructive dog.
>
> KAREN STROHMEYER
> *Bristle Ridge Llewellins*

English Setters require at least one hour of vigorous exercise each day, but this does not just have to be walking. Playing games with your dog, such as catch or tug-of-war, will count toward the dog's overall amount of exercise in a day and is a great way to stimulate his brain.

A couple of laps around the park or local pond will not only give you a workout but will help your dog burn off excess energy. Switch things up by going for a hike or snowshoeing, and your pooch will be happy to accompany you wherever you go. You will find your Setter's love of life contagious, and without even realizing it, you will be more active than ever with your new best friend by your side.

Older English Setters still love to walk and explore their surroundings and will keep going forever, which means they may be getting too much exercise. Over-exercising an older Setter means it is likely to suffer from painful joint or muscle issues, which will take longer to repair due to age.

Life Expectancy

> "
> *The average English Setter's life span is 12 to 15 years. Keeping a senior Setter fit and active will help it live a long and healthy life! Regular yearly veterinary check-ups will help catch any potential health issues early so you can be proactive in treating them.*
>
> JULIA CRAWFORD
> *Crown Setters*
> "

The English Setter has an average life span of 12 years, although some have been known to live well into their late teens. This active breed is prone to health concerns like canine hip dysplasia, hypothyroidism, and epilepsy. These conditions can be treated if caught in time, so your veterinarian may recommend annual thyroid and hip exams for your dog.

Setters are generally healthy and hardy dogs, and the leading cause of death is cancer in their golden years. Quality of life and diet will directly impact your English Setter's life span. Obesity can cause serious health problems in this breed, such as joint problems, heart disease, back pain, and digestive disorders. Even though it may be tempting to share your food with your furry friend when he looks at you with those big soulful eyes, too many treats may cause extra weight gain and future health issues.

Is an English Setter the Right Fit for You?

Owning an English Setter is not just a privilege; it is a serious responsibility. Your dog will depend entirely on you for food, shelter, and so much more. When you share your life with a dog, you need to be committed to giving him the best life possible.

English Setters are excellent pets for both veteran and first-time pet owners. But, as with all dogs, certain breeds are best suited for families with certain characteristics.

Are English Setters aggressive?

English Setters are very gentle, but they are very protective and will bark at strangers who dare to step onto their territory. However, this breed is not considered to be a guard dog. They will quickly calm down when their master lets them know everything is fine. If you live in a condo or noise-free neighborhood, you will need to work on rewarding quiet behavior to avoid alert barking from getting out of control.

Are English Setters good with small children?

The docile personality of English Setters makes them extremely tolerant of any shenanigans children might try and pull with dogs, such as tugging on ears or pulling the tail. English Setter owners will still need to teach the child how to respect the dog's boundaries.

Are English Setters high maintenance?

Your Setter will require a bath every two to three weeks to keep him clean. Unless your dog is a show dog, you can easily trim his hair for easier maintenance. The rest is basic care and will be discussed in further detail in chapter 12 of this book.

Here are some general questions to ask yourself to see if you will make a good match for an English Setter:

- Can I give my English Setter at least one hour or more of vigorous exercise a day in addition to playing, training, and socializing?
- Do I have enough energy to keep up with my English Setter?
- Will there be someone in the house most of the day so that my Setter is not alone for extended periods?
- Can I reciprocate the unfailing love that my English Setter will show me day after day?
- Am I disciplined enough to train my English Setter to be obedient?
- Is there tension in my home? Are there frequent arguments or fights that may stress out my English Setter?
- Do I have the time and energy to properly socialize my English Setter?

If you decide that an English Setter is the ideal choice for you and your family, you are not getting just a pet — you are gaining a new member of the family who will be dedicated to showing his new people how much he adores them and depends on them.

> **"**
>
> *The beauty of an English Setter is that they offer the best of both worlds for an avid hunter or the occasional outdoors person. While they shine in the field, Setters can just as easily enjoy a quiet afternoon by the fireplace. An English Setter is a continuous seeker of affection and is well suited to a companion who enjoys the constant attention they will receive from their pup. The English Setter will need activity on a regular basis, so it is important to keep this in mind when deciding to join forces with one.*
>
> JEFFREY GILLASPIE
> *Tinker Kennels, LLC*
>
> **"**

CHAPTER 2

Choosing an English Setter

Congratulations on making the exciting decision to bring an English Setter puppy or adult dog into your home. Selecting the right dog can be fun, but it also requires some careful thought —even more so if you are looking for a hunting companion that is true to its breed.

Before you even see your future English Setter, you need to look beneath the surface, beyond those soft, warm brown eyes. Often this is referred to as the "Iceberg Principle," which involves learning about the dog's bloodline, its siblings and parents, and possibly, a breeder's reputation and ratings.

In this chapter, we will discuss everything you need to know so you can find the best English Setter for your lifestyle.

Purchasing or Adopting

> 66
>
> *Know what you are capable of. Puppies are a lot of work, and English Setters typically calm down around two to three years of age. A retired show or breeding dog or a rescue might be a good option if you want to avoid the craziness of raising a puppy.*
>
> SHANNON TORBORG
> *SenterStone English Setters*
>
> 99

The question every new pet owner asks themselves is this: "Should I adopt or buy a puppy?"

Before you can start looking for your new English Setter, you will need to choose between adopting versus buying a dog or a puppy. Neither option is better than the other, as there are pros and cons to both options.

You should never feel pressured to buy or adopt your new furry friend. However, being well-informed about your options will help you make the best choice for you and your family.

Adopting a Shelter Dog

An adult English Setter doesn't have the same cute factor as a puppy, but it can prove to be more manageable for first-time pet owners. Often, a dog that has been given a second chance at a loving home has a boundless capacity to love. Plus, as an added bonus, you will bypass the challenge of training a puppy.

Pros to adopting an English Setter:
- Adult English Setters are more likely to already be trained in the basics like potty training. It should be noted that this is not a foregone conclusion and should be confirmed with the shelter.
- The majority of shelter dogs are already neutered/spayed and microchipped.
- In adult dogs, personality and temperament are more evident, so you can get a better idea of how they will fit with your family and lifestyle.
- You are saving the life of an adopted Setter by giving him a new forever home and making space in the shelter for another dog in need.
- Adult English Setters are likely to have less energy than a puppy. That's not saying your Setter will be low energy, just that the hyperactivity of a puppy may have subsided.
- The love and appreciation from a shelter dog are incomparable!

The costs for adopting a dog can be considerably lower than buying a puppy from a reputable breeder. According to the Animal Humane Society, adoption fees for dogs can run between $120 to $650, depending on the shelter. On the other hand, purchasing an English Setter from a reputable breeder can cost $1,000 and up.

Challenges to adopting an adult English Setter:
- Some dogs may have had a traumatic past, which could lead to challenging behavioral issues.
- Bad habits can be ingrained in adult dogs and may be difficult to break.
- Finding a younger English Setter in a shelter can be more difficult than adopting an older English Setter. Age often is accompanied by health problems, especially if previous owners did not look after the dog properly.
- Many shelters have strict requirements for adopting one of their dogs to ensure the animal does not end up in a shelter again in the future.
- After life in the shelter, the dog may have developed phobias about new situations and things such as children, cats, or even the vacuum cleaner.
- Depending on the dog's experiences and previous training, some English Setters may be trained to hunt, but not all older dogs can successfully be trained to hunt later in life.

Choosing a Shelter or Rescue

> *Rescues can serve a purpose and help place many dogs. Watch for those rescues that refuse to adopt to hunting homes or charge very large fees, as they are probably in it for profit rather than for the benefit of the animals.*
>
> KAREN STROHMEYER
> *Bristle Ridge Llewellins*

Photo Courtesy of Yvonne Wale

Animal shelters throughout the United States are overburdened with millions of pets each year. By making the decision to adopt your English Setter, you are making room in the shelter for another dog desperately in need of help. Plus, you are giving your Setter a second chance at finding a loving home. An added bonus is that any costs associated with adopting your pooch will go directly toward the shelter so it can continue providing quality care to other dogs in need.

Many English Setters are patiently waiting for someone to adopt them and take them to their new forever home. The majority of these canines are loyal, devoted, well-trained dogs who just got the short end of the bone for one reason or another and have no place to go.

Before you rush out to adopt your canine companion, though, there are a few things you should consider. Make sure you are adopting a Setter that matches your real lifestyle and not your aspirational one. As mentioned before, English Setters, even if older, are high-energy dogs and need an active lifestyle.

Although you may want to adopt your English Setter from a rescue or shelter, it can seem overwhelming to know where to begin. Start by phoning local veterinarian clinics to ask for recommendations. They often know of dogs who might need re-homing or of reputable shelters in the area that might have an English Setter up for adoption. Another option is to do a Google search online for shelters or rescues in your county or state who specialize in English Setters.

Even though the majority of shelters are honest and great to work with, there are some rescues and shelters that are just out to make a quick buck. They flat-out lie to adopters, leaving them with aggressive, sick, pregnant, or even terminally ill dogs. Adopting your Setter from an unethical shelter can quickly turn into a nightmare.

Here are some warning signs to watch out for when adopting:

The shelter refuses to let you meet your English Setter before the adoption day. Any reputable and trustworthy shelter will let you meet with your future best friend as often as you like, even if you are still thinking it over. Just remember, though — someone can still adopt your English Setter while you are in the "thinking it over" stage.

They refuse to take the dog back. Any reputable shelter or rescue will have a clause in the contract that will permit you to return the dog within a specified time frame if necessary.

They adopt out puppies younger than eight weeks. Federal law states that a shelter or rescue has to vaccinate, neuter, or spay animals before they are put up for adoption. It is considered to be unethical and illegal to spay or neuter a puppy younger than eight weeks in many states.

The shelter provides little or no proof of vaccinations. Avoid any shelter or rescue that is unwilling to provide proof of vaccinations. A reputable shelter will go over the dog's known medical history with you, including what vaccines the shelter administered and when. You will need to pass those records on to your vet so that future vaccines are administered on schedule.

The shelter employees remind you of pushy used-car salesmen. A good shelter is more concerned about the dog's long-term care than about making a sale. It will give you the time you need with the dog to make your decision without feeling pressured.

When you find a shelter that you are interested in, ask for a free pamphlet or information regarding their adoption process, requirements, and information on how to care for your English Setter. Each shelter or rescue organization has different requirements before starting the adoption process.

The following are general adoption guidelines. The requirements will vary from shelter to shelter:
- Most shelters will require you to show a government-issued photo ID proving you are 21 years or older.
- You will need to fill out a straightforward application form or an in-depth questionnaire.
- In some cases, you will need to provide references, such as permission from your landlord, verifying you are allowed to have pets.
- Some shelters or rescues will send a representative to your home to make sure it is safe and suitable for a dog.
- The shelter will observe how you and your family interact with the dog during a meet and greet before taking him home.
- Adoption fees will vary depending on the institution. Generally, the fee covers basic veterinary care, food, housing, and care the dog received while in the shelter or foster care.

WORD OF CAUTION — *once you start meeting different English Setters up for adoption, your emotions will be running high. For this reason, you need to do your research beforehand. Take your time to read the adoption contract before singing, and don't be shy about asking any of the following questions:*

Is the shelter responsible for any immediate health problems?
Some reputable shelters offer two-week health coverage in case a health-related problem occurs. Other shelters expect adopters to assume full responsibility for the canine the minute they sign the contract.

Is your Setter already neutered or spayed?

Most shelters or rescues will include the price of neutering or spaying in the adoption price, but others may charge you extra for the surgery. Always ask to avoid an unwanted surprise later on.

Can the shelter provide you with copies of your dog's medical records or background information?

Find out what kind of life your English Setter had before ending up in the shelter. Be aware the shelter might not know if the dog was abandoned or found. Ask if the dog has any health conditions or dental issues and if it is up to date with its vaccines. Be sure to ask the estimated age of the dog.

What is the shelter's return policy?

Many shelters have rules in case the adoption does not work out. The contract often will state the adopters have to return the dog to them, even if it is years later.

What are the dog's personality and temperament like?

You can inquire about how the dog reacts around other dogs and children or if he is easily startled by sharp, loud noises. Is there anything in particular that makes the dog anxious, scared, or aggressive? The shelter should be able to inform you about the English Setter's training and whether he is potty trained and obeys basic commands.

Can you spend time with the dog before adopting him?

Some shelters or rescues let a potential adopter bond with the dog before signing the contract. If so, ask to take him out for a few walks on and off the leash. Take the dog for a car ride to see how he reacts.

By asking questions, you will have a better understanding of your English Setter and his background so that you can care for his needs and provide a safe environment for him. Plus, you will be better prepared to meet the shelter's requirements and will increase the probability of having many happy years with your Setter.

Photo Courtesy of David Weaver

If you are still on the fence about whether you should adopt your English Setter, here are a few common myths about adopting a dog:

Shelter dogs were abandoned because they have behavior issues – More than often, dogs are given up because of an unexpected change of circumstances, such as divorce, allergies, moving into housing that does not allow pets, financial issues, or lack of time.

Shelter dogs have emotional baggage – Rescue dogs have a past, but their history often is a blessing in disguise as they are already potty trained and have received basic obedience training, saving you time.

I cannot find a shelter or rescue that has English Setters – The majority of shelters maintain a waiting list for specific breeds, so ask to be added to their list. An excellent option is the A Better English Setter Rescue (ABSER), a nonprofit organization dedicated to finding English Setters in need of a loving forever home.

I do not know what I am getting – The shelter should be able to tell you in great detail about your English Setter's personality and temperament. On most occasions, the shelter will be able to tell you the reason why the original owner had to surrender the dog to a shelter. The only time the shelter will be unable to provide extra information is when the dog was found as a stray on the street.

Beware of Puppy Farms

> Be cautious of any breeder who wants puppies to go to their new homes shortly after weaning. Dogs learn how to be dogs from being around other dogs, particularly when they're young. We keep our litters together for 12 weeks so that puppies have the opportunity to learn about canine dynamics.
>
> JOHN MCILTROT
> *Seranoa Kennels*

A puppy farm is often referred to as a puppy mill. Puppy mills are inhumane, mass-breeding facilities where puppies are bred in poor conditions, increasing their risk of ill health and resulting in high vet bills for the owner.

Puppy mills are only concerned with churning out puppies for profit and completely ignore the needs of the pups and their mothers. When choosing to buy your English Setter, avoid pet stores or online websites, as the majority of these puppies come from puppy mills. Often, puppy mills sell through social media, online classified advertisements, and flea markets.

Mother dogs will spend their entire lives in a cramped cage with little personal attention, and when they are unfit to breed, they will simply be dumped on the side of the road or killed. Many dogs never leave the confinement of the so-called breeding facilities alive, whether it's a concrete pen in a shed or in a cage in someone's garage. They live and die in a few square feet of pure misery.

Due to a lack of sanitation and medical care, the majority of puppy mill dogs suffer from health issues and are prone to hereditary conditions, such as respiratory disorders and heart diseases. There are more than 10,000 puppy mills in the United States alone, and they sell more than two million puppies each year.

Puppies from puppy mills also have a difficult time adapting to a normal home environment, and often grow up into anxious, aggressive, and fearful dogs. Lack of early socialization skills can cost thousands of dollars to treat.

Most puppy buyers usually have no clue of the dreadful conditions their puppies start life in or the conditions the parent dogs are left behind to endure. If the buyers do, they believe they are saving the puppy, but the puppy mill market gains another sale, and the demand continues in the lucrative puppy mill trade.

Warning signs to look out for before purchasing a puppy
- The seller does not ask any questions, and you can pay for the puppy up-front without any previous screening.
- Look for the seller's profile online. If they are advertising many litters from different breeds, then it is a red flag.

- Beware of offers to meet somewhere convenient, e.g., a car parking lot or a gas station that is separate from the puppy mill.
- The breeder is located in another state but is willing to ship you the puppy, no questions asked.
- Puppies are sold when they are under eight weeks or younger.
- The seller makes no future commitment to you or the puppy. Reputable breeders always require you to sign a contract promising you will return the dog to them if you are unable to care for it in the future.
- Copy and paste the seller's phone number into a search engine. If the number is being used on lots of different sites, then this is likely a deceitful seller.

As with everything in life, it is important to remain vigilant and to do plenty of research before signing the contract with the seller.

Researching Reputable Breeders

Good English Setter breeders pour their heart and soul into each and every breeding. They have health-tested their own animals. They have competed in various events, such as conformation, field trials, hunt tests, and obedience competitions. Breeders put their money where their mouth is in this regard, proving that their dogs are healthy enough to breed, have great genetics, and have been evaluated against other dogs.

SHELLEY AND STEVE GARLAND
PineWalker English Setters

Responsible breeders do not sell their puppies to the first person who shows up. A reputable breeder will NEVER sell their puppies through a pet store or any other way that does not allow them to meet with you and thoroughly evaluate you to ensure you are a good match for one of their dogs.

Breeders not only connect you with your adorable English Setter, but you can rely on them throughout your dog's life. Breeders are often likened to being your own private guide, as they provide invaluable information, from choosing the best puppy for you to teaching you how to care for him year after year.

Your English Setter will likely live from 12 to 14 years, so it is worth investing time now to be sure you are working with a responsible breeder who breeds healthy, happy English Setters and keeps them in clean, humane conditions.

You can find a reputable breeder by asking for referrals from your veterinarian or close friends, by contacting local English Setter clubs, or even by visiting a professional dog show. A reputable English Setter breeder will be a member in good standing with the English Setter Association of America (ESAA) and the English Setter Club of America and should be an AKC breeder of merit.

If you are looking for a specific English Setter with a Laverack or Llewellin lineage, the you will need to search for breeders in the United States who adhere to the breed standard established by the AKC. Llewellin breeders will specialize in producing field-type Llewellin Setters that are true to the breed standard, resulting in pups with a high prey drive and that are easy to train. Laverack breeders often focus on show quality, with special emphasis on companionability.

A responsible breeder ...

Keeps numbers small – A responsible breeder only breeds one type of dog and is knowledgeable about the breed's requirements and needs. Often, they will only have one or two litters a year, meaning you will be placed on a waiting list for at least six months or more before you can welcome your pup home.

Wants to know you – Any trustworthy breeder cares about their puppies and wants to know where they are going. They may ask you to fill out an application form to allow them to see if you are a good fit for one of their pups. If you have other pets, breeders may ask for a veterinary reference.

Will require you to sign a contract – Reputable breeders will ask you to sign a contract stating that you will have your Setter neutered or spayed by a certain date. The contract will also state that you will return the dog to the breeder if you are suddenly unable to care for the dog at any point in your life.

Encourage you to visit – Responsible breeders want you to come and see where the puppy was born and raised. The best way to get a glimpse into how your puppy will be as an adult is to observe his parents. During the meet-and-greet session, observe the breeder and the dogs. Does the breeder seem genuinely concerned about the well-being of the dogs? Are they kept in clean, roomy, comfortable areas? How do the dogs interact with the breeder and strangers?

Will show you a full medical record – Responsible breeders will proudly show you a complete record of the dogs' parents' and grandparents' medical records. At the same time, the breeder will inform you of your English Setter's personality traits, behavior, size, and appearance.

Are active in breed-specific clubs – Responsible breeders are often active in local, state, and national clubs that specialize in their specific breed. The majority of them compete with their dogs in field, tracking, obedience, and agility trials or other performance events.

Take the time to find a reputable breeder, and you will be thanking yourself for the rest of your dog's life.

Important Questions to Ask the Breeder

> 66
>
> *Inbreeding, or breeding closely related dogs, is very prevalent. While this can pass on excellent hunting capabilities, too much inbreeding can lead to shorter life spans, poor reproduction, and increased chances for genetically related diseases. Look for an experienced breeder who is aware of genetic diversity. Health testing on a pup's sire and dam can help rule out genetically related diseases.*
>
> KAREN STROHMEYER
> *Bristle Ridge Llewellins*
> 99

Buying an English Setter is a big commitment and investment. Ideally, during your first visit or over the phone, there are some questions you should ask any breeder you may be considering. Their answers matter, as does their willingness to provide them. Any sign of hesitation is a definite warning sign.

Here are a few questions to consider asking the breeder:

What are the parents' temperaments like?

Genetically, parents pass down their personality traits to each puppy. Some may inherit more of mom, and others may be more similar to dad, and of course, some pups are anomalies all of their own. If your pup's parents are prone to aggression, friendliness, submissiveness, or any other personality trait, it is good to know what to expect.

What about the sire and dam caused you to consider them for breeding?

This question can tell you much about the breeder's philosophies. If he simply paired two English Setters together to make some extra cash, he will not have a good answer. A trustworthy breeder will provide a long list of reasons, such as genetic tendency of the pedigree, hunting skills, trainability, intelligence, and personality.

Is the pedigree and health information available?

Make sure the breeder has tested and evaluated both parents and has the proper documentation to prove that neither parent has genetic diseases. A good breeder should have certification of the dam and sire and at least three generations' documentation to show pedigree records and certify the bloodline's health (hips/eyes/elbows).

Can I meet the parents?

It might not always be possible to meet the dog's father, but it is essential to see how the pup interacts with its mother and his littermates. Is the mother aggressive, shy, or well-adjusted? Are the puppies hyperactive or docile? Observe the size of the parents and their temperament. This will give you a general idea of what your puppy will be like.

What health guarantees do you offer?

Health guarantees vary from breeder to breeder, but any reputable breeder will offer a health guarantee. Given the unpredictability of genetics, there is no real guarantee you will get a champion hunting dog, but a health guarantee is a nice backup. Let's say you are sold an English Setter puppy that quickly proves to have serious health issues; you will have peace of mind knowing a refund is in order.

Can you provide references?

Any good breeder will have an extensive list of happy clients who have purchased an English Setter from them in the past. Give these folks a phone call, and ask them the following: What are their likes and dislikes regarding the breeder? What are the pros and cons of the breeder's line of dogs? Also, be sure to ask for a veterinary reference, as any reputable breeder will be in good long-term standing with one.

How old is the mother, and how many litters has she had?

Make sure that the mother was not mated before two years of age and is not older than eight years old. During her lifetime, she should not have been bred more than four times, including this litter. If a C-section was required, she should not have had more than two in her lifetime.

How do you socialize the puppies?

Puppies learn proper social skills from their mother and littermates. Ideally, the breeder is raising the puppies in a family environment, where the pups are exposed to adults, children, and a variety of noises. If the puppy is going to be trained as a hunting companion, be sure to ask what training techniques will be taught before the puppy is 12 weeks old.

Breeder Contracts and Guarantees

Breeder contracts and guarantees are in place to protect purebred dogs from ending up in a shelter.

A reputable breeder will always require anyone who purchases one of their dogs to sign a contract. For first-time puppy owners, the requirement to sign a contract may come as a surprise. We often associate signing a contract with purchases of big items, such as a car or a house, but never a puppy.

For many breeders, contracts are the ideal opportunity to share their philosophies, advice, and expectations with the new pet owner. Breeders are taking a leap of faith as they are entrusting you with one of their puppies. Signing the contract reminds you of the enormous responsibility you are about to undertake.

Contracts vary from breeder to breeder, but they contain some basics, such as the puppy's AKC registration number, the name and the registration numbers of the dam and sire, and the purchase price.

If you have never seen a breeder's contract, here are some common elements:

- In case the buyer is unable to care for the English Setter, then the buyer will return the dog to the breeder immediately.
- If the dog will be used for breeding or as a professional show dog, then the contract will specify the terms.
- The buyer must follow the specified schedule of vaccinations.
- If the dog is not planned to be used for breeding, then the contract will specify when the dog is required to be spayed or neutered.
- Some contracts guarantee against certain genetic health defects, such as hip dysplasia.

If there is anything unclear or that makes you feel uncomfortable, ask before you sign the contract. Ask the breeder to send you a copy of the contract in advance, so you can take your time reading it over without feeling pressured.

Show Versus Pet Contract

You will notice in your contract that the breeder will make a distinction between a puppy that is "pet quality" or "show quality." It should say "show potential," as it is impossible for a breeder to predict whether a puppy will be show-quality when fully grown.

The main differences between a show and a pet contract are the responsibilities attached to each. The breeder will determine which pups in a litter are pet quality or show quality. Pet-quality pups are those the breeder deems unsuitable for being future candidates for showing or breeding. Often, pet-quality dogs will have a limited registration, meaning they can participate in certain AKC events, and their offspring can be registered.

Show-dog contracts can vary depending on the breeder. Some breeders stipulate in the contract that they want to reevaluate the dog at a certain age to ensure the dog is developing as expected. Other breeders require the dog owner to hire a professional handler to show their dog. These clauses may seem strict, but your show dog will be representing their bloodline, so the breeders want to guarantee positive publicity.

If you are planning on breeding your English Setter, then the contract will list all of the health screenings that you will need to perform beforehand. Also, the contract will establish when the breeding will happen and a long list of other details, including financial arrangements.

Inquire About the Parents and Health Tests

All dogs are at risk of inheriting diseases, whether pedigree or not.

Puppies are not toys. If they were, they would be interchangeable, and a defective one would just be a slight inconvenience to change without accompanying heartache. Reputable breeders do everything in their power to ensure their puppies are as healthy as possible, but sometimes things do not work out as planned.

The majority of breeders' contracts guarantee against genetic defects up to a certain age, whereas others only guarantee against specific illnesses such as heart problems. For example, some breeders will guarantee against hip dysplasia only if the owner takes certain precautions, such as not letting the puppy run up and down the stairs until it's a year old, perhaps even longer for larger breeds.

The AKC requires all certified English Setter breeders to complete a hip and ophthalmologist evaluation. Look for a breeder with the Bred with H.E.A.R.T. program, which educates breeders on the best breeding practices and intensive health testing. Look for a breeder who provides an OFA or PennHIP certification on at least the parents.

The dam and sire should be checked for Neuronal Ceroid Lipofuscinosis 8. This is a genetic health condition that progresses as the puppy ages, causing uncoordinated movements, behavioral changes, vision loss, and epileptic seizures.

> 66
>
> *When purchasing from a breeder, please be sure the breeder runs OFA (Orthopedic Foundation for Animals) tests for hips, elbows, and thyroid function, as well as BAER (Brainstem Auditory Evoked Response) tests, which evaluate hearing. English Setters can be born deaf due to their markings.*
>
> JULIA CRAWFORD
> *Crown Setters*
>
> 99

Feel free to ask the breeder to show you any health screening certificates for both parents. Ask the breeder about the medical history of the dog's parents, grandparents, and great-grandparents. Consider carefully whether to purchase the puppy if one of these problems is in the family line:

- Hearing issues
- Thyroid disease, specifically autoimmune thyroiditis
- Cancer — thyroid neoplasia
- Allergies
- Spinal muscular atrophy
- Hip and joint dysplasia
- Eye disease — primary lens luxation (PLL)
- Renal amyloidosis

If you are bringing home a new English Setter puppy, the English Setter Association (ESAA) recommends only purchasing a puppy from a breeder who has already tested the puppy for hip and elbow dysplasia, deafness, and any thyroid issues.

Gundog English Setter Breeders

> *I cannot stress this enough. Find a breeder that breeds pups with high intelligence. Find a breeder that breeds 'natural' bird dogs—dogs that are naturally staunch, naturally retrieve, naturally back, and have natural propensity to find game. Training is very easy and is often not even required if you start with a great prospect. My sires and dams have had almost zero formal training and they produce pups that require the same.*
>
> JIM BROADNAX
> *Southern Setters*

If you are primarily looking for a hunting companion, you will need to look for a breeder who maintains a "dual quality" line. This means the breeder can prove the dogs' past field and show performance. Be sure to ask the breeder if it is possible to see both the dam and the sire. If the sire is off-site, you may be able to do a video conference with the owners to see their dogs in action.

Take the time to personally talk with people who have previously purchased puppies from the line you are considering. If they live in your area, meet those dogs in person so you can get an idea of what their temperament is like. Most English Setter owners love to show off their dogs and share details about their dogs' personalities and training.

If you are looking for a good hunting companion, make sure the breeder is an avid hunter. Dogs bred to hunt ought to come from a history of hunters. If the breeder seems apathetic in regard to this notion, it is a red flag.

A pedigree is very important, as it gives you a glimpse into the puppy's bloodline, siblings, and parents.

Ask about the family history. For example: Is there a history of genetic birth defects, such as hip dysplasia or epilepsy? The breeder should provide health certification and put the return policy in writing.

All gundog English Setter breeders have their own set standards when considering traits. However, the majority of breeders evaluate

Photo Courtesy of
Dawn Gode

breeding stock based on the dogs' natural ability and not just their train-ability. Often, they only breed one or two litters a year and are extremely selective of the parents.

Here are some of the traits reputable gundog English Setter breeders focus on when choosing mates:

Size – Males should weigh 42 to 52 pounds, and females should weigh 38 to 42 pounds.

Hunt – Does the Setter have a strong desire to hunt and search out fowl? Does the Setter easily adapt to all types of terrain and different types of climates? Dogs will be tested on a wide variety of game birds across North America.

Natural point and retrieve – Each English Setter must find game in an effective manner, hold solid point, retrieve to hand, and honor other dogs. Dogs will have been assessed by the National Shoot-to-Retrieve Field Trial Association (NSTRA) for hunting techniques.

Ease of training – Smart, well-behaved dogs generally make more effective hunters. Each parent should possess the intelligence and cooperation to adapt to any type of cover.

Great family companion – Even though English Setters have a high prey drive, they will be companion dogs most of the year, so it is important that they possess an "off-switch." In other words, they should be able to be avid hunters and also quickly calm down when not working.

Ask the breeder if there are dogs in the puppy's background (roughly two to four generations back) from both field and show stock. Most English Setters come from dual backgrounds. Look for a pedigree with DCh. (Dual Champion), FCh. (Field Champion), and Ch. (Show Champion), or combined with the dog's points toward these titles. Look for hunting test titles such as JH, SH, and MH (Junior, Senior, and Master Hunter), which are hunter companion titles.

If you are interested in one of the many activities English Setters are able to compete in, be sure to discuss the details with the breeder. Here are a few of the activities English Setters often compete in:

- **Field Trials** – For a polished field dog or a promising junior
- **Dog Shows** – A show for English Setters who meet the AKC's standard of perfection
- **Hunting tests** – For hunting companions of all levels
- **Obedience Trials** – For Setters trained specifically in obedience
- **Tracking** – For certified tracking dogs who can follow and track a scent on the ground
- **Agility Trials** – For Setters trained to go through an obstacle course
- **Junior Showmanship** – For children ages 10 to 18 with any dog breed; handling is judged, not the dog

Avoid picking litters based solely on the number of pedigrees. These may be an indication of past achievements, but they are not always trustworthy indicators of natural tractability, temperament, and prey drive. Evaluate parents of the English Setter pups on the gundog standards important to your lifestyle needs and the breeder's ability to produce good working dogs.

Seek out sires, dams, and grandparents with strong genetic traits that are passed on to their offspring. Recent research shows that grandsires and granddams prove to have more genetic influence upon the litter than the parents.

Genetics can influence a gundog's natural personality gifts and traits, such as:

- Calm temperament
- Prey drive, tractability, and natural delivery to hand
- Intelligence
- Love of water
- Strong sense of smell and soft mouth

Avoid the following negative hereditary traits, such as:

- Hyperactivity
- Hard mouth
- Excessive roughness or aggressiveness
- Gun shy
- Dominant personality

Positive genetic traits, accompanied by soundness and health, should be the main goal when purchasing an English Setter gundog, not just titles, achievements, color, sex, or size. Inherited gundog traits should be a priority when purchasing a pup.

The North American Versatile Hunting Dogs (NAVHDA) and the National Llewellin Gundog Club (NLGDC) provide a list of reputable gundog English Setter breeders in North America.

When you have identified the litter that you want to see, choose a pup that makes direct eye contact, as this is a clear sign of intelligence and a willing hunting spirit that can be trusted. English Setters are one of the most intelligent dogs, and the breeder should start engaging the pups in learning activities from six weeks of age.

Even though puppies are still awkward, you can observe their "prey drive" from six weeks of age. Look for a strong hunting instinct that can be observed by watching the pup try to retrieve something — does he dash after it or simply ignore it and continue playing with his littermates?

Look at the coat quality of the dam as it will give you an idea of her health and, thus, of the pup's. The coat should have a consistent texture with no bald patches and glossy brilliance to the fur. An English Setter's coat should be fine yet dense, with the hair lying flat with a slight wave.

> "
>
> *I cannot stress this enough. Find a breeder that breeds pups with high intelligence. Find a breeder that breeds 'natural' bird dogs— dogs that are naturally staunch, naturally retrieve, naturally back, and have natural propensity to find game. Training is very easy and is often not even required if you start with a great prospect. My sires and dams have had almost zero formal training and they produce pups that require the same.*
>
> JIM BROADNAX
> *Southern Setters*
>
> "

Male vs. Female

People often have personal preferences as to the sex of their pets. Characteristics such as loyalty, affection, and intelligence are not gender specific. Characteristics vary from dog to dog and not between the sexes. Instead of focusing on the sex of the dog, make sure the dog's personality and energy level is a match for yours.

It is worth mentioning that many of the biological differences between female and male dogs are related to their reproductive hormones, and a dog's behavior is affected by hormones. Once the dog is neutered or spayed, the hormonal behavior will disappear over time.

There are a few hormonal and behavioral differences that you should be aware of:

Behavioral differences – Your English Setter's behavior and per-sonality will be molded by his training, upbringing, and surroundings. However, studies show that dogs tend to get along better with the opposite sex. If you are bringing a second dog into your home, create a balance with one female and one male.

Hormonal differences – Unneutered males have a tendency to roam about the neighborhood in search of a mate. Female dogs that have not been spayed will experience a heat cycle twice a year, producing a secretion to attract male dogs. If you do not get your female English Setter spayed, then you will have to deal with her heat cycle generally every six months.

Heat cycles can impact your Setter's ability to hunt and train with other male dogs, as she will cause the male dogs to become distracted. Also, there can be a messy discharge or bleeding during the heat cycle that is unpleasant.

Physical differences – Male dogs tend to be slightly larger when compared to their female littermates. Female dogs tend to mature faster than male dogs, making them easier to train.

Some hunters prefer a bigger dog to handle while hunting bigger game or battling tough terrain. Others prefer the smaller, compact size of female English Setters as they take up less space and use a smaller crate, etc. However, the size differences between a Setter male and female generally are only two to four inches and a few pounds.

Marking – Male dogs, especially unneutered dogs, have a tendency to mark their territory. Some hunters find this trait to be distracting or even annoying, as it may startle or warn potential prey of your where-abouts. If your Setter is more concentrated on marking his territory, he might not be completely focused on the job at hand. Most hunters are not put off by this and accept it as one of their dog's tendencies.

Spaying and neutering can be advantageous if you want to avoid the risk of unwanted puppies or have a more affectionate and less aggressive dog. However, if you plan on entering your Setter in shows or profes-sional field trials, then you need to remember that neutered or spayed dogs are ineligible.

In the end, it comes down to personal preference and what you consider annoying or not. If you've specifically looking for a hunting companion, most hunters agree that sex does not affect the dog's hunting skills. That said, early obedience training is vital to make sure the dog knows its place and its job, regardless of sex or breed.

Picking the Correct Puppy

> **"**
>
> *I like to look for the dog that is neither the bully of the pack nor the standoffish one, but the one that will wander away and explore on its own and return after it gets out there a bit. Once I identify that puppy, I take it for a walk and watch how it reacts to its surroundings. I love to see it be nosy and try to get into everything. I want to see it go 10 yards away on its own and then look back and realize I am not right behind it and come back and 'check in' with me.*
>
> HOYT RORRER
>
> *Hallowed Ground Gun Dogs*
>
> **"**

Often the breeder will recommend a certain puppy for you, taking into consideration your lifestyle, circumstances, and whether your dog will be a working or show dog. If you have the opportunity to choose your English Setter, here are some suggestions to take into consideration.

Observe how your English Setter interacts with his mother and littermates. Is he the bully of the litter or shy and fearful? How does he react when he is apart from them? Assessing the Setter's reaction will give you a general idea of how he will react when he is left alone for a short period of time.

Puppies raised in a family environment are often more socially adjusted to the typical commotion of an everyday household. Your English Setter should feel comfortable around strangers and not shy away from you. If the puppy seems anxious around the breeder or you, he most likely will grow up to be a nervous dog.

Never get a dog on impulse. An English Setter puppy can be adorable, but he will quickly grow out of the cute stage, and it is entirely up to you whether he grows into a devoted and obedient companion or an unruly, disobedient dog. The more time you put into your Setter's training and socialization, the more you will get back.

Avoid puppies that tuck their tails under their legs or pull away from you when you try to pat them. Shy dogs often grow up into adult dogs who are easily frightened and may snap at younger children.

Give the puppy a quick health check by making sure he is in tip-top shape. Your English Setter's ears should be clean and odorless. The pup should be alert and aware of his surroundings. Even though it is typical for all dogs to have smelly breath, the pup's breath should not be offensive, and his curly coat should look soft, clean, and shiny. There should be no signs of fleas or ringworm.

If the puppies do not look healthy, then walk away. Even though the thought of leaving those adorable puppies behind will be difficult, it will save you from heartbreak in the future.

Choosing a gundog puppy

Basically, the same suggestions above apply to choosing an intelligent, healthy English Setter gundog puppy, but there are a few additional aspects to take into consideration.

Most reputable breeders of well-bred gundogs will ask the prospective buyer a series of personal questions to establish their experience with gundogs in general, hunting with them, training them, and caring for their health as the breeder will want to match the individual puppy to the hunter's lifestyle, needs, and expectations. The breeder may recommend a certain puppy for you. But remember, the final choice is yours. Never feel pressured to buy an English Setter puppy.

Any reputable gundog breeder will be able to clearly and accurately describe the general temperament of the puppy's by seven weeks of age. Often, English Setter gundog breeders will spend several hours a day observing their pups, watching them eat, play, and have puppy fights with each other, giving them insight into the personality of each puppy.

Gundog breeders start testing their puppies for hunting potential before seven weeks of age. They use different types of physical stimulation to assess canine temperament and learning aptitude. For example, the breeder will expose the puppy to a tethered live pigeon or fake bird to see if there is perceptible prey drive to pursue a moving object.

Take a look at the litter together, if possible. Are the pups active, alert, friendly, and inquisitive? Are they well-socialized to people and children and, different noises and movements? Now begin to narrow down the selection. Put aside the pups you may not be interested in and focus on the rest. Many hunters prefer a bolder pup that comes when called. Avoid pups that are reluctant, lethargic, or who shrink back from interactive activities.

Clap your hands. Does the puppy respond with interest or withdraw? As the puppies' mock play together, which ones are prone to picking up objects, such as leaves, sticks, etc.? If a puppy picks an object up in its mouth, call the pup. Does the puppy come with the object as if wanting to share? This is a strong indication of tractability and natural delivery.

Do any of the pups deviate from the litter to explore the surroundings on their own? This is a strong indication that the pup will grow up to use its nose to catch a scent or something of interest.

Desirable physical traits include straight legs, a solid chest, strong short back legs, high tails, and the correct placement of teeth or bite. Choose a pup that will sit still and look at you with his tail wagging.

Once you have chosen your pup, the real fun begins as you are on your way to building your ideal hunting companion. Your new English Setter pup is a clear canvas on which to paint the portrait of a perfect hunting companion. Now it is up to you to train him.

AN INTERESTING FACT

Guide dog trainers have proven that for optimal mental development, a pup needs to leave the litter at six to eight weeks of age. This prevents a pack hierarchy that may cause pups to develop a dominant-submissive personality when they get older.

Choosing a gundog puppy is hard but not impossible if you take your time to research the family history and, the breeder, evaluate the pup's parents, quiz the breeder about the litter, and choose a pup who will mesh perfectly with your lifestyle needs. Any gundog owner will agree that picking the correct English Setter puppy is worth the time and effort.

CHAPTER 3

What to Expect the First Few Months

> Be prepared to spend a lot of time with the puppy initially. The first four months are critical. Take the pup everywhere. Introduce the pup to everything: the woods, field edges, barbed wire, fences, loud noises, being in a crate, riding in a car. Doing all of this in a controlled environment is key, especially with Setters. Pups learn by experience and association. They need to experience as much as they can within those first four months.
>
> JIM BROADNAX
> *Southern Setters*

As the owner of a new puppy, you can expect your life to turn upside down within seconds. You can count on finding your leather shoes chewed apart and waking up in the morning to a barking dog, only to find a variety of liquid and solid deposits on your living room carpet.

Even though the first few months may be a challenge, thoughtful preparation and planning can give your bundle of energy a head start into settling into his new family. Any initial bumps in the road will soon transform into happy memories.

Puppy Proofing Your Home – Inside and Out

> 66
>
> *Make sure your puppy will be safe. It will need to be supervised at all times. Put your puppy in a safe area where it cannot get at anything that will harm it. Puppies like to chew things. Give your puppy safe toys to play with that it cannot destroy or swallow. Have a clean crate where it can go to sleep or feel safe.*
>
> DEBRA BEIRL
>
> *Beirl's English Setters*
>
> 99

Before bringing your new dog home, you will need to puppy-proof your entire home — inside and out.

Dogs, especially puppies, are like toddlers and can get themselves into trouble very fast. All dogs are curious and will investigate every nook and cranny of your house. You will want to take precautions to protect your English Setter and your house from potential disaster. It is extremely important that you take certain precautions and create a safe environment.

Before you bring home your English Setter, get down on your knees and crawl from room to room, looking for any possible hazards at a puppy's eye level. The English Setter's personality is often compared to Velcro. This means that wherever you are, your pooch will be right by your side. For this reason, be sure to pay extra attention to rooms where you will be spending the majority of your time.

In the kitchen

Food is, of course, the most attractive element of your kitchen for your English Setter. Most Setters love to eat, so never leave your pup alone in the kitchen with food on the table. You may want to install a puppy gate to keep your pooch out of the kitchen while you are cooking.

Cabinets and drawers are ideal cubby holes for a pup to crawl into and explore. You can buy childproof latches at the local hardware store, which will help to prevent your curious pup from getting into trouble and,

Photo Courtesy of
James Justus

at the same time, keep him away from harmful cleaning supplies and foods. In chapter 11, you will find an extensive list of human foods that are considered toxic for all dogs.

Your English Setter's nose can sniff out the tiniest morsel of food on the floor, and your garbage bin will be almost impossible to resist. Be sure your garbage bin has a tight lid that tightly closes, or better yet, keep it tucked away under the sink with a childproof lock on the door.

In the living areas

Be vigilant in keeping living areas organized and tidy. Make sure there are no small objects lying around, such as shoes, cell phones, or glasses. All of these items will tempt your curious and teething English Setter puppy. Make sure that all blind cords and power cords are tucked away out of sight or placed inside a chew-proof PVC tube.

If you have a fireplace, your Setter may be harmed by ashes and flames. A quick and easy solution is using a protective fire screen. Another overlooked danger is fire-starter sticks; some dogs cannot resist the temptation of munching on them.

Another hazard is houseplants. Many houseplants are toxic if consumed by dogs, such as lilies, orchids, Christmas cacti, jade plants, ivy, and aloe vera. Place any house plants, on a table, a counter, or inside an off-limits room with the door shut.

Be sure there is nothing up high that can fall on your English Setter if he accidentally bumps into a piece of furniture. If your puppy accidentally displaces a heavy vase, your dog may get seriously injured and/or damage your possessions.

In the office

Your office is full of everyday items that will make your English Setter feel like he is inside a candy shop with many temptations: papers, magazines, paper clips, staples, power cords, and rubber bands, just to name a few. These items might be fun for your Setter to play with, but if swallowed, they can cause serious issues and may even be fatal in some cases. If you are into arts and crafts, be sure that any sharp objects, including needles, are out of reach. Plastic bags and plastic wrap can also cause suffocation.

Wires and cords can be a problem, as chewing on a plugged-in cord could electrocute your dog. Be sure to tuck away any cords to keep them out of your puppy's way.

In the bathroom

Some hazards in the bathroom are quite obvious, such as dental floss, medications, razors, cotton swabs, or soap. These can all be dangerous if eaten or swallowed by your English Setter. Expensive emergency visits to the veterinarian's office are quite common for puppies. Be sure to place all shampoos, conditioners, tissue paper, etc., inside of the bathroom cabinet or on a shelf out of the dog's reach.

Drinking from the toilet never is a good idea for dogs, especially if you use harsh chemical cleansers. Furthermore, sinks and tubs filled with water may present a drowning hazard for your puppy. So always close the toilet lid and keep the bathroom door closed. Tuck away any dangling power cords, and place childproof latches on the cabinets.

In the bedroom

English Setters are scent-oriented and will gravitate toward anything that smells like you. Aside from the threat of your English Setter chewing on your leather shoes, bedrooms are generally benign when it comes to puppy hazards. But to be on the safe side, make sure any jewelry, hair clips, hair pins, and hair bands are out of your curious dog's reach.

Mothballs are another potential hazard. They are extremely toxic to dogs, so if you use them, make sure they are stored in a place your English Setter cannot reach. Dirty, smelly clothes are especially tempting for your Setter, so be sure to place them inside a laundry hamper. English Setters love to crawl and squeeze their way into small spaces. If you do not want your puppy crawling under your bed, then make a temporary blockade with boxes until he learns house rules.

In the garage or the basement

Garages and basements tend to be storage areas for just about everything, including pesticides, rodent poison, fertilizers, antifreeze, solvents, coolants, gasoline, and so on. The simple solution is to place these items inside a closed cabinet or on a high shelf. The same is true for smaller items, such as bolts, nails, and screws. If you live in a colder climate, be aware that many de-icing compounds are made from harmful chemicals, so look for a product that is pet-safe.

In the laundry

English Setters are tempted to chew on and even swallow dish towels or stray socks, which can lead to serious gastrointestinal issues and a costly veterinarian bill. Washers and dryers can seem like a tempting

Photo Courtesy of
Scott Berg - Berg Brothers Setters

place for a short nap, and you may not notice the sleeping dog if you put in a load of clothes. Quick fix: keep any appliance doors closed at all times. Make sure laundry detergents, cleansers, bleach, and fabric softeners are up on a shelf and not on the floor.

In the yard

English Setters love the great outdoors and the plants in your flower garden. There are a number of indoor and outdoor plants that can cause gastrointestinal issues such as diarrhea and vomiting. Some of the most common outdoor plants that are toxic for your dog are daffodils, foxgloves, tulips, birds of paradise, and lupines. Be sure to block off access to your plants while your puppy is roaming the yard. You can find a more extensive list of toxic plants for dogs on the Animal Poison Control website.

Compost, mulches, pesticides, insecticides, fertilizers, and other garden chemicals can cause health issues for your pooch. Your best line of defense is to use products on your lawn and garden that are pet-friendly.

Walk through the grass in your bare feet, looking for any objects that could potentially harm your puppy, and removing any rocks, nuts, or pinecones. Just as fireplaces can be a danger indoors, ashes and flames from firepits and barbecues can be hazardous. When you are barbecuing, keep an eye on your English Setter and keep the lighter fluid out of reach.

If your yard is fenced, check to make sure that there are no holes that your pet can squeeze under and escape. If you have holes in your fence, block them off with boards or chicken wire. Your Setter can squeeze through a space much smaller than you would imagine. Be sure your fence is high enough so your English Setter cannot jump over it.

If you have a swimming pool or pond, be sure to block off access. Even though your English Setter can swim, he could still drown if he falls in and is unable to get out. Also, many of the chemicals used in maintaining swimming pools and ponds are toxic. If your English Setter drinks the water, it could cause an upset tummy or diarrhea.

Better safe than sorry

As a general precaution, put away anything of value or that could be a chewing or choking hazard (puzzle pieces, Air Pods, small toys, etc.) when you are not around.

Open doors and windows are great at letting in fresh air, but they can also tempt your English Setter outside into the world of cars and other risks. Make sure, if your dog can get outside on his own accord, that he will only be heading into a safe, enclosed place, such as a fenced-off backyard.

By taking time to puppy-proof your home, you are setting your dog up for success. As your Setter gets older, he will learn basic obedience training and what is expected of him, so you will not need to be so vigilant.

Shopping List

> *An exercise yard with a tall fence is perfect. A large bed for your dog to call its own is a plus for naps. A large crate is the best for developing good manners while home alone and during the night when all should be sleeping. English Setters are soft-mouthed dogs and may enjoy a rag doll, rope, or sock to play with.*
>
> ERIC AND MARDELLE MAUCK
> *Tekoa Mountain Setters*

Once you bring your new dog home, whether he's an adult or a puppy, you will not want to leave your furry bundle of joy alone while you go shopping, so make sure you get the following items beforehand.

The most indispensable item on the list? Your unconditional love. It may sound cheesy, but it is true.

Appropriate food – Puppies need proper nutrition to grow into healthy adult dogs. When you pick up your English Setter, the breeder or shelter will often give you a few days' worth of the food they were feeding your dog. To avoid tummy upset during what is already a stressful time, gradually transition your dog to a new food by mixing the two foods together.

Clicker – An essential training tool for training your English Setter from day one, a clicker is a handheld device that makes a clicking noise, used in positive-reinforcement training.

Crate – Crate training provides your English Setter with a safe place to call his own while minimizing accidents on the carpets and destructive behavior such as chewing on the furniture.

There is no need to buy a puppy-sized crate and then another crate when the dog is adult-sized. Instead, save some money and time by getting a crate that is designed for your English Setter when he is fully grown.

The crate should provide enough room for your Setter to stand up, turn around and stretch. In chapter 6 of this book, we will discuss everything you need to know about crate training.

I personally prefer metal crates for the following reasons:
- Wire crates can easily be collapsed and can take up less space in storage. Plastic crates only come in two pieces, and they take up more room.
- Some puppies can feel claustrophobic in a plastic pen, as there is less visibility. Wire crates provide a clearer view, allowing your pup to see everything around him. When the dog needs quiet time, you can easily place a blanket on top of the crate.
- The majority of wire crates come with a divider that allows you to adjust the size of the crate as your puppy grows.
- The plastic tray on the bottom of the crate makes for easy clean-up as it simply slides up. Plastic crates need to be taken apart to thoroughly disinfect them.

Doggy treats – Doggy treats play a vital role in training your four-pawed companion. Look for treats that are soft, chewable, and low in calories and sugar. Remember that while treats help with bonding and reinforce good behavior, they should never make up more than 10% of your pup's overall diet.

Food and water dishes – Your English Setter should have his own food and water dishes. Even though you may decide to only put out your Setter's food dish at meal times, fresh water should be available at all times. If you find your dog devours his food too fast, consider investing in a slow-feeding bowl to teach your dog to eat at a more appropriate pace.

Shampoo and grooming tools – Even if you plan to get your Setter professionally groomed, you should still have all the basics at home. Dog-friendly shampoo, a comb, a brush, and nail clippers are essential grooming tools. If you live in an area with skunks, it is always handy to have a neutralizing skunk shampoo on hand. You can find more information on how to groom your English Setter later in this book.

Photo Courtesy of
Tracy Wiles

Collar, leash, harness, and I.D. tags – Walking your new English Setter is one of the best ways to bond, stay active, and socialize your dog. You will need a secure and sturdy leash and collar from day one. Collars can be adorned with an identification tag that includes your contact information in case your Setter gets lost. A no-pull harness will teach your energetic Setter not to pull while on his walk. Trust me — your English Setter will love his harness just as much as you do!

Pee pads – Pee pads are essential for potty training, even if you are planning on training your English Setter to go outside. In the beginning, your puppy will have a hard time not urinating, so you can place the pee pad in an area close to his crate and slowly move it toward the designated bathroom area.

Poop baggies – Being a responsible dog owner means picking up after your puppy. Look for poop baggies that are made from durable material and are easy to dispose of. It's even better if they are made from biodegradable materials.

Puppy bed or blanket – The crate will provide a sense of security for your pooch, but a soft, warm blanket will make it feel like home. Look for an orthopedic mattress designed for the crate size. Also, your puppy will greatly appreciate having a soft, fluffy bed to relax on while watching television with his new family.

Puppy gate and playpen – This can give the puppy an area to play that is safe. This comes in handy when you are busy, have company, or have to leave the puppy alone.

Puppy toys – All dogs need mental stimulation, including your English Setter, no matter how old he is. Toys are a fantastic way to bond and interact with your pooch. Look for toys designed for puppies during their teething stage. Consider interactive treat toys and puzzle toys to keep your dog engaged when you cannot be with him.

Stain and odor remover – Puppies do not come potty trained, and even if you adopted an older shelter English Setter, he might need to be reminded about proper indoor potty etiquette. You need to anticipate accidents. Look for a stain and odor remover that is designed to destroy pet urine enzymes. These enzymes are like a red flag calling out for your dog to return to the exact same spot to urinate again.

Toothpaste– You will need to get your English Setter used to having his teeth brushed from the very first week of bringing him home. Never use human toothpaste on your puppy. It contains an artificial sweetener called Xylitol, which is extremely toxic for dogs. Instead, look for toothpaste specifically designed for large-sized dogs. You can find more information on how to brush your pup's teeth in chapter 11 of this book.

By being prepared for your new Setter's arrival, you will be able to concentrate on bonding with him as soon as you bring him home. Besides everything that you need to do to make your English Setter feel like a member of the family, do not forget to capture your memories together with your camera or phone.

Establish Puppy House Rules and Daily Routines

You have just taken your puppy away from the only world he has ever known, leaving his mother and littermates behind. Your dog just had a frightening car ride and has now arrived in a strange, new world with new smells, sounds, and people. Your English Setter needs to learn how to live in this new environment. Helping your English Setter grow into a well-behaved and well-mannered family member is the responsibility of everyone in your house.

Have a family meeting

Before bringing an English Setter into your life and home, it is extremely important to sit down with all of the members of your household and agree upon a set of rules for your new dog that everyone has to respect. By this, I am not referring to a set of rules just for your dog but for every human in the house.

House rules only work if every single person sticks to them 100% of the time. Otherwise, your English Setter will be confused and will not know what is expected of him. For example, it will be impossible to tell your pooch that he is not allowed upstairs if your children occasionally let him come upstairs and sit on the bed while munching on doggy treats.

English Setters are very easy to train, but once they get away with something, they will have a hard time accepting being told "No" the next time. Everybody has to be on the same page when it comes to house rules — no exception ever! Below are a few topics to discuss with your family before bringing your new dog home:

Should you let your English Setter up on the furniture?

There are a few things to consider when deciding whether or not your English Setter will be allowed on the furniture.

- English Setters are a medium-sized breed and take up a fair bit of space; in other words, they are not lap dogs, even though they will try to cuddle up on your lap.
- English Setters love water, rolling in mud, and other smelly unmentionables whenever they get the chance. So, there is a high probability your pooch will jump on the furniture when he is wet and dirty.
- English Setters are a medium-shedding breed, and if your dog is allowed on the furniture, there will be some hair transfer onto your clothes when you sit down.

It may be cute to have your English Setter puppy snuggling up with you on the sofa. However, if you allow this when he is a puppy, it will be extremely hard to change this habit when he becomes a 38-to-48-pound adult dog.

Your options are to never allow your English Setter on the furniture or always let him on the furniture. Instead of banning your dog from all furniture, you may decide to only let him up on a certain chair or couch.

Where in the house is your English Setter allowed?

Most pet owners prefer that their dogs do not roam freely about the house, especially if their puppy is not potty trained yet. Some restrict their dogs to the ground level only and do not allow them to go upstairs. Others block off access to the kitchen, pantry, laundry room, baby's room, or any rooms where fragile items may be.

If you decide to establish rules like this, you will need to use baby gates to restrict your Setter's access and make sure the entire family is consistent in never letting him into those areas. Personally, I initially restrict a puppy's roaming range and gradually open up the house as he learns proper in-house etiquette.

Will you feed him table scraps from under the dinner table?

English Setters love to eat. Even if you give your dog a treat just once in a blue moon, then he will learn to stare, drool, and beg constantly. Even though this might not be a problem for you and your family, many of your guests may find it disturbing.

Begging is one of the hardest bad habits to break, so it is best to avoid it completely. If you decide to give your English Setter table scraps or treats, the best option is to take them to your dog's food dish and never feed him from the table.

Who will be responsible for him throughout the day?

Before you bring your English Setter home, you will need to decide who will take care of the different tasks involved in caring for your dog, such as what needs to be done, when, by whom, and how often.

Here are a few things you will need to consider:

- Who will take your English Setter for exercise and when?
- Who is responsible for feeding your bundle of energy?
- Who will brush your English Setter, brush his teeth, trim his nails? When and how often?
- Who will take the lead in the obedience sessions, and how often?
- Who will be on clean-up duty for your dog's toilet area in the backyard?

To avoid forgetting and/or potential arguments about who has not done what, once you agree, draw up a schedule of who is responsible for what and when. Try to get the entire family involved in caring for your English Setter, as it builds a stronger bond and relationship between each family member and your dog.

Establishing a routine and house rules is essential for your English Setter. Your pooch will be eager to adapt to his new family and to understand what is expected of him. The more consistent the entire household is at following rules, the sooner your dog will figure everything out.

Preparing Your Current Pets and Children

> 66
>
> *Before bringing home their new English Setter puppy, I tell families to teach everybody in the family that their personal items need to be picked up. English Setters will chew/swallow literally anything. Anything within their reach, including on top of tables and counters, is fair game to them.*
>
> SHANNON TORBORG
> *SenterStone English Setters*
>
> 99

If you have any pets who freely move about the house, be sure to assure them of your love. Before leaving to pick up the new dog, take your current pet(s) for a walk and give them a few yummy treats. Allow them to have access to all of the areas where they were previously allowed; otherwise, they will think you are punishing them. If you have a cat, ensure it will have access to high areas so as to observe the new dog from a comfortable distance.

Create a new puppy sanctuary, which includes a crate and an enclosed puppy pen. Allow the resident pets to explore the area freely before bringing home the new dog. If possible, ask the breeder to give you a piece of cloth that has the new puppy's scent. Let your current pets smell the scent, as this will help them embrace your English Setter quicker.

Nothing excites children more than a cute, lovable little puppy. They just want to hug him and squeeze the bejesus out of the little bundle of fur. For this very reason, it is vital that you sit down with your children before you bring home your puppy and teach them how to pet, hold and pick up your new puppy.

First impressions have never been more important, so plan ahead for a smooth transition.

One of the best ways to teach younger children how to pick up and pat a puppy is by doing a few practice sessions using a stuffed toy. Explain to younger children that even though your English Setter looks like a stuffed bear, he isn't a toy. Even though they will want to play constantly with the new dog, tell them that he will need time to explore his new surroundings and rest.

Children tend to yell when they get excited, which can frighten the new puppy. Do practice sessions with your children, helping them to use softer indoor voices to avoid startling the English Setter.

Golden rule: Never leave your puppy and children alone together, even if it's only for a short period of time. Their relationship needs to develop under supervision, rewarding calm and gentle behavior.

The Ride Home

The ride home is all about safety, reducing stress, and catering to your new best friend's needs.

The first car ride home should not be taken lightly. It is an opportunity to get off on the right paw and start bonding. For the journey home, there are a few things you should consider. This includes such things as safety inside of the car, water and toilet breaks, and the possibility of car sickness.

Before heading out to pick up your English Setter, you will want to bring along some doggy treats, a chew toy, a blanket, a leash and collar, poop baggies, and pet-friendly cleaning supplies (in case there is an accident). Make sure you bring along some bottled water, portable food, and a water dish, if the trip is longer than two hours. Also, do not forget to bring any paperwork pertaining to the breeder or shelter contract.

You should expect some whining and crying from your English Setter on the drive home as he was just abruptly taken away from everything he ever knew and loved. To reduce the chance of travel sickness, ask the breeder to make sure your puppy has an empty stomach for the trip home.

No food should be given to your pooch two to three hours prior to traveling to prevent car sickness. If the trip home is longer than three hours, be sure to bring along a dish to give the dog a handful of food in case he gets hungry. English Setters love to eat, and your dog will be no exception; he will clearly let you know he is hungry by whining or barking.

Before hopping in the car and driving off with your new English Setter, take him on a short walk away from the breeder, his mother, and littermates so he can get used to being with you. An added bonus to taking him for a short stroll is that you give your pooch an opportunity to relieve himself before getting into the car.

Let your new English Setter explore the car at his own pace by letting him crawl around the car with the engine turned off. Once he is inside the car, leave the doors open and turn the car on so he gets used to the sound of the engine. Show him his crate and blanket, and when he goes inside, give him a doggy treat.

But how should you transport your new dog home? Should he be placed inside a cardboard box on the floor or in a traveling crate? Or should he sit on your lap and be allowed to roam about the car freely? Is it better for him to sit in the back seat versus the front seat? Here are some common concerns:

Your safety – Having a loose puppy roaming about the car presents a very real danger of causing an accident. All puppies are curious by nature, and if they are not secured inside a crate, they can easily and dangerously become wedged under the pedals while you are driving.

Your English Setter's safety – Younger pups lack coordination, and if allowed to wander around on the seats while the car is moving, they could possibly fall to the floor and hurt themselves. In addition, if you have to come to a sudden stop or swerve around a corner, your English Setter could be thrown off balance and be seriously injured.

Front or back seat – In the United States, children who are seven years and younger are not permitted to sit in the front seat. In case of an accident, the airbag is instantly activated, releasing a punch that could seriously injure or kill a child. In the case of a baby English Setter, the force would, without a doubt, be fatal.

Crate or cardboard box – Placing your English Setter in a box is a recipe for disaster, as he could easily climb over the edges and start gallivanting around your car. Your best choice is your only choice — using a crate.

If the crate is small enough, you can place it on the floor in the rear passenger seating. If not, you can place it on the back seat and secure it with the seatbelt harness. Fully line the crate with absorbent paper in case of accidents; this will facilitate clean-up and keep the mess off your pooch. Place a chew toy or two inside the crate to keep your dog preoccupied. He most likely will ignore it and cry, but it is worth a shot!

Points to consider when choosing a travel carrier:

- **Find the correct size** – A 12-week-old English Setter weighs approximately 12 to 14 pounds. A full-grown English Setter will weigh between 35 to 42 pounds and range from 17 to 20 inches in height. The carrier or crate should be big enough for your pup to stand up in and turn around.
- **Design matters** – Look for a dog carrier that has passed third-party crash tests and comes highly reviewed. A poorly designed dog carrier can be hazardous in an accident.

Photo Courtesy of Stuart Casey

- **Choose a style** – There are two basic styles of travel carriers for dogs — hard and soft. Hard covers offer superior protection for your dog and are preferable if traveling long distances. Soft covers offer less protection for your dog but are easier to carry.

Two are better than one. If you have company on the ride home, you can take turns sitting in the back of the car beside your English Setter. Setters tend to bond quickly with people they encounter early on. Plus, remember that this is the first time your dog has been on a car ride and separated from his family, so being alone can be a terrifying experience.

The need for water and toilet breaks. If it is a long trip home, your pup will need to stop for water and toilet breaks approximately every 30 minutes or so. It is best to combine these two events, as your pooch will need to urinate a few minutes after drinking water.

Whenever you stop for a water and toilet break, make sure your English Setter is on his leash and tightly held before you even open the door. A nervous puppy could easily bolt in panic, as he will not understand what is happening and may be scared.

Avoid spots that are frequently visited by other dogs. This is because your English Setter puppy hasn't received all of his vaccinations yet, and you do not want to risk him picking up a disease. As an extra precaution, carry your English Setter, only put him down to do his business, and then carry him back to the car.

Your puppy may get car sickness. It is normal for puppies and older dogs to suffer from motion sickness on their first car trip. Be prepared by bringing along some paper towels, baby wipes, plastic bags, and deodorizer to clean up after any accidents. Watch for your dog pointing his nose toward the floor, lips wrinkled up, drooling, and heaving.

Go straight home with no unnecessary stops! Your new English Setter is having the most stressful day in his life, so do not make it harder than it already is by taking him to strange places and passing him around to strangers to meet him. You want to get him home quickly so he can start the process of settling into his new forever home. This is not a time to stop and grab some groceries or stop off for a quick visit with friends.

Additional considerations. Cover the pup's crate with a blanket to help him feel more secure, or open the window a crack to let in fresh air. Puppies have a difficult time regulating their body temperature and are prone to hypothermia and hyperthermia. Make sure the inside temperature of your car is comfortable, and never leave your dog alone in the car.

Make your Setter's first journey together with you a positive one. Avoid creating emotional scars that could resurface later on in life, such as separation anxiety. Talk to your dog in a soft, calming voice throughout the trip home to make him feel safe. If you decide to play music in the car, choose relaxing tones that transmit tranquility.

The First Day

Even though you are overjoyed at the prospect of finally having your new English Setter at home, remember, he is overwhelmed and exhausted.

Before introductions to your family, the very first thing you want to do is take your new dog straight to his designated bathroom spot, whether it is inside on pee pads or a spot outside. As soon as you arrive home, take him there, place him on the ground, and wait for your English Setter to do his business. This may take thirty seconds or even as long as 10 minutes. Be patient, and when your pooch finally goes, praise him profusely.

Keep your Setter's home coming low-key and stress-free. Be sure to phone your friends and family ahead of time to let them know you will not be having a meet-and-greet the first day your pup comes home. The fewer new people your dog has to meet on his first day, the better.

A dog from a shelter might arrive sleep deprived or stressed, so do not be surprised if the first thing he does after exploring his surroundings is fall into a deep slumber. Your adopted English Setter will need a short period of time to adjust to his new routine and structure, no matter if he was in the shelter for a few days or a couple of months. He will need to learn new habits and rules as he settles into his new forever home.

If you have other pets, now is not the time for first introductions. Shut them in another room, away from your new dog, as things are stressful enough. Of course, your entire family will be excited to say hello to your new dog, but make sure you have instructed everyone to remain calm and avoid loud voices. It is especially important to instruct your children on how to act in advance, as their excitement can easily startle your puppy. Explain that they need to stay calm and gentle during the first introduction.

After getting out of the car and giving your pooch his first bathroom break, play with your puppy in an enclosed safe area, preferably near his crate, food, and water dishes. Let your Setter take his time sniffing his surroundings and getting used to his new little world.

Everyone can take a turn stepping into your pup's enclosed space and getting down to the puppy's level by sitting on the floor so that they are less intimidating. Let your English Setter come to them instead of having them chase after the dog and scoop him up, as this may frighten your little pup.

All of this stress, excitement, and mental stimulation most likely has exhausted your dog. As soon as the first introductions have ended, put him to bed for a short while. Trust me; he is going to need it. You may have to coax him into his crate with a treat or two.

As for your pup's behavior on his first day, he may run around like a little hurricane, smelling anything he can stick his nose into, barking and bouncing from one spot to another. On the other hand, your pooch may be completely overwhelmed and retreat into his crate. Give your dog the space he needs to accept his new world on his terms. Never force your dog to do something he does not feel comfortable doing.

It takes an average of two to three days for your English Setter to embrace his new home, love his new family, and recognize his name.

If you normally work on the day you plan to bring your English Setter home, make sure you request time off, so you can spend as much time with the puppy as possible. After all, it is the first day that you embark on an incredibly special friendship!

First Night

If you have raised a puppy before, then you know this is when the real challenge begins. At night, your pooch may feel lonely and may vocally demonstrate this by whining.

Your English Setter is still a baby. Up until today, he has spent his entire life near his mother and littermates. All the sights, noises, and smells that once comforted him are gone and have been replaced with strange new ones. To help your puppy settle into his new home quicker, ask the breeder to give you a piece of bedding or a snuggle toy that smells like the pup's mother and littermates.

Puppies tend to sleep between 16 to 20 hours a day, but they have near-hourly bathroom needs. When your English Setter wakes up, he will start whining or crying to let you know that he has to go to the bathroom. You will not have much time to get him to his designated potty spot. So, have a spot close by and run!

Some pet owners prefer to place their pup's crate inside their bedroom or close by so they can hear him wake up. Once you pick a sleeping spot for your English Setter, do not move it until your dog is fully trained.

Place your Setter's crate in a draft-free area and put a blanket over it to make it seem cozier. Try placing an old-fashioned alarm clock under his bedding. The constant tick-tock sound resembles the sound and vibration of his mother's heartbeat. Another option is to place a hot water bottle under the dog's blanket to keep him toasty warm at night.

Do not be fooled by those big brown eyes! Your Setter needs to learn nighttime is for sleeping and not playtime. If he barks, take him on his leash to his designated bathroom area. After he relieves himself, praise him and take him back to his crate. Do not give him any treats or playtime. Put him back in his crate, and he should go back to sleep almost immediately.

Your new pup's bladder has not built up enough control to get through the entire night without needing to go to the bathroom. It will take a number of weeks before you will be able to sleep through the night without having to rush him to his bathroom spot. Expect to get up at least five to six times the first few nights to take him to the bathroom.

Under no circumstances should you take your puppy to bed with you. English Setters are Velcro dogs and love to be as close as possible to you. Once your pooch starts sleeping beside you in your bed, it will be almost impossible to break this habit. It may be difficult to avoid cuddling with him when he starts whining at night, but it is important to leave him in his crate.

Choosing a Vet

How do you know what type of veterinarian is best for your English Setter? Once you choose a vet, how do you know if you made the right choice?

Whether you are a new or veteran dog owner, unsure where to begin, or are looking for a refresher on finding a new veterinarian for your bundle of energy, this section will help you find the perfect vet. Choosing the right vet for your English Setter is something you should consider carefully.

Ask for recommendations.

Word of mouth is one of the best ways to find a reputable veterinarian in your locality. Be sure to ask fellow dog lovers for advice on different options in your area.

Find a veterinarian with expertise treating dogs.

Not all veterinarians are created equal. Some veterinarians specialize in certain types of animals, such as cows, horses, pigs, and other non-canine pets. You definitely want a veterinarian whose expertise is in treating and caring for dogs. Be sure to ask the vet how much experience he has treating dogs like your English Setter.

Look for licensed personnel.

Most of us just assume that all veterinarians are licensed professionals, but that is not always the case. Make sure the vet is licensed in your state as a veterinarian and not just as a registered veterinary technician. On the American Animal Hospital Association's (AAHA) website, you will find a list of accredited and licensed veterinarians in your locality, as well as an evaluation of the facility, staff, patient care, and equipment.

Consider cost and location.

If an emergency occurs, will you be able to get to the vet's office quickly? Choose a veterinarian whose office is less than one hour's drive from your house and ask if they do house calls to your area. Costs can vary from vet to vet, so be sure to inquire about their prices to make sure they are a good fit for your budget.

Look for a clean facility.

Ask to have a look around the office to check the level of cleanliness. If the place seems dirty, dingy, or foul-smelling, then that is a sign to move on. A veterinarian's office is a medical facility, so it should be just as clean as a hospital or clinic for humans.

Inquire about their approach to medicine and pets.

Most vets have different approaches when it comes to pets and medication. Be sure to have a brief discussion with the potential vet to see if his philosophies about wellness and prevention match with yours. If they are not on the same page as you, then you should move on.

Both you and your dog should feel comfortable.

Being comfortable around your vet is vital, as you should feel comfortable talking to him about your dog's health and other concerns. The same applies to your English Setter because he needs to feel at ease around the vet, especially since the vet will need to touch your dog to examine him. Some signs your dog is uncomfortable around the potential vet are uncontrolled shaking, anxiety, fear, and aggressiveness when the vet draws close to your dog.

Personal referrals are a great start, but you should still take time to research the veterinary clinic and its staff. The vet you choose will play a significant role in your English Setter's life, so take your time looking for the right one.

If you have any problems with the vet, you initially chose, do not hesitate to switch facilities. Veterinary clinics expect clients to come and go.

However, before you depart, be sure to request a complete copy of your English Setter's medical file. You can ask that your dog's health records be faxed or mailed to either you or your new vet.

First Vet Visit

Once you have found a veterinarian you feel comfortable working with, book an appointment for a meet-and-greet for your English Setter before his actual visit for his vaccines. Any reputable veterinarian will be extremely busy and will not have time for drop-ins unless it is an emergency. Therefore, make an appointment and arrive early, so your English Setter can get used to the clinic's scents, noises, and surroundings.

Photo Courtesy of Michelle Ball

This will allow your puppy to associate positive memories with the veterinarian's office. The employees may slip your English Setter a treat or two. Many pet owners who skip this step end up with dogs who are absolutely petrified of going to the vet's office.

When you go in for your English Setter's first real vet visit, be sure to take along any paperwork regarding your dog, such as his vaccination and health records from the breeder or shelter. Most likely, this paperwork will stay in your Setter's personal file at the veterinarian's office. If you want copies for yourself, make photocopies before going to the vet's office.

What should you expect during the first vet visit?

You will be allowed into the examination room with your English Setter. Be sure to bring along some of his favorite treats. Be calm and relaxed. While talking to your pooch, use an upbeat, happy voice, praising his good behavior.

If your shelter dog or puppy has not yet been microchipped, ask the veterinarian if it would be possible to do it on your dog's first visit. You can find more information on microchipping in chapter 13 of this book.

The veterinarian will weigh your English Setter, check his temperature through his rectum, examine his eyes, ears, mouth, paws, teeth, genital region, and fur. Then the vet will listen to your dog's heartbeat and lungs using a stethoscope. The veterinarian will palpate your dog's lymph nodes and abdominal areas. Once the general examination is finished, the vet will administer any vaccinations and dewormers required. In chapter 13, you can find more information about why you need to deworm your dog.

The vet will most likely discuss any future medical procedures your English Setter might need, such as spaying or neutering and microchipping. If you have any questions regarding your pup's general health, now would be a good time to ask. Your veterinarian will give you a vaccine schedule for your English Setter. Be sure to place future dates on your calendar so that you don't forget.

CHAPTER 4

Socializing Your English Setter

English Setters are often called "gentlemen" in the canine world, but these good manners do not happen overnight. Your dog needs to learn how to act properly in various situations.

Dog socialization is the process of making your pooch feel comfortable in the presence of other dogs, cats, humans, unfamiliar environments, and situations. Socialization teaches a dog to trust the world it lives in, helping the dog live a happier, more relaxed life.

Why Socialize Your English Setter?

> *Most Setters are extremely friendly and love to meet other dogs! When socialization starts at a young age, adults will have all the tools to appropriately meet and greet new dogs and be able to recognize the boundaries the other dog may set. Socialization should always be closely monitored, and the more exposure at a young age to as many different-looking breeds as possible, the better! Many great breeders start this process before the puppy ever goes to its forever home.*
>
> KATIE KILLIAN
> *English Setters of the Eyrie*

Socializing your English Setter teaches him to be well-behaved around other humans and animals. Socialization helps your dog feel comfortable within a wide variety of situations and helps him feel confident in new situations.

The idea behind socializing your English Setter is to help him become acclimated to different types of sights, sounds, and smells in a positive, memorable manner. Proper socialization will prevent your pooch from being fearful of the mailman, children, car rides, etc., and help him develop into a well-mannered, happy companion.

HELPFUL TIP
Noisy Guard Dogs

Although English Setters are often described as "merry" and "mild-mannered," they can make surprisingly good guard dogs. Between their large size and propensity for barking, these fluffy companions love to watch out for their families. However, these family-loving dogs tend to turn barking into a full-time job if it attracts your attention. Therefore, setting clear expectations about barking at a young age is essential. English Setters crave human attention and will turn to loud and destructive attention-seeking behaviors without clear boundaries and adequate exercise.

In general, well-socialized dogs are more enjoyable to be around. This is because they feel more comfortable in a wide variety of situations than poorly socialized dogs. They are less likely to be aggressive or fearful when presented with something new. Poorly socialized dogs can be a headache, as they often react with fear or aggression when they meet unfamiliar people, animals, dogs, or new experiences.

What age is best for socializing your English Setter?

Puppies handle new experiences best between three to 16 weeks of age; after that, they become more cautious of new situations. Even if your dog is older than 16 weeks, though, continued socialization and introduction to new situations and people are essential, as they will reinforce good behavior.

However, socializing your English Setter before the age of 16 weeks can be a challenge as he has not received all of his vaccines. You will need to be extra cautious when exposing your puppy to unknown animals or even walking in an area that is frequented by other animals.

Unfortunately, if you wait to socialize your Setter until he is old enough to be completely vaccinated, you are missing out on vital training opportunities.

Photo Courtesy of Cy Black

If you adopted an older English Setter, you might have missed out on crucial puppy socialization, but remember, it is never too late to teach an old dog new tricks. The key is slowly reintroducing your older English Setter to sights, sounds, smells, people, and animals with careful supervision and a huge dose of positivity in the form of praise and treats. With patience, you can help your Setter overcome all of his fears.

Socializing your English Setter is a necessity and requires planning. The more positive experiences your pup is exposed to, the better!

Try not to stress out when exposing your English Setter to other dogs, people, or situations, as your puppy can pick up on that. Take baby steps and avoid doing too much at once. Stop socializing if you notice your dog feels overwhelmed.

Take into consideration the type of lifestyle you plan to give your English Setter and make a list of any sights or sounds he might encounter on a regular day. For example, consider some experiences, such as trains, garbage trucks, crowds, cats, crying infants, a schoolyard full of screaming children, and more. While it might be impossible to expose your pooch to everything he might encounter in his lifetime, the more bases you cover, the better.

When socializing your Setter, try the following:

- Introduce your English Setter to one new situation at a time. This will help to avoid overwhelming him. For example, if you plan a puppy play date, organize it in your backyard or a park that your dog is already familiar with.

- Immediately after a new experience or meeting a new person, reward your English Setter with a few treats and generous praise.
- If your English Setter seems uncomfortable or wary of the new experience, such as hearing a group of children playing in the playground, move further away and distract him by playing catch, moving gradually closer each time.
- Always follow any new socialization experiences with praise, patting, a fun game of catch, and of course, a special treat.

Socializing your English Setter is not optional. It is an essential part of your English Setter's training and is a life-long process that will need to be reinforced throughout the years. Never force interactions with strangers, other dogs, animals, or children. Always let your dog establish his own terms for discovering and accepting new situations, environments, and people.

Socializing an Older Dog

Even in dog years, age is nothing but a number! Contrary to popular belief, it is possible to socialize an adult English Setter. However, socializing an older dog is more challenging because it is not starting with a blank slate. Many older dogs are hesitant about new situations and experiences.

Start slow.
Avoid overwhelming your pooch. Before introducing your older Setter to a new pet, person, or place, make sure he is feeling calm. In the beginning, make sure first introductions are in a controlled environment and be ready to intervene if needed. Make sure your pooch knows commands, such as "come" and "stay," in stressful situations.

Be positive.
Be prepared to generously praise your dog for his good behavior. Remember you are trying to help your dog break old habits and

overcome past traumas. Being social can be rough on an older pooch, so make sure your dog feels encouraged.

Set realistic expectations.

Your dog may never accept all new situations, dogs, pets, or people. Most dogs do not love everything and everybody. Your goal should be

Photo Courtesy of
Stuart Casey

that your dog can feel comfortable enough and safe in day-to-day experiences that he will encounter, such as veterinary visits, grooming, seeing other dogs in the dog park, or hearing fireworks.

Introducing Your English Setter to Your Resident Dog

English Setters are social animals who tend to love the company of other dogs. However, it can still be tricky when introducing the new dog to current family pets. First impressions have never been more crucial, especially if your resident pooch is used to being the only dog contending for your attention.

Your older resident dog has already declared your house his territory and may feel the need to defend what he rightfully considers to be his property. Depending on your new English Setter's energy level and personality, your old dog may be submissive, act fearful, or, worst-case scenario, fight back.

According to the Humane Society, more than 40 percent of US households that have pet dogs have more than one dog. The majority of those dogs in a multiple-pet household did not arrive at the same time. So, if you are bringing your English Setter into your pack, what are the dos and don'ts of the first introduction?

 DO

Prepare your house beforehand. Prior to bringing your new English Setter home, put away anything your resident dog may be protective of, such as his food bowls, bones, beds, and toys. Make sure your new puppy has his own designated area for his items. Even if your resident dog has never been possessive in the past, it is best to be vigilant.

Use a leash. Introduce your new English Setter to your current dog while on the leash. This will allow the older dog to feel as if he is in control of the situation. Also, if there are altercations, you can quickly pull your puppy out of harm's way without causing a huge commotion. Keep the leash slack so that your dogs do not feel as if they are being held back.

Choose a neutral area. The initial meeting should occur in a neutral environment, such as a park or a walking trail. It is preferable to avoid first encounters in your house or even in your front yard, as your resident dog may become territorial. Ask a family member to meet you at the meeting spot. Expect your dogs to sniff, circle, play, urinate, or even ignore each other. Keep the first instruction short, followed by the next step.

Go for a walk together. Once the dogs walk together side by side, tolerating each other, then you can go home. First, enter the house with your current dog, and then bring the new dog inside your house. By doing this, your resident dog is essentially inviting the new dog into his territory as his guest.

 DON'T

Do not force interactions. One of the biggest mistakes pet owners make when introducing their new dog to their older resident dog is simply tossing them together and hoping for the best. Also, do not place the dogs in the same crate. This is a recipe for disaster, as both dogs could end up seriously hurt.

Do not get involved. Once your dogs are both inside the house together, there may be altercations between the two of them, but do not become irritated or annoyed with your older dog. It is natural that the older dog will try to put the new dog in his place. Stay calm and let them establish a hierarchy among themselves.

If your older pooch is being a bit of a bully to your puppy or vice versa, place them in separate areas and do not give them toys when they are spending time together. Teach your younger pup to respect the older dog's personal space. Establish a quiet retreat for your older dog where he will not be disturbed or harassed by a puppy demanding attention.

Do not forget to show affection to your older dog. Small puppies can be quite annoying for older dogs, and older dogs can feel a tad bit jealous of the attention you are giving the new dog. Do not forget to cuddle your older dog with extra love and attention to reconfirm that you still love him. Do not expect the dogs to embrace each other instantly; often, it can take up to six months before a new addition to the household is accepted or tolerated.

Don't get two puppies at the same time. Dog behaviorists, trainers, and breeders discourage adopting siblings as their deep bond impedes their individual ability to learn basic obedience skills and form a connection with their human family. Often this is referred to as littermate syndrome, as the sibling dogs assume their interactions with each other are adequate. Littermate syndrome causes intense separation anxiety when the dogs are separated from each other and results in fearfulness of unfamiliar people, situations, and other dogs.

Helpful suggestions to ease the tension between your dogs:
- Confine your English Setter to an established part of the house that is far away from the older dog's crate and feeding area. Be sure to make any changes at least a week before bringing home your new dog and allow your older dog to sniff out the new dog's area.
- After your dogs have finished eating or playtime, place your new puppy inside his crate and close the door. Ask your older dog to come over and investigate the new dog on his own terms.
- Give your older dog the royal treatment! This will prevent his feelings from being hurt. Never let the new dog push past him for your affection or praise. Your older pet deserves and needs to feel he is still loved as much as he was before.

Cats and Dogs

Here are suggestions to help your English Setter and your cat get along:

Use positive reinforcement. Never ever yell, hit, or throw something at your cat or dog to stop them from fighting as this will make the situation more uncomfortable and stressful. Instead, look for opportunities to reinforce good behavior, such as the animals tolerating each other from different sides of the room. Offer treats for any type of good behavior around each other to teach them that good things come when they tolerate each other peacefully.

Play games together. Play games with each pet separately, with the other pet observing within close proximity. Once your cat and dog appear to tolerate each other, even if it is from a distance, play games with each one simultaneously, such as playing with a string, hide-and-seek, or scavenging games. Just a word of caution: be careful not to play any games that may get either pet overly excited or hyper.

Give them their space. Even though you want your English Setter and cat to be best buds, it is never a good idea to force them together. Instead, keep your cat and dog separated if there is any sign of aggression, fighting, or stress. Cats and dogs need some time and space apart from each other during an argument.

Keep them safe. While teaching your English Setter and cat to like each other, you need to take into consideration their physical safety. For first introductions, you will want to play it safe instead of sorry, as you do not really know how either of your pets will react. Provide high places for your cat, so it can escape. For your dog, use two levels of safety, such as a leash and a baby gate. If your pup gets too excited, ask him to lie down or distract him with his chew toy.

Use sensory cues. Cats and dogs are both highly scent-oriented. Swap out beds, blankets, or towels to help your dog and cat get used to each other's scent without the pressure of seeing one another. Another helpful sensory cue is to let them listen to each other's sounds from a safe, comfortable distance so that when they are closer together, a bark, growl, or hiss will not frighten the other pet.

Give your cat its own territory.

Cats like to feel safe and protected. Set up a "sanctuary" for your cat that cannot be accessed by your English Setter. Create several safe spots for your cat around the entire house to allow your cat to confidently navigate the shared space without crossing paths with its canine roommate.

Most cats are natural climbers, so take advantage of your home's vertical space to create an easy and quick escape route for your cat. Install shelves, buy tall cat trees, or place a cat bed on top of a bookcase. By doing this, you give your cat an opportunity to observe your English Setter from a safe distance.

Photo Courtesy of Kim Ciaputa

Make sure your English Setter cannot access your cat's litter box. Cats enjoy privacy while doing their business, plus some dogs enjoy snacking on cat feces, which is a bad habit for your English Setter because he can contract intestinal parasites. These parasites can cause a long list of health problems, such as vomiting, diarrhea, anemia, and weight loss.

Baby gates are an excellent option to keep your English Setter out of your cat's base camp, but since English Setters are known for being escape artists, keep the litter box in an open space and use an uncovered box. This way, your cat will not be surprised and cornered mid-squat.

To prevent disastrous mealtime encounters, schedule regular mealtimes for your cat and dog; in other words — no free feeding. Place bowls at separate ends of the house or place your cat's food dish up high on a table or countertop where your English Setter cannot find it.

Keep a close eye on your cat's toys. Dogs tend to love the scent of catnip even more than cats, which can prompt competitive fighting and bickering.

The following steps will maximize the chances for success:

- Before you bring home your English Setter, make sure your cat is up to date with her vaccinations and is parasite-free. Plan to keep your pets separated for at least three days after the new arrival. The goal is for your cat to get used to your dog's presence without face-to-face contact. Even though they cannot see each other, they can smell and hear each other.

- Feed your cat and dog on opposite sides of a closed door. This will help your cat to associate the presence of the new dog with something pleasant, such as eating. If your cat seems skittish about eating close to the door, then place her food dish a few feet away and slowly move it closer each day or until your cat is comfortable eating next to the door.
- Begin face-to-face meetings in the common area of your house. Keep your English Setter on a leash and distract him with a chew toy, and let your cat come and go as she wishes. Do not restrain either pet, as that could result in injury. Reward your cat with treats and praise, then do the same with your dog. If either pet shows signs of aggression, redirect your pet's attention by tossing a play toy, etc.
- Be prepared to supervise your pets' interactions for at least the next few weeks, perhaps even longer.

There is no need to be alarmed if there are altercations. If your cat bats its paw or growls at the dog, it is simply communicating its boundaries to your new dog. With time, your cat will learn to co-exist with your English Setter, and your dog will learn to respect your cat's space.

Reassure your cat that you love it by giving it extra attention and treats. Cats like to do things on their own terms, so never force your cat to meet and greet the new dog, especially if he is still a puppy, as it will not end well.

Recognize your cat has a definite personality. If your cat acts like it barely tolerates the new dog, then it means she has accepted your English Setter. Remain watchful to ensure all of their interactions go smoothly — especially when your pooch hits his rambunctious "teenager" stage.

Options if Your Pets Don't Get Along

Every pet owner's secret dream is to come home and find their pets cuddled up together on the couch. Unfortunately, pets do not always get along, especially if they are different species. If you find your pets cannot be friendly, keep them separated for a few days, then reintroduce them to each other.

Reasons why pets may not get along:

Hormonal – Many disagreements between pets often are related to hormonal changes. An easy fix for this problem is to make sure that all of your resident pets are neutered or spayed, as this will keep any aggression at bay.

Food – Al animals, no matter their species, have a built-in instinct to protect their food. If your pets tend to become aggressive around meal-times, place your pets' food dishes in separate parts of the house and feed them at the same time.

Jealousy – All pets need to feel loved and cherished. An easy solution for this problem is to designate quality time with each of your pets alone, without the other pets watching. This will ensure each pet that you love it, and you will never replace it.

Dominance – Rivalry among pets is normal, especially if you bring a new pet into the household. Only one pet can be the leader of the pack, and this is something they need to figure out on their own terms and time schedule. Once your pets have established which pet is the leader, respect their decision by feeding the boss first.

A good relationship between your pets may take a few days to establish, or it may take a couple of years. Fights will happen, especially during the first few weeks, as they determine who will be the dominant leader in your house. One method to make your animals back off from fighting is to douse them in water. Trust me; they will back off immediately.

If you fear your pets' behavior toward each other may cause harm to each other, you, or even another person, it is not unreasonable to think about giving up one of your pets. Some pets cannot and will not tolerate other pets and are happier living in an "only child" environment.

But, before you consider such a drastic decision, there are lots of behavior specialists out there who are willing to extend you a helping hand to encourage your pets to get along. A certified dog or cat trainer or a board-certified veterinary behaviorist will be able to diagnose and treat your pets' stress, anxiety, phobias, aggression, and reactivity toward each other. Often extreme misbehavior occurs because the pet is suffering from an underlying medical condition, so be sure to check with your vet.

Ask around

Perhaps you have come to the difficult decision to give up one of your pets. If so, first ask a friend or family member if they would like to adopt your pet. If you ask around, you will be pleasantly surprised how many people would be thrilled to give your pet a new forever home. Just make sure the home is suitable for your pet by visiting ahead of time.

If you did not have luck with the above alternatives, then think outside of the box and contact dog trainers or your veterinarian to see if they know of any good homes that are searching for a good pet.

Seek out rescue groups

Most localities have active rescue groups dedicated to fostering pets in a caring home until they can find their forever home. One of the main advantages of a rescue group is you are assured that your pet is going into the home of someone who not only loves pets but understands how to take care of them. There is also the option of looking for rescue breed-specific groups. If you are considering surrendering your pet to a shelter, you need to make sure it is a no-kill facility.

Socializing with Other Animals

Do you have smaller pets, such as hamsters, rabbits, guinea pigs, gerbils, geckos, etc.?

English Setters have a high prey drive and usually consider small animals as prey rather than buddies, but the two species can live together peacefully. Before you introduce your English Setter to your small critters, it would be helpful if your dog has previously learned some basic commands, such as sit, come, and stay. These commands will guarantee your English Setter will be well-mannered and make a good first impression with your small critter.

Before a meet-and-greet with your smaller pets, take your English Setter out for an invigorating run or hike to tire him out. A hyperactive dog will not make a good impression on your smaller pet.

Make sure your tiny critter is confined to its cage. Bring your English Setter close while on a leash. Command him to sit and stay next to the cage and reward your dog for any calm, non-aggressive behavior. Allow him to sniff at your small critter through the cage, then reward him once again for any good behavior. If your dog tries to snap or bark at the small critter moving freely in its cage, walk away with your dog and try again later.

After the initial introduction, continue having your pets meet for a few minutes at a time, lengthening the time of each meeting. Always keep your English Setter on a leash and your small critter confined until your dog shows no sign of aggression. Once this happens, let your small critter run about its enclosure freely while your English Setter observes on his leash. When your dog neither shows any interest in chasing after the critter nor displays any signs of aggression, then you can try letting him off his leash. Never forget to praise and reward your dog's good behavior.

English Setters are bred to hunt small animals, so a small rodent, such as a rabbit, guinea pig, or hamster, is an almost irresistible temptation. Even if your dog shows no signs of aggression or prey drive around your small critter for an extended period of time, he could still harm it, even by accident. Never leave your English Setter unsupervised with your small critter.

> "
>
> *Initially, keep playdates short. Remain vigilant and monitor the puppy's body language at all times. Puppies tire long before they are ready to stop playing. Grumpy, tired puppies start to snap and snarl and learn bad habits and don't get invited back for another playdate. A few minutes short is far more constructive than one minute too long. You want positive interactions.*
>
> MARK D. DENEKA
> *Twilight Setter Kennels*
> "

Socializing with Strangers

According to the AKC, the English Setter rates four out of five on the scale of breeds that are considered the friendliest to strangers.

However, even the friendliest dog can become aggressive if not properly socialized. To avoid this happening to your English Setter, it is vital you expose him to a number of different types of people, such as men, women, children, men with beards, people in a wheelchair, and so on. But the quantity of those experiences is not as crucial as the quality of each of these encounters.

If your English Setter only spends time with you and your immediate family, over time, he can become wary of anyone who is not his family. For this very reason, it is crucial you diversify your pup's social calendar.

If your English Setter has not received all of his vaccines, have a meet-and-greet party at your house for him by inviting friends and family over. Ask them to dress up, wearing a wide variety of clothes such as uniforms, raincoats, face masks, hats, and gloves, etc. Before introducing your English Setter to someone new, tell them ahead of time so they can pamper him with love and affection, and be sure to slip them a treat or two for your pooch.

Remember, Rome was not built in a day. Take your time introducing your English Setter to everyone on your list. Start off slow, first with friends and family, then integrate a stranger, such as the postman. Avoid taking your dog to busy public areas too soon, as he may become overly excited or fearful of strangers in general.

Start off with meeting people in neutral, familiar environments, not a beer garden with a live band playing, as it can be overwhelming for your pooch. Instead, plan your meet-and-greet while on your walk together, in your yard, at a dog-friendly café, or in a small store. Once your English Setter has acclimatized to these situations, you can try standing outside of a busy supermarket with more people.

Here are some suggestions to help your English Setter become acclimated to all sorts of people:

- Stay calm and confident during meet-and-greets, even more so if your English Setter is frightened. If your dog is skittish or agitated, don't make a big deal about his behavior, as it will cause him to become more upset.

- When asking strangers to pat your English Setter, ask them to pat him where their hands can be seen, such as the dog's chest or under his chin.

Photo Courtesy of
Karen Lishinski

- Use treats and praise to give your English Setter a positive association with meeting strangers and experiencing new situations.
- Enlist a different dog walker or dog sitter each week to expose your English Setter to a variety of caregivers during the day.

Your English Setter should be exposed to the following people within his first few months with you:
- Neighbors
- Family and friends
- Groomer and vet
- Unfamiliar people wearing different styles of clothes (hoods, jackets, face masks, sunglasses, uniforms, hats, and so on)
- Postman
- Anyone who regularly comes to your house

Follow your English Setter's cues. Interactions should be long enough to make a positive impression but not so long that you wear your buddy out. Even simple new experiences can be overwhelming for your puppy, so keep them short and sweet!

Know your dog. An English Setter is very happy. Never just turn your dog loose in a group of strangers. A traumatic experience can last a lifetime. Some other dogs don't like 'happy.' Always have your dog on a leash, so you have control. Any socializing should be gradual and positive. See how your dog reacts to other dogs or people, and you will know whether to kick it up a notch or slow the process down a little. Just keep it positive!

ERIC AND MARDELLE MAUCK
Tekoa Mountain Setters

Socializing with Children

Even though English Setters are noted gundogs, they are also exceptional family dogs because of their love of children. Your Setter's high energy means he can keep up with children's hyper-activity. However, as mentioned earlier, first impressions make long-lasting impressions, and this statement could not be truer when introducing your dog to small children.

English Setters are very gentle, but with their exuberant personality, they may accidentally knock over a small child while playing. Attentive supervision and training can prevent mishaps.

Dogs and children need to be properly prepared for first introductions and taught proper manners. If adequate training and supervision do not take place, it may create a dangerous situation for both the dog and child. An overly enthusiastic child can easily injure your English Setter puppy. Likewise, a scared or overly excited puppy could bite, scratch, or seriously hurt a child. These tragedies can be easily avoided if you are willing to put in the time to properly socialize your English Setter with children.

How to educate children on how to behave around your English Setter:
- They should pat the dog gently.
- They should never force attention on the dogs; instead, let the dog come to them.
- They should know the dog's crate is not a play toy or a place for hide-and-seek. It is strictly off-limits. If the dog goes inside, leave him alone.
- They should not approach the dog while he is eating or chewing a bone.
- They should leave the puppy alone while he is sleeping.

Make sure there always is an adult around to supervise interactions. Young children should never be left unattended with your English Setter.

Children can often mistake your puppy for a cuddly, stuffed toy, so it is important to remind them how to properly handle your dog. A general rule of thumb is to teach them to treat the puppy as they would another child. They should not pull the dog's ears or tail, climb on the dog, or engage in rough play. Here are some suggestions to consider when socializing your dog with children:

Create a calm environment. Before the meet-and-greet, make sure everyone is in a good mood. Never encourage a grumpy, cranky child to meet your English Setter or vice versa. A boisterous, rowdy child will frighten your dog.

Take it slowly. Children tend to have jerky movements and high-pitched voices when they get excited, which can easily frighten your Setter. Before first introductions, show the children how to walk, talk, and approach your puppy. Tell them to use their inside voices and use gentle hands while patting the dog. No poking, grabbing, pulling, or squeezing the puppy. Keep introductions short and sweet!

Supervise. No matter how well your English Setter and children get along, never ever leave small children alone with the dog without proper supervision. Accidents happen within seconds, and the only way to prevent them is by regularly supervising them.

Let your English Setter set the pace. If your English Setter is nervous around children, let him set the pace. Instead of handing your puppy to the child to hold, ask the child to sit on the ground and place your English Setter nearby. Ask the child to play with something, and let your curious puppy come and investigate. As your English Setter's confidence grows, let the child pat him and eventually hold him.

Keep it positive. When your pooch is behaving properly around small children, generously praise him and give him a treat or two. Positive reinforcement will teach your dog that good things happen whenever children are around. Soon he will seek out children and be on his best behavior.

For the best success with his first encounter with a small child, choose a moment when your English Setter is tired, perhaps after a walk or playtime.

Suggestions for a smooth first encounter with small children:

1. Ask the child to sit on the floor with his legs crossed. Place your English Setter nearby and have the child place his hand out with a treat for the puppy.

2. Once the puppy sniffs out the little person, you can gently pick up your puppy and place him on the child's lap. Remind the child to use his inside voice and to talk softly. Generously praise your English Setter and give him a reward. Instruct the child to gently pat the puppy using soft, gentle strokes.

3. Your English Setter most likely will curl up and go to sleep. If not, he will decide to move on and explore his surroundings. If the latter happens, tell the child not to grab or pull the puppy back to his lap. Doing so could frighten and maybe even hurt your small English Setter.

4. If your puppy decides to explore his surroundings, let him do so for a minute or two, then direct his attention to the child by repeating steps one and two. If the dog runs away again, be sure to reassure the child that the puppy likes him, but he is very curious.

5. Do not forget to praise and reward your puppy every time he sits and plays with the child. Positive reinforcement is the key to laying a healthy foundation for a healthy relationship between your English Setter and children of all sizes.

CHAPTER 5

Laying a Solid Foundation for Training Your English Setter

C hildren need to learn the alphabet before learning to read, as it will become a foundation that will set them up for success throughout their lives. Similarly, your English Setter will need to learn the A-B-Cs of basic training and boundaries, as it will become the foundation upon which all future training will be built.

Your primary job is to introduce your little puppy to his new world in a positive way. In this chapter, we will discuss how to avoid common training mistakes and how to nip bad behavior in the bud.

Photo Courtesy of
Trisha and James Litzinger

Common Puppy-parenting Mistakes

> *Positive-reinforcement training and making sure everyone in the home is on the same page when it comes to training a pup is important—don't have one person allow a pup on furniture and another not allow that. Some Setters are very 'soft,' and a harsh word is all you need for a correction; others are too smart for their own good and will give you the sad eyes and train you to give in. As with any breed of pup, consistency in training, with positive reinforcement and lots of love, will help a pup thrive.*
>
> JANIS FLAHERTY
>
> *Blu'Star English Setters*

There is an old English saying, "To err is human," which means we all make mistakes whether we want to or not. That saying could not be truer than when it comes to puppy training. Often, these training errors are not life-threatening, and they can be amended. But they definitely will slow down the entire training process, causing irritation on both ends of the leash.

Here are some of the most common mistakes people make while training their puppy.

Giving too much freedom

First-time puppy owners often make the mistake of giving their new puppies too much freedom by letting them run around without boundaries. All of that extra freedom leads to unwanted accidents on the floor or chasing your puppy around the house to retrieve the headphones he just stole. Not only is this frustrating, but you are teaching your puppy bad habits that will have to be corrected later on down the road.

Puppies need structure and diligent supervision. Whenever you let your English Setter wander around freely, someone should be watching him 100 percent of the time. It helps to let your dog wander with the leash attached to his collar or harness. Your pooch can drag the leash behind him, and you can quickly grab it if you need to gently redirect your pup's attention. English Setters have a tendency to wander, so this is a behavior you will want to nip in the bud.

Not enough practice

Many dog owners make the big mistake of assuming their dog has learned everything in his obedience classes. But fast forward a few weeks, even a few months, and the dog has forgotten everything he has learned. What happened? Dogs, just like us, get rusty. Be sure to reinforce your dog's skills daily; all you need is a few minutes each day.

Through repetition, a skill is practiced and rehearsed until it becomes easier. Remember, when it comes to your English Setter, practice makes perfect!

Giving attention for the wrong behavior

Your English Setter will repeat behavior that results in praise or treats. This may seem like a simple concept, but many first-time pet owners totally get it wrong, as they forget to reward their dog's good behavior and instead give him loads of attention only when he does do something wrong.

For example, your English Setter is quietly playing with his chew toy inside of his crate, but you are busy sending a text message. When you look up, your pup has started chewing on your shoes. Suddenly your English Setter is getting all sorts of attention from you to make him stop chewing on the shoes. What did you just teach your puppy? When he plays with his chew toy, he gets ignored, but when he chews on your shoes, he gets a whole bunch of attention!

You need to be proactive in rewarding your English Setter when he is doing the right thing. Is your pooch walking calmly on the leash? Good boy! Is he sitting patiently while you serve his breakfast? Good boy! Look for opportunities to praise good behavior. If your dog's behavior is undesirable, like jumping up, barking, whining, or begging, then the best thing you can do is to completely ignore your dog until the behavior stops.

Inconsistency

Inconsistent training will confuse your English Setter. For example, let's say your pooch is not allowed on the couch. Occasionally you make the exception for your dog to come cuddle with you on the couch, but then you turn around and discipline your pup for sitting on the couch. He will not understand what he did wrong.

Strive to be constantly consistent with your English Setter. For example, every time you come home, do not give your fuzzy ball of fur any attention until he is sitting on the floor and not jumping up. This can be difficult, but consistency will prevent your English Setter from becoming confused and, in the long run, will make the training process easier for both of you.

Lack of patience

Training your English Setter takes time, and you need to remember that every dog learns at a different pace. Avoid getting frustrated while training your dog, as he will pick up on your negative vibes. Training sessions should be upbeat and positive, so make sure your attitude is in the right frame of mind first.

If your English Setter is struggling to learn something, instead of becoming frustrated with him, stop and consider whether this is a good time or if the session has gone on for too long. Remember, training sessions should be short and sweet (about five to 10 minutes) and end on a positive note. If you are impatient and getting irritated with your pup, stop the training session by requesting an easy action that your puppy already knows, such as "sit" and end with a reward.

Just a word of caution: never ever train your English Setter when you are in a bad mood. This is a recipe for disaster. You could easily take your frustration and anger out on your defenseless dog if he makes a mistake. Instead, make a cup of tea and snuggle up with your English Setter on the couch until your mood improves.

Harsh discipline

English Setters are very sensitive dogs. They do not respond well to harsh discipline or punishment. An English Setter who is scolded or physically hit can become very timid, fearful, and over time, may become aggressive. Harsh discipline involves yelling, hitting, use of physical force, leash-jerking, grabbing at the scruff of the neck, and staring down.

Punishing your English Setter is counterproductive, as he will become less responsive to training. Fear of being punished will prevent him from even trying to learn a new command, as he will be confused and worried about what you will get mad at him for next. Rather than punishing your English Setter, reward him for positive behavior.

English Setters thrive on affection, so praise your dog generously and give him treats whenever he does something that pleases you. When you hit or yell at your dog, you are teaching him to fear you; you break his trust and weaken his confidence. There is no place for any type of harsh discipline in training your dog.

English Setters are independent dogs, meaning they will feel free to break the rules over and over again if they think they can get away with it. It is vital you establish your dog's boundaries to reinforce your role as pack leader and prevent your dog from developing dominance-related behavior such as aggression. But being the "pack leader" does not give you the license to treat your dog cruelly or domineeringly. It simply means to lead the pack. Reward your English Setter for obeying the rules, and he will happily continue to do so.

How to Teach an Old Dog New Tricks

> *Setters are not bred to retrieve birds, so they don't always learn to play fetch with toys. English Setters do great with food-puzzle games due to their intelligence.*
>
> JULIA CRAWFORD
> *Crown Setters*

The saying "you can't teach an old dog new tricks" has been around for decades. The truth is, you can teach an old dog new tricks, and it is not that much different from teaching a puppy.

Congratulations if you just adopted an English Setter from a shelter or rescue group! No matter the reason why your Setter landed in a shelter, with a large dose of love, time, and patience, he will soon become a happy, well-adjusted member of your family.

Your newly adopted English Setter most likely already has some level of obedience training; he simply needs a refresher course on what is expected of him in a family environment. There is a small possibility that something from his past may trigger bad behavior, which is why it is vital you take your time to socialize and train your older English Setter.

Give your English Setter time to adjust
All older dogs come with a prior history, either positive or negative — not to mention the trauma of being relinquished to a noisy shelter. Keep in mind that the stress of all of this upheaval, along with whatever your pooch has experienced in the past, can cause him to be wary of new surroundings.

Give your adopted English Setter time to adjust to his new home, surroundings, and family. Some dogs instantly adjust to their new life, while others may take several months before they fully embrace their forever home. If you notice your English Setter is having a hard time adapting, make him feel safe and comfortable. Do not expect him to warm up to his new home immediately; instead, be patient and keep day-to-day activities consistent and predictable.

Establish boundaries

Training your older English Setter starts from the very first day you bring him home. Avoid the temptation of coddling him the first few weeks to make up for time spent in the shelter.

If you let your older English Setter get away with bad behavior the first few days, you will have a much harder time trying to break these unwanted habits later on. This includes letting him beg while you eat dinner at the kitchen table, climbing up on the sofa, or eliminating on the carpet. Be sure to establish your dog's boundaries from day one, and make sure the entire family knows how to enforce them.

Photo Courtesy of
Tom Gibbs

Set a schedule

English Setters thrive on a strict schedule. If your older Setter has spent the last few weeks, or even months, in a shelter, he probably is very stressed as life in the shelter can be very unpredictable. Provide much-needed stability for your English Setter by setting up a daily routine for walking, feeding, playing, and sleeping. In most cases, a well-established routine will help your dog embrace his new life faster.

Assume your English Setter has no training

Treat your older English Setter just as you would treat a puppy coming into your home. Assume your English Setter has had no training, even if the shelter assures you that your dog is well-behaved and had obedience training in the past. Most likely, your pooch will need a few reminders about proper indoor and outdoor etiquette. For more information on how to potty train your English Setter, see chapter 6 of this book.

Your best choice is to assume your Setter does not know anything at all. This way you will be pleasantly surprised when you discover he already knows basic commands such as sit, come, and stay. Be sure to use loads of positive reinforcement methods while training your older pup, and keep training sessions short and sweet.

Start with crate training

Just as with a puppy, you will want to introduce your shelter dog to crate training from the very first day. This way, you can instantly start working on housebreaking and have peace of mind knowing your new dog will not get into mischief when you are unable to supervise him. In chapter 6 of this book, you can find more information regarding how to crate train your dog.

Your English Setter will embrace his crate, as it will give him a place to call his own. Between being relinquished at the shelter, living in the shelter, and coming to your new home, your new dog may feel extremely stressed out. Your dog will thank you for giving him a place to retreat to whenever he is feeling overwhelmed.

A word of caution: crate training may be difficult for some dogs, especially if the previous owner used a crate as a place of punishment or the dog had to spend long periods of time confined to one. Never force your older English Setter into a crate.

Enroll in an obedience class

Just because your shelter Setter may be having a hard time adjusting to his new home does not mean you should put off joining an obedience program. These regular training sessions will help you and your dog bond and help him adapt to his new routine. English Setters crave structure and predictability, so obedience classes are one of the best gifts you can give your shelter dog.

Socialization is another important factor to teach your older shelter dog, as it is important to get him familiar with new environments, people, and other animals. Socializing an older dog should be taken slowly and within your dog's comfort level.

Considerations with training an older shelter dog

There are quite a few advantages to teaching older dogs compared to puppies due to their longer attention span. However, your older English Setter might need a little more motivation than a puppy, especially if his previous owner mistreated him. Even though your English Setter might not be as agile or mentally sharp as a puppy, he still has a built-in desire to please you.

While your English Setter is adjusting to his new home, be sure to supervise him at all times, including inside and outside. Even if your yard is completely fenced in, your shelter dog could become startled by strange noises or smells, causing him to escape. If your dog escapes, he will have a difficult time finding his way home because he is still not familiar with his new surroundings.

Here are some suggestions to consider when training an older dog:
- Keep training sessions upbeat and positive. If you or your English Setter become agitated, anxious, or nervous, then it is best to take a break.
- Old joints do not like doing the same movement over and over again. Avoid asking your English Setter to "sit" 20 times in a row

without taking a break. Doing so may cause your pooch pain and may make him slow to respond.

- Keep training sessions short and sweet.
- Recognize and take into consideration your English Setter's limitations.
- Use verbal and hand signals. Older dogs may be hard of hearing, so the hand signals will help.
- Positive reinforcement is your secret weapon, especially treats. If you are worried about weight gain, chop unsalted, boiled, skinless chicken breast into small pieces.
- Be aware of the temperature. Older dogs are more sensitive to heat and cold than younger dogs.
- Train on soft surfaces. Choose soft surfaces such as carpet, grass, or a yoga mat to make training sessions more comfortable for your elderly English Setter.
- Practice one trick at a time, as multiple tricks may be confusing and frustrating for your elderly dog.

Remember that training sessions should be fun and give you moments to bond with your English Setter. If your dog's health and age prevent him from learning a new trick, concentrate on making him feel comfortable, loved, and cared for.

Obedience Classes

> *Obedience training is a must if you want to have a nice companion. Consistency is the key. Whatever you do, be consistent in the words you choose. The less you say, the faster your dog will learn. An English Setter may try to run the show or even ignore you. Don't fall for it!*
>
> ERIC AND MARDELLE MAUCK
> *Tekoa Mountain Setters*

Whether you have a puppy or a shelter dog, obedience classes can help your English Setter learn to behave correctly at home or while out and about. Typically, obedience classes teach pet owners how to teach their dog basic commands, such as lie down and sit. Also, your English Setter will learn socialization skills required to interact with different people and other dogs.

Before your English Setter begins any type of obedience or socialization classes, be sure he has received all of his vaccinations at least seven days prior to the first class.

FUN FACT

The Longest Tongue

An English Setter holds the world record for the longest tongue on a living dog. Clocking in at 3.74 inches, an English Setter named Bisbee from Tucson, Arizona, has a tongue longer than an average popsicle stick. The Guinness World Record measures a dog's tongue from the tip of the snout to the end of the tongue. Before Bisbee claimed this title, it belonged to a St. Bernard named Mochi, whose tongue measured a whopping 7.3 inches. Mochi held the title for five years before passing away in 2021.

Beginner obedience classes for dogs often will be divided into age groups and will teach your English Setter the following:

- Basic commands, such as sit, lie down, come, and roll over
- Not to pull on the leash while going for a walk
- Not to jump up on other people or dogs
- Not to chew on your furniture
- How to socialize with new people, dogs, and places

Obedience classes are designed to teach basic training. So do not expect them to resolve any major issues such as aggression, separation anxiety, depression, or excessive barking.

The majority of obedience classes will meet for approximately one hour each week for a period of eight to 10 weeks, depending on the program. The success of each course will depend entirely on pet owners having daily training sessions with their dogs, putting into practice what they learn each week. Here are some suggestions to consider when choosing the right obedience course for your English Setter.

Ask for referrals. The best place to start is by asking fellow dog lovers, friends, family, and of course, your veterinarian for recommendations on obedience classes in your locality. In addition, you can also look online for reviews of the obedience course you are interested in.

Check their credentials. Look for an instructor who has credentials from one or more of the following associations: the National Association of Dog Obedience, the Association of Pet Dog Trainers, the National K-9 Dog Trainers Association, and the International Association of Canine Professionals.

Visit a free class. Most obedience classes will let you observe a class or two before signing up for the entire course. If they do not allow you to sit in on a class for free, even without your dog, then that is a warning sign to look for another course. Transparency is essential for the well-being

Photo Courtesy of Stuart Casey

of you and your dog. Be patient in searching for the best choice for you and your English Setter.

Watch out for red flags. Obedience classes are not only about teaching your English Setter new commands but also about socializing your dog with other people and dogs. The class should also be fun and enjoyable for your dog. Never accept an instructor who encourages pet owners to yell or hit their dogs or use potentially harmful techniques or devices. Dogs are very intuitive. If you notice your English Setter is uncomfortable around the instructor, there probably is a good reason.

Pick the right fit. The best dog obedience course should be a good fit for your budget, driving distance, quality, content, and of course, your overall first impression of the instructor. Be sure to take into consideration any referrals you received to help choose the best obedience course for you and your English Setter.

When to get professional help

It can be a challenge to figure out if your English Setter is simply misbehaving or if he has behavioral issues. If your English Setter does have a behavioral problem, normal training tactics may not be enough. There are a few extreme cases where you might need help:

Biting – It is normal for a puppy to go through a biting stage while he is teething. However, when a dog viciously bites and snaps, that is unacceptable. Aggressive behavior cannot be fixed by common obedience classes. In this case, the dog will need professional help from a dog trainer who specializes in behavioral issues.

Separation anxiety – English Setters often suffer from separation anxiety, but the problem can often be corrected by working one-on-one with your pooch. But if you have tried and tried to reprogram your English Setter's bad behavior and he still goes into a destructive panic mode every time you leave the house, then he may need specialized training and medication.

If you need professional help for your English Setter, the best place to turn to is your vet for recommendations.

Unacceptable Behavior from Day One

> *Some English Setters are perfect in the home, while others take every opportunity to shred your slippers or steal your tortilla off the countertop. They are surprisingly long-reaching when it comes to cruising the countertop for any spare food. Usually, if there's some misbehaving going on, it is because of boredom, which means it's time for some quality play.*
>
> JEFFREY GILLASPIE
> *Tinker Kennels, LLC*

Many dog behaviors that we consider to be inappropriate are actually an instinctive part of their canine personality, such as digging, barking, or rolling on a dead animal. For your pooch, these activities are innate behaviors, but you can train your English Setter to at least minimize these habits.

Chewing

> *You must make sure the puppy does not get into trouble—the house needs to be puppy-proof. The most important aspect of this is: do not let the pup get into items he can chew and swallow, which can cause an impaction and can lead to high-cost medical bills and/or death.*
>
> VINCENT GUGLIELMO
> *Chenango Valley Kennels*

Chewing is a natural instinct for your English Setter. Puppies chew to relieve teething pain, and older dogs chew on bones to keep their jaws strong and their teeth clean. However, excessive chewing can quickly become a bad habit if you do not teach a dog what objects are appropriate for chewing and which are not.

SIMPLE SOLUTION: If you catch your English Setter chewing on your shoes or your furniture, do not scold him. Instead, quickly distract him by clapping your hands, then replace the object with an appropriate chew toy. Never give your English Setter an old sock or shoe to chew on, as he cannot tell the difference between new and old ones. The same goes for letting your English Setter puppy chew on you; it may seem cute when he is a puppy, but in a few months, it will not feel cute.

Excessive Barking

English Setters do not like to be left alone, and will vocalize their unhappiness through barking. English Setters are the most vocal of the Setter breeds.

Your dog may bark, howl, whine, or cry. Before correcting this behavior problem, determine why your Setter feels the need to vocalize in the first place. Your dog may be barking out of excitement, boredom, attention-seeking, anxiety, fright, or in response to other dogs.

SIMPLE SOLUTION: If you determine your English Setter is barking for your attention, simply ignore him until he stops barking, then be sure to praise him for being quiet. Do not even look at your English Setter while he is barking, as he will assume you are encouraging his behavior and will bark even More loudly. If your pooch is barking at a stranger, such as the delivery guy, assure your pooch everything is okay and introduce him to the new person, reassuring him there is no reason to be frightened.

Digging

All dogs will dig simply, because they are dogs, no matter the breed. If given the chance, your English Setter will have a ball digging up your flower garden, as it is part of his natural hunting instinct. In general, most dogs dig out of boredom to burn off excess energy, cool off, out of fear, hunting instinct, or a desire to conceal their most precious possessions (like bones or toys). A common myth is dogs outgrow digging, but if this behavior is not corrected, then most likely, it will continue.

 SIMPLE SOLUTION: *Nobody wants a dog who is constantly digging up the backyard. But before you decide to lay down cement, determine why your English Setter is digging, then work to eliminate the source. Perhaps your high-energy pooch needs more exercise or more quality time with you playing fetch or practicing obedience training. If digging seems inevitable, establish an area where your pup can freely dig, such as a sandbox. Train your Setter that he is only allowed to dig in this area.*

Separation Anxiety

Separation anxiety is one of the most common behavioral issues for English Setters and occurs when your dog is left alone for long periods of time. Separation anxiety can be manifested by barking, whining, chewing, inappropriate urination, and even defecation. Often a dog who suffers from separation anxiety will have the tendency to follow his owner around constantly.

 SIMPLE SOLUTION: *True separation anxiety can be extremely difficult to break as it involves dedicated training with professional help. Here are a few simple steps to prevent separation anxiety from developing in the first place.*

- Ask a family member to hide near your English Setter's crate, but out of sight.
- Place your English Setter inside his crate with a chew toy and a few treats. Avoid making a big show about leaving.
- Before entering the house, text the family member who is hiding and ask how your pup is behaving. If he behaved, calmly walk in, greet your dog, and reward his good behavior.
- Each time that you leave, slowly increase the time away until your English Setter learns how he is supposed to act when he is left home alone.

One of the most wonderful traits of English Setters is their devotion to their family, but since some separation from their human companions is unavoidable, some English Setters do better with another canine companion.

Wandering

When they are adults, if you have the ability to let them run in a fenced enclosure, they will love it, but I would not recommend letting a Setter off-leash without solid recall training. Those hunting instincts will kick in, and they will be a mile away before you can catch up.

KAYLA KOZAK
Kei-Rin Kennel

English Setters are escape artists who can and will dig or jump their way out of any enclosure, as they love to wander.

Your English Setter's desire to chase after moving things or follow a scent is simply a display of his predatory instinct. However, your pup's little nose can lead to devastating and dangerous outcomes. You may not be able to prevent your Setter from sniffing out a small rodent or animal, but you can take direct steps to avoid disaster.

SIMPLE SOLUTION: *If you have a fenced-in backyard, get down on your knees to make sure there are no small holes or spaces that your English Setter can squeeze under and escape. If you don't have a fenced-in backyard, then keep him tied up when left outside unsupervised. Keep your dog on a leash until he is trained to come when called and watch out for potential triggers such as joggers. Have a dog whistle on hand to get your Setter's attention when he starts to get too far away.*

Another solution to prevent your English Setter from wandering is to make sure he is getting enough exercise. Often, Setters will roam when they are bored and need to burn off some extra energy.

Jumping Up

Jumping up is another common behavior for English Setters. Puppies learn to jump up to greet their mother; later, they repeat the same behavior when meeting people. Your dog may jump up out of emotion when seeing you or when he is seeking an item in your hand. A jumping dog may be cute when he is still a puppy, but a full-grown jumping dog is not only annoying but also dangerous.

SIMPLE SOLUTION: *There are a handful of different methods to teach your pooch not to jump up when greeting you; however, not many of them are successful. For example, lifting your knee or grabbing his paws and pushing him away often sends the wrong message to your dog. Jumping up is an attention-seeking behavior, so any type of acknowledgment (whether positive or negative) of your dog's actions means you approve of his behavior.*

The best way to teach your English Setter not to jump up is to simply turn around and ignore your dog. Once he has all four paws on the ground and has ceased jumping up, praise his good behavior. Trust me; it will not take too long before your pooch understands what you expect of him.

Begging

> *Don't offer people-food scraps to dogs. It is hard to measure those extra calories and they can add up quickly! It will also help eliminate table begging. Be strong and resist those incredibly persuasive eyes!*
>
> MARK D. DENEKA
> *Twilight Setter Kennels*

Begging is a habit that your dog learns from you, and it is extremely difficult to break. Most Setters love to eat; however, table scraps are not doggy treats and can cause a long list of digestive issues and obesity. English Setters have a tendency to overeat, which leads to unwanted weight that will lead to health complications.

It may seem almost impossible to resist those soft brown eyes, but giving in just once will create problematic behavior in the long run.

 **SIMPLE SOLUTION:** *Before you sit down for dinner or chow down on some pizza on the sofa, tell your Setter to go to his place. If necessary, confine your pooch to his crate or another room. If he behaves, be sure to give him a treat or two after your family has completely finished eating.*

Mounting

Mounting and humping are normal behaviors for both male and female dogs. Your English Setter may attempt to mount moving and inert objects, such as people, other animals, dog beds, and toys, or he will just lick himself. Neutered and spayed dogs may continue mounting or humping because this behavior feels good.

Simple solution: If you notice that your Setter is trying to mount or hump, quickly try to distract him. Play a game, toss him a chew toy, or ask him to perform a trick such as "give a paw." Over time, your dog will forget about this behavior, but only if you nip it in time.

High Prey Drive

Hunters praise English Setters for their high prey drive, but there is a time and place for tracking an animal. Due to Setters' high prey drive, they cannot be considered to be reliable off-leash. Many English Setters will ignore commands if there are natural distractions that are tempting. If a Setter with a high prey drive did not grow up around cats, he might accidentally injure or kill a cat.

If your dog is left to his own devices, his strong prey drive will cause him to chase anything that moves. This can lead to potentially dangerous situations, such as hunting and killing an animal or chasing cars.

SIMPLE SOLUTION: *Never encourage your puppy to chase other animals, even if it is a form of exercise, as your dog will love it, and it will become a habitual behavior. Your dog will not be able to understand the difference between chasing a moving object in the backyard or a moving object on the side of the road.*

Whether you are planning to use your English Setter's prey drive for hunting or not, having your dog come to you is by far the most important command you can teach your dog. Having a reliable recall will save you a lot of heartaches and may save your dog's life. That said, if your older English Setter shows signs of a high prey drive, he should never be left alone with a cat or any small animal.

CHAPTER 6

Basic Training

> *Setters take longer to mature into what will be their prime, so when you are working with a puppy, keep that in mind. I've had only one dog in my life that came out of the chute running and responding like it had been on the job for 10 years. The others all had to develop their tools over a period of a few years, with improvements and adjustments made along the way.*
>
> JEFFREY GILLASPIE
> *Tinker Kennels, LLC*

A re you ready to start training your English Setter dog or puppy? It is essential to start training your dog as soon as possible to sit, stay, come, go to his crate, and go potty outside. Training your dog is something you can do by yourself, even if you are a first-time pet owner.

Training a dog can seem pretty overwhelming, especially if you are a first-time pet owner. However, if you take it step by step, you will find the task far less daunting. In this chapter, you will learn everything you need to help you get started on basics, such as house and crate training.

Crate Training Basics

> *English Setters are prone to chewing for many, many months, so keeping them in a crate when you can't watch them closely or will be away from home is helpful. They'll get used to sleeping in their crate if you keep it near the family. Feeding them in the crate also makes it a positive place to be.*
>
> LIN SELL, MD
> *Linwood English Setters*

Some first-time pet owners may shy away from crate training, believing it is cruel and will isolate their new four-pawed best friend. However, your English Setter's crate is his own private bedroom for resting and sleeping. Dogs instinctively seek out small places to shelter. Your dog's crate is more than an essential tool in house-breaking your puppy; it will also be your English Setter's safe haven.

Crate training is widely accepted by professional trainers and veterinarians to be one of the most effective methods to teach your dog desirable behaviors and help to prevent separation anxiety.

When properly and humanely used, crate training provides many advantages for you and your English Setter.

Advantages for you:
- If you need to travel with your fur baby, many hotels will permit you to stay with your dog if he is in a crate. You will be able to travel with your English Setter safely and be assured that your dog will quickly adapt to any new situations or strange surroundings, as long as he has his familiar "security blanket" — his crate.
- If you are unable to take your English Setter on a holiday, friends and family may be more willing to watch him if he is crate trained.

- You will have peace of mind when you have to temporarily leave your English Setter home alone, knowing your pup is comfortable and safe in his private bedroom, instead of running unrestrained throughout your house and destroying who-knows-what.
- By temporarily confining your English Setter to his crate, you can effectively establish a regular bathroom schedule and prevent unwanted accidents during the night or when your pooch is left alone.
- If you ever need to leave your pooch overnight at the vet or a kennel, you will be at ease knowing he will be comfortable and safe inside a crate.
- Crate training will allow you to confine your English Setter when he becomes overly excited by guests or children.
- Another advantage is that you can place your dog inside his crate during dinnertime, which helps to prevent him from begging.

Photo Courtesy of
Michelle Ball

Advantages for your English Setter:

- Your English Setter will love having a den of his own where he can retreat whenever he is tired, not feeling well, or is stressed out.
- Your English Setter can be included in different family activities, such as picnics, camping trips, etc., instead of being left at home alone.
- Since your English Setter will avoid soiling himself inside his crate, he will learn to control his bowels faster and associate elimination only within a specified location.
- Your dog's crate will spare your English Setter from feeling isolated, lonely, and frustrated at being placed alone in the basement or laundry room. The crate will only restrict him from certain things for his own safety and will not keep him away from his family.

Your English Setter is very social and does not like being left alone. One of the main benefits of a crate is that you can bring your dog with you wherever you go, even if you are busy and cannot interact with him. Your English Setter needs to feel that he is part of your family, and this comes from being with you as much as possible.

Crate training is a fantastic training tool, but it can be abused. Never leave your English Setter locked in the crate all day long, as it is inhumane and cruel. Plus, this can cause emotional distress or promote problematic behaviors, such as barking, chewing, and jumping.

If your schedule requires you to spend the majority of time away from home and your English Setter, you will need to hire a dog sitter to drop by every two to three hours to let your dog out of his crate. This will give him a chance to stretch his legs, relieve himself, and burn off excess energy.

 **A WORD OF CAUTION:** *English Setters do not do well in a working household. They prefer being around their family, and when left alone regularly, they often develop separation anxiety.*

FUN FACT

The Confusing Issue of Llewellin Setters

At first glance, Llewellin Setters and English Setters are the same breeds, but the issue is slightly more complicated. In the mid-1800s, Richard Purcell (later Richard Llewellin) decided to create a smaller type of English Setter that was even more skilled at hunting. In Richard Llewellin's mind, English Setters had become increasingly large and more suited to the show ring than the hunt. Today, all Llewellin Setters are considered English Setters, but not all English Setters are Llewellins. Most casual observers are not able to tell the difference between these two dogs.

Your English Setter is a high-energy dog who will run through mud puddles, bushes, and shrubs and may even roll in a pile of bear poop or two. For this very reason, your dog's crate can become soiled very quickly. Do not forget that your English Setter's crate requires regular maintenance. If not maintained, it can become a breeding ground for bacteria. To avoid this from happening, regularly wash your pup's bedding in hot, soapy water and disinfect his crate using dog-friendly cleaning supplies.

If your English Setter is under 12 months of age, he should never stay inside his crate for more than two to three hours at a time. This is because your puppy cannot control his bladder and bowels for long periods at a time.

Be sure to remove any dangling ID tags, harnesses, collars, etc., as these items can easily get caught on the crate doors, causing injury or accidental strangulation.

Does my English Setter need a bed in his crate?

Generally, I start using old towels or blankets. It is not wise to put an expensive new dog bed in the crate until your English Setter is potty trained and past the teething stage, as the bed will most likely get mauled. One advantage to using towels is they are easy to wash and dry.

Does it matter where I place the crate?

Whenever possible, place your English Setter's crate in a location that is close to the main people area, such as the kitchen, living room, or family room. Your English Setter will feel more safe and secure if he can see you.

In addition, choose a place inside your house that is draft-free and does not receive direct sunlight. To create a den-like environment for your English Setter, place the crate in a corner or drape a sheet over the sides.

How to Crate Train

Make sure your attitude toward crate training your English Setter is 100 percent positive. If not, your dog will pick up on your negative feelings about his crate and feel the same way. Even though you may occasionally use your dog's crate as a time-out, it should never be used as a disciplinary tool or a jail. Your English Setter needs to view his crate as his bedroom or a safe place to retreat to when he is overwhelmed.

One of the best ways to start crate training is simply to start using the crate. Avoid making the common mistake of only using the crate when you have to go out, as this can cause your English Setter to develop a fear of being inside his crate. Introduce the crate when you will are home and use it while you are in the room with him.

If you do not handle crate training properly, your English Setter may come to fear his crate. First introductions have never been more important!

If you follow the suggestions below, your English Setter will love his crate and may even start to go into it on his own whenever he needs some quiet time or rest.

First introductions

Make your Setter's first introduction to his crate as pleasant as possible. Be sure to place a soft, fluffy blanket inside with a couple of chew toys and leave the door wide open or, if possible, remove the door. If you have a piece of blanket with the scent of your English Setter's mother, place it inside the crate to reassure your puppy that the crate is a safe place.

While your puppy is watching, throw in a few treats, then back off and give your English Setter the space he needs to explore his crate on his own. Most English Setters will immediately go into the crate after the treats and start sniffing around.

Some English Setters may be wary of their crate and may need additional enticing, such as placing food and water dishes inside. Your goal is to make your pooch feel comfortable with being inside his crate. This may take a few days. If your dog is claustrophobic, try taking the top off the crate until he gets used to the feeling of an open crate, then try placing the top back on. However long it takes, be patient with your pooch throughout the entire process.

Use during mealtimes

Once your English Setter freely enters and leaves his crate, your next goal is to get your dog comfortable with staying in the crate for longer periods of time. Use your Setter's love of food to your advantage by creating a positive association by feeding him inside the crate.

Try placing the food dish far back in the crate so that your English Setter has to go all the way inside. If your puppy is not willing to go all the way back, place his food dish toward the front of the crate. Each time you feed him, slowly move the dish back.

Closing the crate

Once your English Setter is happy to be sitting inside his crate, then it is time to practice closing the door. Throw in a few treats, and while he has his back to the door and is munching down on his treats, close the door without locking it. Once your pup is finished eating, quickly open the door. Repeat this a dozen or so times, each time leaving your puppy inside with the door closed a minute or two longer.

Extending crate time

Once your English Setter goes in and out of his crate on his own accord, then it is time to start lengthening his time inside. Start with enticing him inside with a few of his favorite treats and a chew toy or two. Once he is inside the crate, close the door. Spend a few minutes hanging out near the crate, then move out of sight by going into another room. This will get your English Setter used to being alone inside the crate with the door shut.

When you return, do not open the crate immediately; instead, sit beside the crate for a few more minutes. Slowly increase your dog's time inside the crate, being sure to reward him after each crate training session.

Leaving and returning

Once your English Setter has mastered all of the above steps without whining, then he is ready for you to leave him for a short period of time. For this stage, it is vital that you do not show any emotion or excitement.

Entice your dog into the crate with a treat and a favorite chew toy. Once he is inside, quickly praise him for being such a good boy and close the door. Go about your business in the house, then go outside, shutting the door behind you. When you come back inside, let your dog out and keep a low-key attitude and ignore any excited behavior your English Setter may be displaying.

Using the crate at nighttime

Before bedtime, take your English Setter to his designated bathroom spot outside and do not come back inside until he has relieved himself. Place the crate near where you are sleeping, so you can hear him when he wakes up to go to the bathroom. If your Setter is still a puppy, he will need to go to the bathroom approximately every two to three hours.

If your English Setter cries from inside his crate during the night, it might be difficult to discern if he is whining to go to the bathroom or whether he wants to be let out of the crate. Ignore him for a minute or two and, if he continues whining, use the word or phrase your dog associates with eliminating himself. If he gets excited, then take him to his designated bathroom spot.

If your English Setter is older, place the crate close to you, so your dog doesn't associate his crate with being socially isolated. Once your English Setter sleeps through the entire night without disturbances, then you can move the crate to another location.

If you think your English Setter is only whining to play with you, resist the urge to give in. Simply ignore him until he stops crying; otherwise, you are basically teaching your pooch that by whining loudly, he can get you to do what he wants. Never yell at your English Setter or pound on the crate, as any type of attention, especially negative, will make things worse.

Once your dog is comfortable with being left in the crate for 15 minutes at a time, you can start leaving him inside for longer periods. If he is still a puppy and not housebroken, never leave him inside his crate for more than thirty minutes at a time. A full-grown dog that is house-trained should never be left inside his crate for more than four hours at a time.

Dos and don'ts of crate training:

 DO

- Do let your dog out as soon as you get home and take him to the bathroom, as this will help your dog realize potty time comes after crate time.

 DON'T

- Do not punish your dog while he is inside the crate; otherwise, he will associate his crate with negative experiences.
- Do not leave your dog inside the crate for more than four hours at a time. Crates are NOT substitute dog sitters. Leaving your dog locked inside for an extended period of time can cause separation anxiety and depression.
- Do not make a big show over your departure. Place your dog inside the crate a few minutes before leaving, and make sure he is occupied with a toy or treat before you leave.

Potty Training Basics

Potty training your English Setter takes time, patience, commitment, and vigilance. Accidents in the house are a normal part of bringing home a puppy. It may take several weeks to a few months to successfully train your English Setter. However, by following the suggestions below, you will learn how to minimize potty accidents.

Try to maintain the routine below for two to three weeks. If your dog stops having accidents in the house, you can start giving him a little more freedom each week. Reinforce good behavior by continually rewarding your English Setter for going in his designated spot.

> *If a dog or pup has an accident in the house, it is the owner's fault, not the dog's. Watch your dog—don't let it go off on its own. Take the dog out a lot, especially the first few weeks. Don't rush it—let the dog find its own place and go. Once it does, play with the dog and give it a treat; don't just snatch the Setter up and take it back in. Make the act of going potty outside rewarding. As soon as the dog goes, it's time for fun and treats! It will pick up on that the first day.*
>
> SHELLEY AND STEVE GARLAND
> *PineWalker English Setters*

Establish a routine and be consistent in sticking to the following suggestions:

Take your puppy outside frequently. Plan on taking your English Setter outside at least every two hours, including right after he wakes up from a nap, during and after playing, and after eating and drinking.

Pick a bathroom spot outside. Choose a convenient location inside your house or outside to be your English Setter's bathroom spot. If you clean up an accident inside of the house, after disinfecting the area correctly (as discussed later in this chapter), take the soiled paper towels and rags to the bathroom spot. The scent will help your English Setter recognize the area where you want him to eliminate.

Reward your English Setter every time he eliminates outdoors. Generously praise or give your English Setter treats every time he eliminates outdoors, but remember to do this immediately after he has finished. Do not skip this step, as it is vital in reinforcing proper bathroom etiquette and the only way to teach your dog what you expect of him.

 **WORD OF CAUTION:** *Before rewarding him, be sure your pooch is finished going potty. Puppies are easily distracted; if rewarded too early, your English Setter may forget to finish his business until he goes back into the house.*

Put your puppy on a regular feeding schedule. What goes into your English Setter on a schedule also comes out of him on a schedule. Depending on the age of your puppy, he may need to be fed three to four times a day. By putting your puppy on a regular feeding schedule, it will be more likely he will eliminate at consistent times, making potty training easier on both of you.

Use a verbal cue. Before and while your dog is relieving himself, be sure to say the command word for bathroom — go potty — to remind him of the task at hand. Do not play with your dog until after he has relieved himself, as puppies get easily distracted and may forget they had to go to the bathroom until they go back inside the house and have an accident.

Bedtime. Bedtime does not mean you can take a break from potty training. Take turns with a family member to get up every hour or two to take your puppy outside to the bathroom. Your dog's bladder is not fully developed yet, and he will not be able to hold it all night.

Supervise, supervise, supervise. Until your English Setter is fully potty trained, avoid letting him roam about your house freely, as this will reduce any opportunities for him to have an accident inside. Use baby gates or tether him with a long leash to prevent him from wandering around unsupervised.

Do not acknowledge bad behavior. If your English Setter has an accident, simply take him to his pad or litter box. Never yell at him or tell him he is a bad dog or give him another type of punishment. Clean up his mess using an enzyme-based cleaner. Remind yourself that the reason your dog had an accident is because you were not paying attention to his signs when he needed to go to the bathroom.

Mistakes happen

Be mentally prepared for your puppy to have accidents inside the house; it is a part of potty training. Here are some suggestions when it does happen:

- Interrupt your English Setter when you catch him in the act.
- Make a startling noise or say in a firm voice, "Outside!" and take him outside right away. Praise and give your pup a treat for finishing up his business outside.
- Clean the soiled area thoroughly.
- Never punish your English Setter for eliminating inside your house. Just clean it up. Do not rub your dog's nose in it or scold him for his accident. This will only make your dog afraid of you or afraid to relieve himself in your presence. Punishing will do more harm than good.

Cleaning up after doggy accidents

Puppy accidents can be a pain in the neck, but they can easily be prevented if you clean up quickly, efficiently, and correctly. Contrary to common belief, your dog is not relieving himself inside the house out of spite or because he is impossible. The majority of potty accidents happen for one of the following reasons:

- Your puppy does not quite understand where his designated bathroom spot is.
- You are not giving your puppy frequent opportunities to go outside in his designated spot.
- Your pup suffers from a medical condition, which will be discussed below.

If you do not thoroughly clean and deodorize where your puppy had an accident, it will lead to more accidents in the same area. Simply wiping up the mess might satisfy your eyes and nose, but there is an enzymatic scent only your dog can smell that will lure him back to the same spot later on.

Follow this three-step cleaning process to deter any future potty accidents:

1. **Protect your own paws:** Before cleaning up your dog's mess, make sure to wear gloves to protect yourself from potential urine and fecal pathogens, especially if your English Setter is not fully vaccinated yet.

2. **Remove the mess:** For any type of accident, pick up any solids with a paper towel or baggy and blot up (do not rub) any excess liquid. Once you have removed the bulk of the mess, follow up by using damp towels or rags to gently blot away the rest of the smaller residue.

3. **Use a good enzymatic neutralizer for doggy accidents:** Avoid using any ammonia-based cleaning products, as they may enhance the urine smell, which will make the spot irresistible for your puppy. The best cleaning products will not mask the scent or simply clean up the accident; they will neutralize the enzymes that entice your dog to pee or poop in that same spot. Look for products that are specifically designed for cleaning up after dogs.

When potty training relapses

Nothing can be more disheartening than to discover your well-behaved Setter regressing to bad bathroom manners. If your English Setter is suddenly relieving himself indoors again, there's probably a good reason.

- **Medical problems** – Bathroom accidents may be a sign of medical conditions, such as urinary tract infections or parasites. Your veterinarian will be able to rule out any possible medical issues.

- **Submissive/excitement urination** – Some English Setters, especially younger ones, may temporarily lose bladder control when they become overly excited. Often, this occurs during greetings or playtime. Involuntary urination or defecation is not a house-training issue, as your dog simply has no control over it and is unaware that he just soiled himself.

- **Hormonal behavior** – As your English Setter matures, he will undergo hormonal changes. Marking territory is a common behavior trait for both male and female dogs. If your dog is marking inside the house, then return to the first steps of house-training. If the problems persist, you can consider using a belly band designed to prevent him from marking.

A belly band for dogs looks like a big Band-Aid or diaper that wraps around your English Setter's rear girth. Often, the belly band has a waterproof shell with an absorbent liner, which prevents any unwanted accidents in your house. Most styles are reusable and machine washable.

- **Climate changes** – During the warmer summer months, your pooch may spend more time outside and, therefore, be able to go potty whenever and wherever he pleases. But on the other

Photo Courtesy of
Dawn Gode

hand, during the colder winter months, your dog may need to be reminded of inside bathroom etiquette.

- **New environment** – Just because your dog is housebroken in your house does not guarantee that he will know how to act when placed in a new setting. If you are traveling or visiting a friend's house, go back to the basic house-training methods until you can trust your English Setter again.
- **Fear or anxiety** – If your English Setter is afraid of loud noises such as fireworks or thunderstorms, he may lose control of his bladder and/or bowels. If this happens, try to isolate the sounds that frightened him and help him learn to associate good memories with those noises.

Tell-tale signs your English Setter needs to go to the bathroom

Puppies under the age of four months do not have enough muscular control to hold the urine or feces. The instant they have to go to the bathroom, they go. If you wait for any tell-tale signs that your little Setter has to go, you will be too late. Instead, you need to anticipate your puppy's needs.

As mentioned before, your baby English Setter will need a bathroom break as soon as he wakes up or after munching a few treats. Puppies also need to relieve themselves after a few minutes of playtime. You are much better off giving your English Setter too many potty breaks than too few because the more often he has accidents inside, the harder it will be to potty train your puppy.

There are some tell-tale signs that indicate a dog of any age has to go to the bathroom. By learning to read your dog's body language, you can learn to tell when he needs to relieve himself. Watch for the following signs to prevent accidents:

- **Sniffing the floor** – Dogs will sniff out an area to go potty. If your English Setter starts sniffing the floor or around your furniture, immediately take him to his designated area and praise him for going potty there.
- **Turning in circles while sniffing the floor** – Sniffing the floor might just mean your pup is searching for something to eat. If he starts turning around in circles while sniffing, however, then

he probably has to poop. Pick him up as fast as you can and get him to his bathroom spot. Again, praise him for a job well done.

- **Barking, scratching, or standing at the door** – Puppies generally are very vocal about when they need to go. If your English Setter starts barking and staring in the direction of the door or his pee pads, then take him to his spot immediately.
- **Whining** – If whining is combined with any of the above behaviors, your dog most likely needs to go potty. Younger dogs who still have not mastered housebreaking will often just sit and cry to tell you they need to go really badly.

Understanding Doggy Language

> *I talk to my dogs. I carry on conversations with them. I ask them questions. I test them by giving commands even when I do not need them to respond. I use this to confirm they understand and remember. I feel like the pups I raise understand the conversations I have them with. I talk to them, and they talk back in their own way. I have not experienced this with other breeds. A new owner should expect the pup to have a great capacity to learn and should not be afraid of asking a lot out of the dog.*
>
> JIM BROADNAX
> *Southern Setters*

Understanding what your dog is trying to tell you will help you develop a deeper bond of trust and respect. Plus, it will help you predict your pup's behavior and prevent issues before they even occur. To communicate better with your English Setter, here are some tips on reading dog body language.

Tail wagging – Tail wagging is frequently misinterpreted. Pet owners believe a wagging tail means their dog is happy, which is often true, but it can also mean a dog is in pain, aroused, nervous, or overstimulated. To decipher your English Setter's emotions, look at the wag speed and direction as well as the position.

> **EXAMPLE** *A fast, twitch-like wag generally means your English Setter is aroused, alert, and possibly irritated. A long, slow, side-to-side tail wag shows your pooch is relaxed and happy to see you.*

Tail position – Even though your English Setter's tail may be stubbed, it still holds clues about his emotional state. If you get to know your dog's neutral tail position, it will be easier to recognize when his emotions have shifted.

> **EXAMPLE** *If your dog's tail is pointing to the ground or tucked between his legs, he may be stressed or scared. If your dog's tail is pointed up, it means he is assertive, confident, and perhaps even aggressive. If your English Setter is relaxed, he will hold his tail in a neutral position.*

Posture – Your dog's posture can tell you a lot about his mood and intentions. A common behavior in Setters and other gundogs is a raised paw, which is a pointing behavior that indicates nearby prey. But it can also indicate your dog is uncertain about a situation.

> **EXAMPLE** *If your dog shifts all of his weight forward as if he is going to lurch, it is a clear indication something has captivated his interest. Or if he is in the same position but growling, it could mean he is being protective or even aggressive. If your dog is cowering and hunched toward the ground, he is trying to look smaller and submissive.*

Facial expressions – Your English Setter has some very expressive facial expressions, but they can be easy to misinterpret. For example, humans tend to yawn when tired or bored, but dogs yawn when they are stressed out.

> **EXAMPLE** *Lip-licking may be an indication your dog thoroughly enjoyed his meal, but it can also be an indication he is anxious. Ever notice your English Setter smiling? If your pup's smile is accompanied by a loose and wiggly posture, then he is trying to tell you he is happy. On the other hand, if his smile is more of a snarl with teeth and growling, then your pooch is not a happy camper.*

How Do You Become the Alpha?

> "
> *Your Setter will be far more interested in what its nose smells and in what it wants than it will be interested in you. You have to be more interesting, smell more interesting, and offer something the dog can't get on its own. Think about training a cat—it's quite similar. Setters know what you want, and they may or may not do it—depending on what else has their attention at the moment.*
>
> SHELLEY AND STEVE GARLAND
> *PineWalker English Setters*
> "

Wolves operate as a social hierarchy, with one leader and his or her followers. The alpha or pack leader is often the strongest and establishes the rules for the rest of the pack. Just because your English Setter is domesticated and docile does not mean he has lost his hierarchical instinct. Trust me; your innocent-looking Setter will push the boundaries to see who is the boss.

English Setters may be easy to train, but they will attempt to be the alpha dog. Your English Setter will not do it by fighting or snarling his way to the top, but he will do it by charming you into doing things his way. If you want your Setter to be a joy to live with, you need to be the one in charge.

Your English Setter has to know that you are in charge, and he must obey your commands. Being the alpha leader does not give you or anyone the right to punish or physically hurt your dog. By being the leader, you are simply establishing that your rules protect your dog. A word of caution: if you lose your patience and get visibly upset with your dog, in the eyes of your English Setter, you have lost your position as the alpha leader.

You will discover that your Setter will gravitate toward whoever is in charge. However, maintaining dominance is easier said than done. During your dog's adolescent years, he will test your dominant position before deciding to be a submissive, obedient dog.

If you are wondering if your dog sees you as the boss or alpha dog, ask yourself if you relate to any of these situations:

- Your dog walks over to the treat jar and starts to whine.
- Your English Setter does not move off the couch or floor when asked to move.
- Your pooch does not come when repeatedly called.
- Your pup defends his possessions and will not let you near them.

Your Setter drops a toy at your feet when he wants to play.

If you answered yes to any one of these questions, then your English Setter is giving you commands and does not see you as his boss.

Before you can prevent dominant behavior, you need to recognize when your dog is trying to be dominant or when he is just acting like a rambunctious teenager or is very excited.

- **Never feed your dog before you eat** – The alpha dog always eats first. If your dog does not see you eat, at the very least, you should make him wait before he gobbles up his kibble.
- **Walk through doors or gates before your dog does** – You will need to get the whole household on board for this one. Each family member should let you go through the door or gate first,

and if they are alone with the dog, then they should go through first and then the dog.

- **Walk ahead of your dog on walks** – In a pack, the alpha dog walks at the front of the pack and leads the rest of the dogs. Once your dog is leash trained, you will need to take the lead and not vice versa.

These suggestions will help rein in your English Setter and make sure you stay in control:

Establish the rules and limitations

English Setters are extremely intelligent, which means your dog will challenge your authority. Never physically punish your dog; instead, firmly correct any bad behavior by redirecting his attention to appropriate behavior, such as chewing on a toy instead of your furniture.

EXAMPLE *The moment your dog is allowed to come and go as he pleases, he is basically telling you that he is the boss. This even applies to lying on the floor. Alpha dogs will never walk around members of the pack. If your English Setter is in your way, gently tap him with your foot and remind him where his spot is for napping.*

Be consistent

A good alpha leader is fair and makes the rules clear through consistent communication. Have a family meeting with everyone in your household to decide on the ground rules for your English Setter and make sure everyone is diligent in enforcing them. Your dog can be submissive to two or more humans, but he will favor one over the other when listening to commands.

Remember that being an alpha leader is not about punishing your dog with excessive force. If you are not consistent and fair, you will never see the results you want.

> **EXAMPLE** *If your English Setter is going to understand what is expected of him, the entire family needs to be on the same page. If one person says, "Sit," and another says, "Sit down," your puppy is going to be very confused, and it will take twice as long to teach him this command.*

Establish a routine

Your English Setter loves routine! The structure of a well-established routine is the best gift you can give your dog as it teaches him what to expect each day. Be consistent with feeding times, daily walks, naps, and bathroom breaks. Your English Setter will thrive with a daily routine, as he will not need to worry or wonder what is or is not about to happen next.

> **EXAMPLE** *Sticking to a regular bathroom schedule while house-training will prevent accidents in the house. If a dog feels a certain urgency to go to the bathroom, he is more likely to "hold it" if he knows and trusts that you are going to be giving him an opportunity soon to relieve himself.*

Stay calm yet assertive – In nature, the alpha dog takes charge of every situation by taking the lead. He is not nervous or doubtful. Remember, your English Setter is a highly sensitive dog and picks up on your emotions. If you are uncertain or fearful, your dog will interpret it as a sign of weakness. He will think he needs to protect you and become your leader.

Being the alpha dog does not mean being aggressive, cruel, or physical. You should never shout or scream at your dog. You would never hit your children or scream in their faces when setting boundaries, and you should never do this to your dog. Be calm but direct.

> **EXAMPLE** *If your English Setter starts chewing on your furniture, say a firm NO. Then distract him with a more appropriate chew toy. Once he is chewing on the toy, praise and reward him.*

Common questions about alpha dog dominance

What does it mean when your English Setter puts his paw on you?
There are a few reasons why your pup may place his paw on you. Perhaps, your pooch is demanding your attention or telling you he thinks it is time for dinner. Experts state that your dog is showing dominance because he is telling you what to do. Even though this type of behavior may seem cute and affectionate, it should be discouraged. Instead, follow your regular feeding regimen and give your English Setter plenty of attention.

However, if you are petting your English Setter when he puts his paw on you, he is simply returning the affection, and this is perfectly acceptable behavior.

What does it mean when your dog is sitting on you?
Generally speaking, your dog sitting on your lap is not a sign of dominance. It is a gesture of good faith and your dog's way of telling you he wants to be close to you. But if he barks or growls at other pets or family members while sitting on your lap, then this could be a sign that he is taking on the dominant role and you need to be more assertive.

Should your dog sleep in your bed?
If you like sharing your bed with your dog and your dog is potty trained, it is unlikely it will cause him to take on the alpha role. However, be aware that humans and dogs have different sleep patterns, and English Setters are natural spreaders. This behavior may affect your sleeping pattern, in which case it is recommended to avoid this behavior from day one.

Rewarding Positive Behavior

In the 1980s, a dog trainer named Ian Dunbar developed a reward-based obedience training program. Ian Dunbar is considered by many to be the "father of positive reinforcement training." Dunbar's methods revolutionized the dog training industry so that there was no longer a need to use force, cruelty, or punishment. Positive reinforcement focuses on rewarding right behaviors and ignoring bad behaviors.

Fear aggression often results from force/punishment-based training. This fear aggression is even more common in dogs that have a soft personality, such as your English Setter. A fearful dog may lash out at the first sign of fear, which often means biting, as that is your dog's only real option for self-defense.

Positive reinforcement is one of the most effective ways to train your English Setter. When using this method, you give your pooch a reward to reinforce good behavior. For example, you ask your English Setter to sit, and he immediately does it, so you give him a treat. You are rewarding his good behavior.

Positive reinforcement teaches your dog that positive actions equal rewards. This reward can be in the form of verbal praise, scratching behind his ears, a game of fetch, or a delicious treat. Your dog's brain observes the cause and effect. He realizes, "If I sit, I get spoiled! Wow, I need to sit every time they ask me!" And practice makes perfect.

It might take a few practice sessions for your English Setter to notice the pattern of COMMAND + OBEDIENCE = REWARD. If you want to get the most out of positive reinforcement training, there are a few Dos and Don'ts to follow:

 DO

Immediately reward your English Setter's good behavior

Despite the fact that your English Setter is highly intelligent, he has a short attention span and lives in the moment. This means you will need to reward your pup's good behaviors immediately. For example, if you are house-training your Setter, be sure to reward him every time he does his business outside.

Keep training sessions short and fun

Your goal is to teach your English Setter that good things happen when he obeys you. Make training sessions short, fun, and positive — leaving each class on a good note. For example, if your pooch struggles at learning a new command, end the session by asking him to perform a command he has already mastered.

Wean from treats

Treats are an excellent tool to motivate your English Setter in the beginning, but you will eventually want to wean him off all of those extra treats and switch to more praise and affection. Over time, your dog will forget about those high-calorie treats and just want to please you.

 DON'T

Make it complicated

Keep commands simple and clear. Instead of teaching your English Setter to "sit down here," simply say, "Sit." Choose specific and simple commands.

Be inconsistent

It is useless to reward your dog for staying off the couch but then later let him come on the couch for a cuddle. This type of behavior will confuse your English Setter, and he will not be able to decipher what you actually want. Additionally, everyone in your household needs to understand and abide by the rules for your dog; otherwise, he may run himself ragged trying to figure out how to behave with each member of your family.

Stop correcting your English Setter

Many pet parents assume that positive reinforcement means they cannot say no to their dogs. This is not true. If your English Setter is acting out of sorts, a firm NO is one of the best ways to correct his bad behavior. Of course, you should never yell, scold, hit, grab, or hurt your English Setter in any way.

How to Reward Your English Setter

Positive reinforcement creates the ideal environment for your English Setter to learn. Since there is no verbal or physical punishment involved, he can relax. Studies have shown that relaxed dogs learn faster and perform better. Positive reinforcement focuses on building a bond between you and your dog based on mutual respect. Your English Setter wants to do the right thing so that he gets a reward or two.

Knowing which rewards to give your Setter can make training sessions more stimulating and fun for both you and your dog. Here are several ways to reward your pup's good behavior:

Praise and attention

There is nothing your English Setter loves more than being praised and getting attention from you. A pat on the chest or a scratch under his ears is just as rewarding for your dog as a handful of treats. Instead of giving him your undivided attention, make him work for it first.

EXAMPLE *Ask your English Setter to sit down. Once he does what you have requested, then give him some cuddle time. If he does not do what you requested, then walk away, and when you return, try again. This exercise teaches your pooch that certain actions do or do not generate attention.*

Games

Often, pet owners forget that games are another fun way to reward their pups. Initiate a game your dog enjoys immediately after your dog does something which pleases you. Games stimulate your dog's brain in the same way as yummy treats.

EXAMPLE *Ask your pooch to sit, and once he sits, offer him the ball and start playing fetch. During the game, you can teach him the command Leave It or Drop It. Once he drops the ball, tell him to sit down again and when he does, start playing fetch again. Your English Setter will love this method, and it will reinforce proper behavior.*

Treats

Treats are one of the most popular rewards for positive reinforcement, as they are fast and easy to dispense. Plus, it is gratifying to see our little four-pawed companions happily devour their snacks. However, the downside to treats is they are high in calories, which can be an issue if your English Setter has a weight problem.

 *Treats are ideal for training sessions with your English Setter when you are teaching him to learn a new behavior or command.*

> 66
>
> *The English Setter breed is a very soft breed and does not respond well to heavy hand or yelling. You can teach your Setter the basic commands in no time at all, as long as you do this over very short sessions with low voice tones and no yelling. The Setter loves to be rewarded with affection and treats for completing a task. If you yell at or raise your hand to this breed, it will shut down on you and will not respond well. Be gentle and loving all the time, but be consistent. This breed will try you.*
>
> HOYT RORRER
> *Hallowed Ground Gun Dogs*
>
> 99

Picking the Right Treats

Food is a powerful motivator for your English Setter, which is why it is an essential element for obedience training.

With obedience training, you are asking your Setter to understand a verbal or visual cue and then perform the desired behavior. This may seem pretty straightforward to you, but for your pooch, it can seem extremely complicated. This is because dogs do not communicate this way naturally. However, by harnessing the power of something very primal for your English Setter — food — you will be able to make learning a new command much easier for him.

Picking the right treat to motivate and encourage your English Setter is essential. Enticing treats for dogs come in a wide assortment of flavors, sizes, textures, and shapes. Some training sessions require a more appetizing reward with a stronger scent, such as meat and cheese.

> **"**
>
> *English Setters are not always biddable dogs due to their independent nature, but with positive reinforcement, they can easily be taught basic obedience. I warn new puppy owners that using kibble or store-bought treats may not be enough of an incentive while training a puppy; they may need to use more high-value rewards during training sessions.*
>
> JULIA CRAWFORD
> *Crown Setters*
>
> **"**

However, many treats your English Setter loves are often high in fats and sugars. These fats and sugars may be a hidden cause of weight gain, health issues, or dental problems.

It can be easy to lose track of the number of treats you hand out throughout the course of the day. Depending on your English Setter's activity level, a 10-pound puppy may burn only 300 calories each day. If one medium-sized doggy biscuit contains roughly 20 to 30 calories, just two or three of these can quickly become an overindulgence.

- Choose treats that are specially formulated for dogs to avoid tummy upset.
- Choose treats that have added nutrients or benefit your dog's teeth.
- Keep track of the calories you give your dog each day in treats and subtract these from his total daily caloric intake.
- Try to keep treats under 10 percent of your dog's daily intake.

Remember, your goal is to reinforce whatever type of behavior preceded the treat, so be careful not to unintentionally reward hyperactive

*Photo Courtesy of
Stuart Casey*

behavior. Wait until your English Setter is calm and in the right frame of mind to reward him.

Reward each step toward the desired behavior. Many new pet owners make the mistake of waiting until their dog performs the entire command before giving the treat. You want to reward progress, no matter how insignificant it seems.

For example: if you are trying to teach your English Setter to sit, but he only lowers his butt partially, still give him a treat and generous praise. When he does it again, give him another treat. Eventually, your English Setter will associate the cue word with sitting and then getting a yummy treat.

Due to the wide variety of treats available, try to make wise choices. Be sure to read the ingredient label and check for fat content. Ask your veterinarian for recommendations about the best type of treats to use for rewards for your English Setter. Here are some useful tips to help you choose the best reward for different training situations:

- **Small-sized treats** – Smaller-sized treats can quickly be gobbled up, making them ideal for keeping your English Setter motivated and attentive during training sessions. If your dog spends too long chewing a treat between repetitions, cut the treat in half.

- **Soft and smelly treats** – Soft, smelly treats will be your English Setter's favorite treats. These treats are better suited for training your dog to do more complex commands, such as "roll over" or "leave it." Or perhaps you have stepped up your pup's training sessions to a public area with more distractions; this type of treat will keep him motivated.
- **Chewy treats** – Some training sessions will need the treat to last a little longer, such as crate training or learning to stay still on the couch. For these occasions, a chewy treat is ideal as it keeps your dog distracted for a longer period of time.
- **Switch it up** – Dogs can become bored with the same old treat. For training, mix a bunch of different treats together in a baggie to keep your English Setter intrigued, especially if he is struggling to learn a new command.

Clicker Training – It Really Works

> *Positive-reinforcement training with a clicker is best. An English Setter likes praise. They have a naturally soft demeanor.*
>
> JENNY KURZ
> *Wild Bird Setters*

In the late 1990s, clicker training began to gain popularity as an effective alternative to cruel and negative training methods that relied heavily on pain, fear, and intimidation. Unlike traditional training techniques, clicker training is an easy and effective training method that works on dogs of all ages, including older dogs.

Clickers and markers are some of the fastest ways to create a common language with your English Setter. A clicker (or a marker) is often combined with other positive reinforcement methods. Your English Setter does not know what you want him to do, so you need to mark his behavior. A clicker marks the exact behavior you approve of and want the dog to repeat.

What is a clicker?

A clicker is a small, handheld device. It has a thin metal strip inside that makes a distinctive clicking sound whenever you push down on the button. You can find a good-quality clicker at most pet supply stores; an added bonus is that they are quite inexpensive. If you prefer, you can download an app on your phone that duplicates the clicking sound.

In positive reinforcement, we use a short marker word to show our approval. A common marker word used by many trainers is "Yes!" So, when you ask your English Setter to sit, the second his butt hits the ground, you would say, "Yes!" The clicking noise takes the place of a marker word. The clicking sound is faster than you can say, "Yes," much more effective than training with treats, and healthier for your dog's waistline.

The clicker allows you to communicate effectively with your dog by showing him exactly what you like about his behavior and solves the problem of having to dig a treat out of your pocket in time to reward him. In clicker training, the clicking sound over time will replace your "yes" of approval. When you ask your English Setter to sit down, the instant his butt hits the ground, you activate the clicker, followed with a reward as quickly as possible.

How to use a clicker:

1. Choose a calm and quiet place to help your English Setter stay focused without any distractions, such as your backyard. Choose a moment when your dog is hungry, preferably before mealtime. Do not forget to have a handful of treats in your hand or pocket.
2. Teach your Setter the meaning of the click. Click the device, immediately say the marking word, and give him a treat or two. Repeat two or three times each day until he associates the sound with a treat.
3. Start using the clicker in training sessions to reinforce good behavior. Once your English Setter learns the positive effects of the clicking sound, the noise starts acting as a reward in itself.

Once you and your dog have mastered clicker training, you can move on to more complicated commands and even tricks.

A clicker creates an unmistakable, distinct sound that only occurs when you are actually holding the clicker and training your dog.

A further advantage to using a clicker over a marker word is that neutral sounds, such as the clicker eliminate the stress or confusion your English Setter may feel around trying to figure out your mood.

How to use the clicker for basic and advanced commands:

1. At the exact moment your English Setter completes the desired action, press the clicker. Then reward him with a treat and with praise.
2. Be aware that if you do not click at the exact moment your dog performed the new behavior, he might not associate the new action with the treat.
3. For more complicated commands or tricks, you can click and reward for small steps toward the desired behavior. For

example, if you are teaching him to fetch the ball and bring it back to you, click for fetching, then click again when your English Setter brings the ball back.

A clicker will not replace high-calorie treats, but with time you will be able to wean your Setter off them, as the sound of the clicker is a reward in itself. However, this does not mean you can stop using treats. You will still need to give your dog an occasional treat; otherwise, the clicker will stop being as effective.

If you have an older English Setter with teeth or weight issues, a healthier option to doggy treats is to give him a few pieces of unseasoned cooked chicken or turkey breast during the clicker training sessions. Remember, your dog lives in the moment, so when you click the clicker, immediately give him a treat, so he can learn to associate the clicking sound with a treat.

Test your English Setter when he is playing or distracted by clicking the clicker. If he immediately stops whatever he is doing and looks at you, then you know he is ready to start being weaned off treats. If your pooch does not acknowledge the sound, then you know you need to spend extra time training with the click-treat combination.

One of the most common mistakes with clicker training is that pet owners forget to give their dog verbal praise. Your Setter will associate the clicker sound with a yummy reward, but he still needs your verbal approval.

Tips for successful clicker training
- Try using a clicker with a wristband, as it will stay tethered to you and prevent you from accidentally dropping it.
- Place the treats in a baggie. You only have two hands, and a baggie allows you to keep the treats close at hand yet still hands-free.
- Keep all of your clicker-training sessions short and sweet. English Setters learn better in bursts of five to seven minutes instead of longer sessions.
- The clicker is not a remote control to cue your English Setter into doing something. The clicker only marks the moment your dog does something worth rewarding.

- Keep the clicker in a safe place, out of reach of mischievous children who will think it is a toy.

Gundogs and clicker training

There is some debate about gundogs and clicker training. Some trainers believe clicker training is a betrayal of traditional training methods. On the other hand, other force-free trainers consider clicker training to be a valuable tool when training your gundog.

More and more hunters prefer using a clicker while training their English Setter, as this gets them predisposed to the sound of the safety pin of the shotgun. When the dog hears the click, he will instantly become alert and focus on the direction of the gun barrel.

Clicker training is based on a scientific principle called operant conditioning, which means that the animal's actions can reliably be predicted by the chance of those actions being repeated over and over again. Undesired behaviors are essentially ignored and never rewarded, naturally extinguishing bad habits.

There are some challenges involved in clicker training your gun dog, but it is not impossible. Successful clicker training has to be combined with rewards. For example, if you want to train your English Setter for off-lead walks in the woods with lots of gamey scents, such as rabbits and other things to chase, you will need to have an even more attractive treat prepared for your dog than the ones he could catch for himself.

Many hunters start off by using a long line for the first several weeks before letting their dog off the lead. However, a long line can be difficult to manage for a novice trainer in certain terrains and can easily become tangled up in bushes and shrubs.

There are many opportunities in the field for distractions; therefore, clicker training must be introduced before field training and carefully monitored to maintain high standards.

Mental Stimulation

Your Setter is extremely intelligent, which means he will get bored easily. A bored English Setter may develop destructive behaviors, such as barking, chewing on furniture, digging up the garden, or trying to escape from the yard.

English Setters often start exhibiting boredom by barking when their daily physical and mental stimulation needs are not being met. In other words, your dog barks constantly because he has nothing better to do. One of the best ways to eliminate boredom barking is by increasing your dog's stimulation.

> *English Setters are very quick to pick up new commands and are often looking to practice what they know! Be consistent in what you're trying to train and once they have the basic portion of that skill down, add in another skill!*
>
> KATIE KILLIAN
> *English Setters of the Eyrie*

Here are some creative ways to keep your English Setter mentally stimulated and keep misbehavior at bay.

Teach him a trick or two. Your English Setter will love to learn a new command or two as it will give him a mental challenge and a chance to bond with you. Once you move past the basic commands, then move on to more advanced commands. Even older dogs will benefit from training sessions, often helping them become less anxious and calmer around other dogs.

Play together. Play an interactive game together to challenge your English Setter. Keep your dog engaged with a game of doggy dominos or dog memory. If you cannot play with your dog, then give him a chew toy that lets you hide a treat inside.

Run errands with your English Setter. Even a quick errand to the mailbox, grocery store, or friend's house will leave your English Setter feeling quite stimulated. (Remember, you should never leave your dog alone in the car, even if it's just for a few minutes.) Your English Setter will absorb the new sounds, scents, and situations. By the time you get home, your pup will fall right asleep, even though the outing was not physically taxing.

Give him a task to do. Your English Setter was originally bred for hunting. It's in his blood. A hearty game of fetch or Frisbee will leave your English Setter feeling satisfied. Take a tennis racket and a few balls to the park and hit the ball as far as possible; your English Setter will bring your ball back again and again, like it's his job.

Socialize your pooch. Every time your pooch meets a new person or fellow canine, he is being exposed to new butts to sniff, new faces, and new sights. Taking your English Setter to a dog park gives him an excellent opportunity to engage his senses. Or take your dog for a walk down Main Street; he will love all the attention from everyone wanting to stop and pet him.

Rotate your dog's toy collection. You would not enjoy playing with the same toy day after day. So, why should you expect your dog to love the same toy he has been chewing on for months? Give your English Setter a toy to play with, and when he becomes bored with it, replace it with another one. Keep all of his toys in a box and rotate them out. Your pup will love it when you switch up his toys, just as if he is getting a brand-new toy.

CHAPTER 7

Expanding on Basic Training

Training your English Setter will teach him basic good manners, such as politely greeting guests when they arrive, walking properly on the leash, and coming when called. By teaching your dog these basic commands, you are setting him up for a happy and safe life. Plus, a well-mannered dog is loved by all!

Many of the misunderstandings between dogs and humans are related to a communication gap. However, obedience training takes time; think of it as a marathon and not a short sprint. Some commands your pooch may learn in a day or two, and others may take a few weeks to master.

Benefits of Proper Training

> **"**
>
> *The sooner you start training, the better! Make sure the pup understands what you want. Take a simple exercise and make sure the dog has it down pat before you add on to it. They also train us with their sad eyes and the sorry, pathetic look they give us! If you ask your Setter to do something, make sure the dog doesn't get away with not doing it. If they learn they can just give you 'the look' and then not have to do something, they won't. You'll then get a pup that will try to outsmart you all the time.*
>
> JANIS FLAHERTY
> *Blu-Star English Setters*
>
> **"**

Photo Courtesy of
Scott Berg - Berg Brothers Setters

If your dog is constantly disobedient or exhibits serious behavioral issues, it can become a source of stress and discouragement for both you and your English Setter. Training your dog is your responsibility, not just for your peace of mind but for your dog's best interests.

Your English Setter's behavior reflects directly on you as his owner. No matter your dog's age or temperament, he can benefit from a little extra instruction.

Here are five reasons why you need to train your English Setter:

Training benefits both you and your English Setter. When you train your dog, he is not the only one reaping the benefits. Regular training sessions with your pooch help you to understand your dog's needs and personality, making you an even better owner.

Training keeps your English Setter safe. The more easily you can control your English Setter by using basic commands, the better you can protect him when unrestrained. A dog who bolts when he is off the leash is likely to run in front of a car and get hit or even escape out the front door before you are ready to leave.

Training helps your English Setter to be more sociable. Obedience training teaches your English Setter his limits, boundaries, and how to behave in social situations. As a result, other people and dogs will enjoy being around your dog.

Training makes traveling a breeze. Nobody enjoys being around a disobedient dog. A well-trained dog will obey your commands and also those of others. Training will make boarding easier, either at a kennel, a close friend's house, or a relative's home.

Because you can teach an old dog new tricks. Old dogs can learn new tricks. It is never too late to improve your English Setter's education. With a little extra patience, an older dog can learn just as well as younger dogs.

A well-behaved dog experiences less stress and anxiety, interacts better with others, and over time, will form a stronger bond with you. One of the best gifts you can give your dog is your time and energy to train him, which will make him a happier and healthier dog in the long run.

Basic Commands

> *They are intelligent and sensitive. Don't move too fast, but be consistent with your commands. Once they know what you expect, they are eager to please you.*
>
> DON OLSEN
> *Ashuelot Sunset Setters*

Your English Setter will love the chance to bond with you while learning these basic commands. It is fundamental you begin teaching your dog these commands as soon as possible, as it will help him grow up into a well-behaved dog.

If your English Setter is older, most likely he has already learned these commands in the past but may need a refresher course. Be patient with your older pooch as he may be dealing with mobility or hearing issues. Remember, training your English Setter, no matter his age, is an excellent way to spend time together and have fun!

English Setters are very intelligent and are eager to please you, so use that to your advantage. With a large dose of love and patience and a couple of dozen doggy treats, you should be able to teach your pooch to sit, come, stay, etc., in a few weeks.

Avoid training your dog when you are grumpy, upset, or irritable, as your English Setter will only pick up on your foul mood. Start training your English Setters in an enclosed area with zero distractions; as he masters different commands, move to a new environment, such as a park or a spot along your walking route.

The following commands can be combined with clicker training, as discussed in the previous chapter.

As we noted earlier, keep commands simple. Say "sit" instead of "sit down here."

When training your English Setter, pay close attention to the tone of your voice. Never yell at your dog, as he has exceptionally good ears and can hear you very well. A loud, angry voice is not going to teach him anything except the fact that you are upset. Patiently show your dog what you expect of him; speak in a soft, kind voice, and praise him affectionately.

FUN FACT

What is "Setting"?

English Setters adopt a distinctive stance while hunting, referred to as "setting." English Setters track their prey through air scenting. Once the dog locates its quarry, it "sets" or freezes and crouches down to alert the hunter of the bird's whereabouts. English Setters are often referred to as "birdy" because of their instinctive interest in birds.

Sit

If the Setter is going to be a hunting dog, it is recommended to not teach sit right away, as we want them to stand their birds on point and not sit in the field. This may require more repetition and practice, but the breeding is there for them to do it.

GREG AND CARLA FRYAR

High Fly'n Kennels

Once your dog knows this command, he will be much calmer and easier to control. Plus, the sit command is the foundation for other commands, such as "stay" and "come."

1. Hold a treat near your dog's nose.
2. Slowly move your hand up, allowing his head to follow the treat, which will cause his bottom to lower to the ground.
3. Once your English Setter is in a sitting position, say "Sit," and give him the treat and affectionately praise him.

Repeat this sequence a few times a day until your English Setter has mastered it. Then start asking your dog to sit before dinnertime, while going for walks, or in any other situation you want to teach him to be calm.

Stay

The drive to catch prey is very strong in the Setter. When the dog is scenting or sees movement, it is easily distracted and its focus is no longer on you. 'Whoa,' 'wait,' 'stop,' or any other command that requires the dog to stop immediately is necessary for its safety.

KAREN STROHMEYER

Bristle Ridge Llewellins

The stay command is similar to the sit command, as it makes your dog easier to control in certain situations. This command is handy for moments when you need your pooch to stay out of the way as you clean your house or if you do not want him to overwhelm your houseguests.

1. Tell your English Setter to sit.
2. Once he is sitting, then open the palm of your hand in front of you and say, "Stay."
3. Take a few steps back. Reward him with a yummy treat and affection if he stays sitting.
4. Gradually increase the number of steps you take backward each time before rewarding your dog.
5. Always reward your English Setter for staying still, even if it is only for a few seconds.

This command teaches your dog self-control, so do not be discouraged if it takes a little longer than you thought. Most dogs, especially English Setters, prefer to be on the move, exploring their surroundings instead of simply sitting still and waiting.

Down

This can be a challenging command to teach your English Setter, as it requires him to get into a submissive posture. Be sure to keep the training sessions for this command fun, upbeat, and positive. Also, never forget to praise and reward your dog once he successfully follows through on the command.

1. Tell your dog to sit.
2. Use a particularly delicious-smelling treat and hold it out in front of you in a closed fist.
3. Place your closed fist in front of your Setter's nose. When he sniffs it, slowly move your hand toward the floor so that he follows the treat.
4. Slide your hand along the ground in a vertical line toward you to encourage the dog's head to follow.

5. Once your English Setter is in the down position or lying down, say "Down," give him the treat in your hand, and generously praise him.

You will need to practice this command daily until your dog has mastered it. If your pooch tries to lunge toward your hand, say a firm "No" and take your hand away. Never push the dog into a down position; instead, encourage him every step of the way until he figures out how to please you.

Come

> You must teach the pup its name and to 'come.' Two of the most important commands are 'stay' and 'come here.' This can be done with a leash and then a check cord. Once you're confident the dog will come back consistently, try letting it go in a confined space, such as a fenced-in yard. Once this is accomplished you can start letting the dog run in a field for exercise or play.
>
> VINCENT GUGLIELMO
> *Chenango Valley Kennels*

This command is a godsend for times when you lose your grip on the leash or when your dog catches the scent of something and runs off before you can stop him. This command is quite easy to teach and will keep your English Setter out of trouble.

1. Put a leash and collar on your English Setter.
2. Get down to your dog's level and say, "Come," while gently tugging on the leash.
3. When your pup comes to you, be sure to reward him with treats and affection.

Once your English Setter has mastered coming to you with the leash on, then attempt the same sequence without the leash and in a safe, enclosed space.

Off

"Off" can easily become confused with "down." The Off command is used to teach your English Setter not to jump on people or to climb on certain furniture. The goal is for your dog to keep all four paws on the ground.

1. When your dog jumps up, say a firm "Off" and point to the floor. Once he is standing with all four paws on the ground, reward his good behavior.
2. If you find your English Setter on the couch, and he is not allowed to be there, say a firm "Off" and encourage him to come to you. When he comes, reward him with a treat and praise.

Another way to avoid this bad behavior is by simply ignoring it. When the dog jumps up on you, turn around and act like you are leaving. Wait a few seconds, and then try again. Reward your dog when he does not jump up on you.

Leave It

This command can keep your English Setter safe when his curiosity gets the better of him, such as when he smells something on the ground that may be potentially dangerous for his health if he eats it. The goal of this command is to teach your dog that he will get something even yummier if he ignores the other item.

1. Place a treat in each of your hands.
2. Open one of your hands with the treat inside and say, "Leave it."
3. Close your fist again; ignore any behaviors such as licking, sniffing, pawing, or barking at your hand to get the treat.
4. Once the dog stops these behaviors, give him the treat from the other hand.
5. Repeat until your English Setter moves away from the fist when you say, "Leave it."
6. Next, give your Setter the treat in the other hand only when he looks up at you and away from your closed fist.

It is vital to maintain constant eye contact with your English Setter during this command session. Make sure you always have a smelly, yummy treat in your second hand, and in the other hand, just an ordinary piece of kibble.

How to Teach Your Dog to Walk on the Leash

> *English Setters love going for walks with their people, so teach them early to walk nicely on a leash by doing consistent, short training exercises with lots of treats and praise. We do not recommend harnesses, as these teach dogs to pull; it can be damaging to their growing bodies if they are allowed to pull.*
>
> KAYLA KOZAK
> *Kei-Rin Kennel*

Some English Setters are quick to embrace their collar and leash, while others tend to shy away from them.

Whether you live in an urban or rural setting, your English Setter is going to need to learn to use a collar and leash. Often the breeder will introduce your English Setter to a collar when he is only a few weeks old. The first thing you need to do is make sure you have all of the right equipment for training your pooch to walk on a leash.

Below is just a short overview of the different types of collars and leashes available and their uses:

Standard collar – This is your basic collar, often used to place your dog's ID tags, etc. English Setters are expert escape artists, and they will easily slip their head out of a standard collar.

Muzzle harness – Often, this type of harness is used for training sessions for show dogs. The general idea is to keep your dog from following his nose.

Back harness – This style of harness is great for smaller breeds such as your English Setter. This style of collar prevents a dog's airway from being damaged when he pulls. Also, it prevents your four-pawed friend from sliding out of his collar.

Martingale collar – This collar option is for dogs who have the tendency to pull on the leash. It is a double-looped collar, which tightens when your dog pulls on the leash. There is no need to worry about choking, as the collar only tightens enough to be uncomfortable.

Standard leash – The classic leash comes in a variety of styles and lengths. It can be a rope style or a flat band.

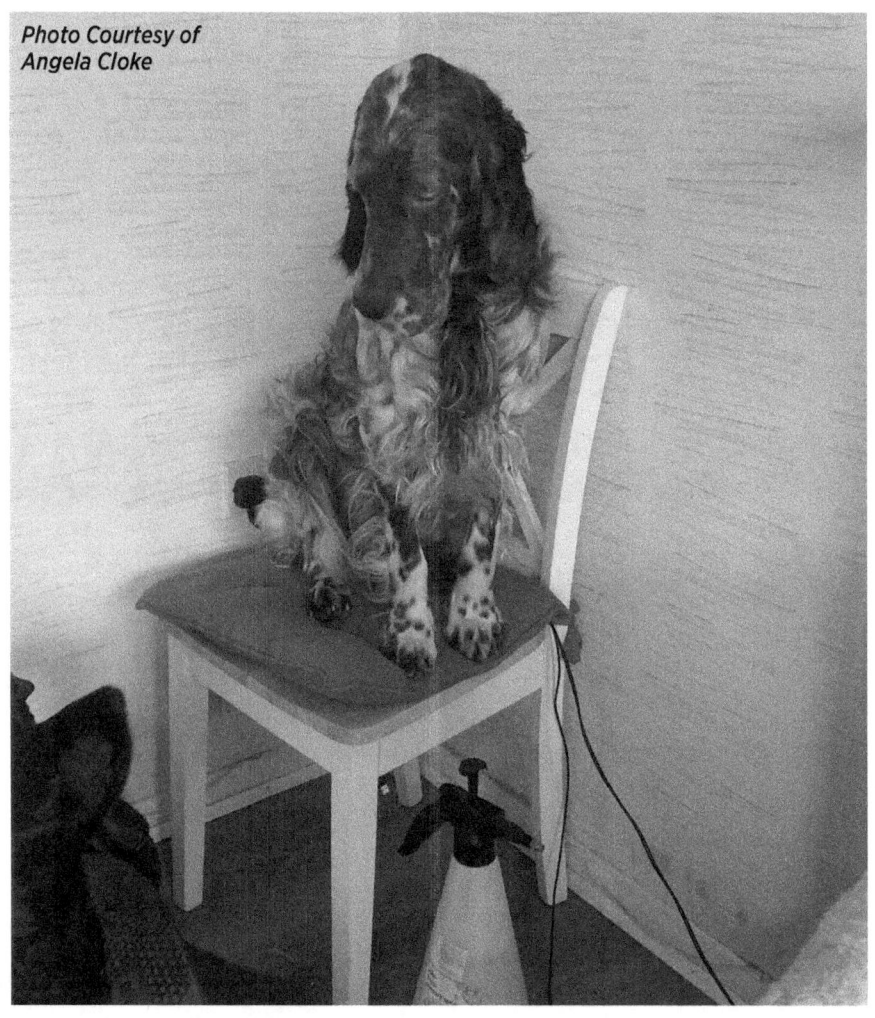

Photo Courtesy of Angela Cloke

Retractable leash – A retractable leash has a coiled-up compartment, allowing you to let out as much length as desired or lock it so your English Setter cannot go any further.

The following steps will help you train your pup to use a collar and a leash:

Go to a neutral space, such as your living room or backyard, and let your dog sniff the collar. Put the collar on your dog when he is distracted. Once he is used to the collar, attach the leash and let him run around with it behind him while in the house. Just keep an eye on him to make sure he doesn't get the leash caught on anything and possibly hurt himself.

Take your English Setter for a walk around the block or to a neighbor's house. This will allow your pooch to get used to the leash and collar while in a safe environment. If your English Setter walks without pulling, give him praise and treats.

Now you are ready for a real walk. When you start walking, if your English Setter pulls or tugs on the leash, do not painfully pull back on the leash. Just stop walking and say, "No." When your dog stops pulling on the leash, give him a reward and affection.

How to Teach Your Dog to Walk Off the Leash

> *Their drive to seek out birds also makes them unreliable off-leash. English Setter owners should have a fenced-in yard and take care in training their dogs to recall while off-leash.*
>
> JULIA CRAWFORD
> *Crown Setters*

Setters love to run, play, and explore their surroundings without feeling hindered by their leash. However, letting your energetic dog off the leash can quickly turn into a massive headache for you, not to mention be dangerous for him.

Your dog must be properly trained to behave on the leash before you even attempt training your English Setter to walk off the leash.

Consider the risks

Before you let your English Setter off the leash, you should consider some factors that may jeopardize the safety of your dog and others. For example, many cities and towns have leash laws in place to keep everyone safe. If you choose to break the law, be prepared to pay expensive fines and maybe even get a citation.

Even the best-trained dog can get distracted. A loose dog may act out of sheer instinct if he encounters another dog, cat, or prey animal. An unleashed dog may end up getting lost, be hit by a car, ingest toxins, get in a dog fight, or be attacked by a wild animal, among other things.

Also, it is important to remember that not everybody likes dogs, and some people may be terrified of a loose dog. Some dogs may sense this fear and react unexpectedly.

Photo Courtesy of Amber Vick

Master basic commands

There is no way you can completely guarantee your dog's safety when he is off the lead. However, advanced obedience training can decrease any chances of your English Setter getting hurt. You need to teach your Setter that freedom comes with obeying the rules. You need to trust that your off-leash dog will stay right by your side or can easily be called to your side.

Here is a checklist of basic commands your English Setter should have mastered before being left off the leash:

- Loose-leash walking
- Leave it
- Drop it
- Look
- Stay
- A reliable recall
- Come

Potential distractions

As your English Setter becomes more comfortable and obedient being off-leash, you can start to work your way up to more challenging environments, such as a hiking trail. Before letting your dog off the leash, make sure he is allowed to be, as many public parks or state parks have regulations for dogs. For your pup's safety, never let him off the leash in a crowded public area or around traffic, regardless of the leash laws in that area.

No matter how well trained your English Setter is, always carry a leash with you for the unexpected, such as a surprise encounter with a wild animal. Remember that your Setter has a very high prey drive, and it may be almost impossible for him to resist the temptation of following a scent.

Here are some tendencies that put your dog in danger when off the leash:

Squirrel chaser – Does your English Setter love chasing small animals such as rabbits, cats, squirrels, or grouse? Chasing after animals could cause your dog to get separated from you and perhaps even get lost.

Car chaser – Dogs that chase cars, motorcycles, or bicycles are at risk of being hit or causing a car accident.

Aggressive or hyperactive around other dogs – Dogs who are aggressive or get excited when other dogs are around can cause unwanted dog fights.

Wanderlust – Some English Setters love to explore their surroundings, and your dog's sniffer can quickly get him excited so that he runs away and completely ignores anything you say or do.

Afraid of noises – Some dogs are frightened by loud noises such as thunder, fireworks, or even a car backfiring, which may cause the dog to run off.

Training can help to minimize these tendencies, but they may never completely vanish. If you know your English Setter cannot resist a certain situation, then you will need to keep him on the leash. Remember, always put your dog's safety first.

Overcoming Common Dog Training Problems

> **"**
>
> *My advice would be to work with someone that has trained Setters. They are very different from other field dogs and require a different kind of training.*
>
> SABRINA OAKES
> *Sevenoaks English Setters*
>
> **"**

Unfortunately, when it comes to basic training cues, not every dog responds the same. Here are some suggestions on how to overcome some of the most common dog training problems.

Minimize distractions

If you are training your pooch in a dog in a new environment that is full of strange smells and new stimuli, you will not get far. Your dog's needs must be fulfilled before training. So, give your dog time to explore and sniff his new surroundings.

Readjust your goals

Always adapt to your English Setter's pace, and not the pace you wish him to go at. If your puppy cannot "stay" for 10 seconds, then readjust your goal to five seconds and reward based on his behavior. The more your dog feels like the winner and gets rewarded for his positive behavior, the faster the cue is reinforced.

The same goes for distance. If you're training your dog on recall or to "stay in place," how far can you or your dog be from each other to reasonably follow the cue? Ask yourself: what is a comfortable distance away from your dog to avoid him from being distracted? The rule of thumb is if your pooch cannot perform a cue two times in a row, then maybe you should shorten the distance to make it easier.

Do not underestimate the power of rewards

If your English Setter repeatedly ignores your treats, then your treat selection is not tempting enough. Remember, Setters are motivated by positive reinforcements, such as a mouth-watering reward. Sometimes a certain treat will lose its enticing power over time, so try something new.

Master your timing

The correct timing of your marker word or hitting that clicker just right can be difficult to master. The marker word or the clicker should not be heard while your English Setter is still moving into position or while you hand him his treat. The correct timing is just as your pooch completes the desired behavior. Consider the marking and feeding as two separate parts in rewarding your dog's behavior.

Let your English Setter decompress

Puppies and recently adopted dogs may need up to six months to fully decompress into their new environments. Focus on building a positive rapport and trusting relationship. Observe your dog's body language; if he seems tired, take a break from training and play together.

Physical discomfort

Sometimes an underlying condition, such as a sore paw or a toothache, may be the reason your pooch does not want to be touched or perform any cues. If you notice any behavior changes in your English Setter during training sessions, consult with your vet.

CHAPTER 8

Introduction to Training for Fieldwork

As long as anyone can recall, man has always fared better in his pursuit of game with the help of a canine.

English Setter – A Versatile Gundog

> " Some of the best bird dogs I have ever hunted behind have had very little to no formal training. You want to see your puppy begin to climb over tree limbs and explore all areas of the woods. Both you and the puppy have to become confident in each other's ability to have a fun time in the bird woods. Just remember, the hunter's idea of a good time needs to be watching good dog work. The English Setter's idea of a good time is spending time with its family in the bird woods and occasionally catching some bird scent.
>
> HOYT RORRER
> *Hallowed Ground Gun Dogs* "

The English Setter is typically worked in a swampy area or moorland to hunt a variety of gamebirds and small animals.

The English Setter's hunting style and characteristics hold true to that of their ancestors, by squatting to the ground in an attempt to catch the scent of their prey. Once a Setter catches a whiff of its quarry, the dog "sets" – crouching in the prey's direction with the front paw lifted off the ground. In the past, this position would allow the hunter to get close enough to throw a net over the dog and prey, but since the emergence of game shooting, this positioning allows the hunter to anticipate where the quarry will be flushed out and get in position to take a safe shot.

Why do English Setters make good gundogs?

If you have ever been lucky enough to shoot quarry with English Setters or have seen them in action, you will agree that they are a complete joy to behold. Here are some comments by experienced owners of English Setter gundogs:

The president of the English Setter Club says: "English Setters have been part of my whole life and have been part of my family's life for several generations."

Another proud owner of English Setters states, "Their keenness to find game is second to none. They also have an amazing ability to adapt to different terrains, conditions, and people."

English Setters are not headstrong, have good manners around other dogs, and naturally understand what a gun range is. They are considered to be one of the most versatile show and field dogs.

Pointing and Setting

Pointing and setting Setters tend to roam around, often out of the shotgun range of the hunter. When the dog finds a bird, he will crouch down, get into the setting position, and point toward it, often with one of his front paws lifted and his head pointing toward the bird. The hunter will walk toward the area the dog is pointing to flush out the bird.

Many hunters prefer to keep their English Setters within gun range, as the dog may spook the birds, causing errant flushes of a certain area. Even if the Setter does not retrieve, he will sniff out the downed bird, re-point the bird's location, and run down any crippled birds.

Photo Courtesy of David Weaver

Flushing

Flushing English Setters work next to the hunter, often within shotgun range, and are taught to flush the birds out into the air so they can be shot. The Setter will locate pheasants, quail, doves, grouse, ducks, etc., and flush the birds out of hiding.

Often the English Setter will establish a tight zigzag pattern that covers the immediate ground within the range of the gun and will check in with his handler frequently. Even though English Setters are not natural retrievers, they can easily be taught to retrieve the bird.

Choosing a Hunting Puppy

If you are planning on buying an English Setter, you are mostly paying for natural instinct. But before taking the plunge and getting a hunting dog, there are a few things to watch out for. Your goal should be to set yourself and your English Setter up for success, and the best way to do that is by finding yourself the best dog in the first place.

In chapter 2, we discussed how to find a reputable gundog English Setter breeder, but here are a few reminders when choosing your hunting companion.

Buy the best quality English Setter you can afford

Well-bred English Setters cost a pretty penny, as they come from a bloodline, such as the Llewellin lineage, predisposed to accomplishing a certain task. Another advantage is that this breed is highly trainable and intelligent enough to learn the job and has the disposition to handle the pressure of high-stress training.

Additionally, a well-bred English Setter comes with a health screening, which often costs the breeder money but ensures that puppies will live long and healthy lives.

The cost of the well-bred English Setter will be only a small portion of the money you will invest in your dog. Good quality food, vet visits, training (if you go the professional route), boarding, etc., will add up over the next 10 to 15 years that you own your Setter. A well-bred hunting English Setter may cost $1000 or more, but it will save thousands of dollars in vet bills later in life.

Buy an English Setter from a pedigree you want

If you want a hunting English Setter, then look for one with a field pedigree. Field-trial and hunt-test parent dogs will have been measured against other dogs by hunting standards. A field pedigree assures you that your dog will have the smarts, trainability, and natural instincts to find game.

A top-notch field pedigree will include the puppy's parents and grandparents having earned the title of Versatile Champion at least once in their life. Often, gundog breeders will be long-time members of the North American Versatile Hunting Dog Association (NAVHDA).

Finding a breeder that specializes in English Setters with the Llewellin bloodline can be tricky because, over time, some dogs have been bred with the Lavarick lineage, so be sure to do your research. If you are not interested in an English Setter from a bloodline, look for a dog that comes from hunting stock. Ideally, the breeder will let you watch the pup's parents hunting.

Choose an English Setter with genetic testing

It may cost more money to buy an English Setter who comes from parents who were genetically tested before breeding, but it will eliminate a long list of genetic mutations that can cause future health issues. Many mutations will not appear until your English Setter pup is two to three years old, such as blindness, kidney failure, and neurological disorders, just to mention a few. Genetic testing may cost you money, but it will save you time, money, and heartache in the long run.

Male vs. Female

Some hunters firmly believe that male dogs are easier to handle and better team players. And females tend to range further and are harder to control. However, other hunters believe completely the opposite when it comes to female and male English Setter gundogs.

Basic Gundog Training

> *When developing a gundog or field trial prospect, slow and steady wins the race. Plan your training, and don't let your expectations distract you from what is actually going on. Observe, understand, and proceed—when a trainer builds every new lesson on a concept the dog already understands, the journey goes a lot smoother for everyone.*
>
> JOHN MCILTROT
> *Seranoa Kennels*

Whether you are new to hunting or an experienced hunter, it can be overwhelming to raise a working English Setter, but getting started is not as challenging as it sounds. The key to training your Setter to be a hunting dog is to choose one single training method and stick with it.

Basic obedience training is essential to create a perfect hunting dog, but without exposure to actual hunting, your dog will never develop into a hunter. Your young Setter must gain experience, spending ample time actually hunting during the first two years of his life. This means you will

Photo Courtesy of Amber Vick

need to spend weeks in the field to ensure your English Setter interacts with game as often as possible.

Your English Setter will learn to hunt in the woods, not your backyard. Running through swamps, swimming across creeks, trekking through the bushes, and being exposed to different types of elements are all aspects of being a hunting dog. As your English Setter's personal trainer, you should plan on spending at least an hour in the field, two to three times each week, for your dog's first year of his life.

Raising a hunting dog takes time, energy, money, and patience. Many first-time field dog owners prefer to purchase a young, already partially trained gun dog. Many field English Setter breeders and trainers sell one- to three-year-old dogs that are already trained in obedience and have experienced one or two hunting seasons. These dogs are quite a bit more expensive than a puppy, but the initial foundation has been laid for you, and you will be able to take the dog hunting with you immediately.

Puppies
Basic obedience training is essential, as your English Setter will need to be obedient. One of the biggest mistakes first-time gun dog owners

HISTORICAL FACT
Bird Dogs

English Setters were bred to assist with bird hunting around 400 years ago and are often still used for this purpose today. The birds in question were game birds such as grouse, pheasant, and quail, but English Setters are still known to take a keen interest in birds today. Despite their laid-back demeanor, this bird dog heritage can translate into a high prey drive for some English Setters. Use caution when introducing your English Setter to small animals in your home, including cats, rabbits, or pet birds.

make is trying to rush their dog through learning a bunch of complicated commands when the dog hasn't yet mastered the basics.

Force yourself to take it slow with your English Setter pup, as he will have a very short attention span. Focus on one command at a time and work your way through all of the basics, such as sit, come, down, stay, and drop it. If you plan to use your English Setter as a pointer, you will also want to teach him the "Whoa" command.

How to teach the "Whoa" command

As with any training exercise, it is best to train according to your dog's temperament. If your English Setter has a bold personality, you may want to consider starting to train this command before he is four months of age. Before you take your Setter into the field, it is vital he knows this command and obeys it.

1. Place your English Setter on a bench and tell him, "Whoa." If he moves, physically pick him up so that his feet are off the ground. Put him back on the bench, repeat the command, and pick him up when he moves. Most dogs learn this step in a week.

2. Place your English Setter on a bench and say, "Whoa." Take a few steps back from him. The first few times, your pooch will try to follow you – but do not let him. Pick him up and place him back on the bench, but do not repeat "Whoa." Only give the command once, and reinforce it by returning the dog to the bench. Practice this step for two weeks or until he stays in place while you walk in front or behind him.

3. Place your English Setter on a short lead and have him walk beside you. Tell him, "Whoa," and then pick him up and place him on the ground when he moves or lunges.

4. Once he stays still when you pick him up after hearing "Whoa," say the command but do not pick your dog up; instead, continue to walk forward or around your dog. If he stays still, then you can try the command with the leash attached in a secure, closed-in area. Every time he disobeys and moves after hearing "Whoa," pick your English Setter up, place him back in the original spot, and repeat.

The purpose of the "Whoa" command is to teach your dog to stop moving, perhaps to avoid bumping into a bird or prevent your dog from running across the cattle grate, etc.

Before introducing a new command, backtrack to an older command that your pooch has already mastered, as this will help him be more confident, which means he will be easier to train. Do not forget to end each training session on a positive note. For your English Setter, it may involve a simple retrieve or two.

Photo Courtesy of
Scott Berg - Berg Brothers Setters

Photo Courtesy of
Karen Lishinski

Older dogs

Perhaps you have a two or three-year-old English Setter who has loads of potential but is not quite the hunting partner you desire. Often this happens because the dog was allowed to develop some bad habits when he was younger.

Bad habits are like weeds; it is difficult to keep them in check. Weeds tend to grow back unless they are uprooted, and even then, they always seem to want to grow back. Your older dog's bad habits can become a chronic issue.

If your pooch seems to fall into this category, you will need to start from the beginning. This may seem counterproductive, but you need to be 100 percent sure that your dog has mastered everything. Otherwise, his behavior will give you a constant headache. One advantage to backtracking with obedience training is that your older dog's attention span will be better than a puppy's.

Whether you have a puppy or an older pooch, you need to make time to train your English Setter daily. Training your dog does not take more than 15 minutes a day to practice different drills and commands. Short training sessions are preferable over long, once-a-week sessions.

Measure progress

I find it helpful to keep a ledger of my weekly and monthly goals for my English Setter, as well as our daily progress. It is easy to forget where your English Setter is during the training process, and notes in the ledger will help you. If you keep a ledger, you can compare your dog's performance from one day to another.

Keeping a ledger and paying attention to your Setter's skills will help you to grasp his strengths and weaknesses. If you notice that your pup is a little slower at learning things, then it is a sign that you need to slow down. If your dog is struggling, do multiple training sessions each day with ample play breaks between drills, and your dog will eventually retain the commands he is struggling to learn.

The E-Collar Debate

> *Most English Setters (including show Setters) love to hunt. However, they are emotionally 'soft' dogs and do not do well with heavy-handed trainers or those who rely on electronics to instill new lessons. I highly suggest you ask around and find a trainer who has worked successfully with Setters.*
>
> LIN SELL, MD
> *Linwood English Setters*

An e-collar is an electric training aid, often referred to as a shock collar, zap collar, or remote training collar. The collar has a wireless receiver that the dog wears close to his neck, and the wireless remote may be controlled by you or a stationary location. The idea is to teach the dog the difference between good and bad behavior by sending an electronic vibration through the collar.

E-collars use something called electronic stimulation, which is the same technology used if you have ever visited a physical therapist or chiropractor. The electronic stimulation is not an actual electronic shock but more of a pulsing wave sensation. Most e-collars have vibration and intensity settings ranging from low to high, so you have control over what your pooch feels.

In the past, shock collars were more intensive.

E-collars have been used for decades in field-training dogs of all sorts. Some gundog trainers are against the use of e-collars, and others swear by them. Some e-collars have GPS settings so you can track your dog and his movements.

The use of hand-held e-collars is banned in Denmark, Norway, Sweden, Switzerland, Slovenia, the United Kingdom, Germany, and Australia. These countries consider hand-held e-collars to be barbaric devices, as they are often abused and can create fear, aggression, and anxiety in a dog. Even though shock collars may aid in suppressing unwanted behaviors, they do not teach the dog proper behavior.

E-collars are often considered to be a form of negative reinforcement, as the desired behavior is enforced by a negative outcome when the dog does the opposite. Many dog trainers compare this type of negative reinforcement to not wearing a seat belt while driving the car; the car will make an annoying ding ding sound until you put your seat belt on. The ding-ding sound will stop when you perform the desired behavior, which is the same principle applied to the function of e-collars.

If you are considering using an e-collar to train your English Setter to work in the field or just to prevent him from running out of the yard, I highly recommend consulting with a professional to incorporate this into your training program. It is essential you completely understand how and when it is appropriate to use the e-collar.

PROS

Adjustable intensity – The majority of e-collars give you the flexibility of using either a warning beep or vibration intensity. This option can be comforting if you are on the fence about using a shock collar.

Fast results – Many field trainers prefer using e-collars because it only takes a few times to correct bad behavior, and after that, using only the beeping sound is warning enough. E-collars are also very effective at keeping your English Setter in the yard, which keeps him safe while having freedom. However, if your English Setter is on the stubborn side, he may take longer to train.

Affordable – One of the main reasons that gundog owners prefer using e-collars for training their dogs is because it is more affordable than paying for a professional dog trainer. E-collars range in price from $80 and up, depending on the features, such as adjustable warning/vibration levels, remote controls, a range of distances, and a number of collar sizes.

Off-leash – In field environments, e-collars provide the ability to communicate with your pooch, guide him, and help him avoid potentially dangerous situations.

CONS

The shock – In the past, e-collars were called shock collars, but due to negative marketing, companies changed the name. However, many pet owners still associate e-collars with the word shock, and you still are using aversive behavior modification. More and more field trainers are opting to use positive training methods over negative reinforcement.

Fear – There are reports that some dogs develop an extreme fear of objects, people, or certain situations they associate with the electric vibration of the e-collar. One pet owner I know used a low-vibration collar on a dog to prevent him from leaving the yard, and then the dog refused to go outside and started urinating inside the house.

Overcorrection – For this very reason, I do not recommend leaving your English Setter unattended while wearing an e-collar, as it could malfunction. It could unnecessarily confuse your English Setter by "correcting" a problem that was not even there.

No positive reinforcement – E-collars do not reinforce good behavior with praise, treats, and affection. Whatever training method you decide to use, never underestimate the power of a reward, verbal approval, or affection.

E-Collar Training – How to Get Started

Before you start using an e-collar to train your English Setter, he should know basic commands such as sit, come, and whoa. Your dog should immediately obey these commands without needing you to repeat them two or three times.

If your English Setter does not obey basic commands, then he is not ready for e-collar training.

Collar conditioning

Long before you start e-collar training, you want your English Setter to recognize that the collar goes on at the beginning of his day. It is part of your dog's daily outfit – nothing more. You want your English Setter to associate the collar with going on walks, going outside, and playing. The collar is part of his everyday life.

At this stage, the power switch stays off unless you are actually training your English Setter or you are in a situation where you need to enforce a command.

One of the keys in e-collar training is selecting the correct stimulation level. Each collar will come with at least three different adjustable levels. The sensation level should be adjusted to a level that the dog understands as part of his training. It should never be painful.

When training, you will want to tighten the collar just a notch so the contact points actually touch the skin. My recommendation for Setters is that you should be able to slip two fingers under the collar comfortably; three fingers is too loose. Never over-tighten, as the constriction may cause muscular strain.

First introductions

Ask your English Setter to sit in front of you. Put the stimulation level on the lowest setting. Slowly increase the setting until you notice your English Setter seems to be slightly annoyed with something, such as the buzzing sound from a fly around his head. You want to see a vibe of confusion, not a yelp or cry of pain.

If your furry companion vocalizes, his ears turn down, or if he tucks his tail between his legs, it is an obvious sign the stimulation is too high. Dogs feel pain, but their reactions to pain are different from humans'. Dogs' natural instinct is to hide pain and act stoically, to protect themselves and not seem vulnerable. If you see a reaction, it is a level of discomfort that would be unacceptable to humans, making it definitely unacceptable for your best friend.

Coming when called

Now that you have established the baseline stimulation level for your pooch, you can start teaching him the come command using the e-collar. However, it is imperative that your English Setter already obeys the verbal command, "Come."

Put your dog on a long leash, at least 20 feet in length. Tell your Setter the "Sit" command, and once he is sitting, walk backward about 10 to 20 feet. Stimulate your dog collar using the baseline stimulation level while giving the "Come" command enthusiastically. Gently nudge the dog's leash to come toward you.

When your English Setter is within arm's length, release the stimulation button on the e-collar. Generously praise your pup. Let your dog know that this is exactly the type of behavior you approve of.

The goal of this training exercise is to teach your English Setter that the annoyance will go away when he obeys your command.

You will need to do this practice training in various different situations and environments. Start off in your backyard, then move to a place with more distractions, such as the dog park or near a playground. If your English Setter does not come, be prepared to slightly increase the stimulation level. Never underestimate the power of generous praise, affection, and yummy rewards each time your dog comes when asked.

The dos and don'ts when using an e-collar

The e-collar is a powerful tool, as it gives you the ability to enforce a command at a distance. Many hunters prefer using e-collars for this reason as it improves communication between them and their dogs despite the distance.

However, this powerful tool is often abused. Never turn up the stimulation level past the point of being annoying to being painful. If your English Setter is not responding, it is more than likely your training methods have failed along the way. Take a step back and reinforce more simple commands. If your dog is having a bad day, there is no need to make it worse by using the e-collar. Give your dog a break, and do not even turn the collar on. Never take your frustrations out on your English Setter, who adores you.

If you have a professional trainer in the area, who specializes in training hunting dogs, take a few classes with them to learn how to ethically handle your English Setter. If you misuse your dog's e-collars, it can cause more behavioral problems than they can actually solve.

Photo Courtesy of Cy Black

Introduction to the Gun

> "
>
> *Don't shoot over or around Setters until they have been properly introduced to birds. Get them on birds early, introducing deep cover and obstacles, and anything they may encounter in the field. Build confidence in the field before doing too much obedience, as Setters are bred to run, point, and hold the bird until the hunter arrives. The natural ability is bred into them, so don't push a pup too young. Let it mature into the work.*
>
> GREG AND CARLA FRYAR
>
> *High Fly'n Kennels*
>
> "

One of the important aspects of introducing your English Setter to the sound of gunfire is to take it slowly and not rush anything.

If your pup is confident and has already mastered all of his basic commands, such as sit, come, whoa, and stay, then you should be ready to introduce your dog to gunfire noises by seven to eight months of age. If your pooch is on the timid side and still needs to master basic commands, then leave things until he is at least one year of age. Also, your pup should have mastered walking by your side and be able to obey the stop command or whistle before you even think about firing a gun in the vicinity of your English Setter.

The majority of gundog trainers prefer to wait till a dog is at least eight months old, as the dog's hearing will have fully developed by then. If you have any questions, contact a local professional gun-dog trainer to evaluate your English Setter. It is better to be on the safe side than to end up with a dog who has lifelong problems with hearing gunshots.

How to introduce gunfire noises

One of the first steps is to start getting your English Setter acclimatized to loud, cracking noises without being startled.

Start by dropping empty metal food bowls on the floor near your English Setter to desensitize him to loud noises. Clap your hands when you are walking up behind him. Make loud background noises and observe your dog's reaction each time. Teach your dog to associate loud, startling noises with something he enjoys, such as being walked or fed.

Some gundog trainers like to fire an older air gun without pellets at a considerable distance from their dog to give off a realistic "crack" sound. Over a period of weeks, the trainer will repeat the process but move a little bit closer to the dog each time. Over time, they switch it up with an actual shotgun, again at a considerable distance, maybe starting with a starting pistol and graduating to finally a .410 with a short cartridge.

Remember the following when introducing your English Setter to gun noises

- Do not fire a gun in close vicinity to your dog to gauge his reaction to the loud sound.
- Take things gently, and do not rush things.
- Don't introduce your English Setter to gunfire until he is at least seven months of age.
- If your pooch shows any signs of anxiety or nervousness, then you will need to take things even slower.
- Get your English Setter used to the sight of the gun by carrying around an un-cocked air rifle over your arm during training practices so that when the time comes to fire it, he will not be alarmed.

Some gun dog trainers use party poppers to introduce their pups to gunfire noises and bangs. You can buy a bag of a hundred or so for about $10 at any supermarket or dollar store. They make a loud banging sound but are still soft enough not to frighten your pooch. Pop the party poppers at a considerable distance and come a little closer each time.

Starting pistols are ideal for the next step for training your English Setters. Many professional trainers prefer to fire the pistol inside their game bag, so it muffles the sound of the shot. Be careful of shooting a dummy launcher too close to your dog. There are numerous stories of gundogs being so badly spooked by dummy launchers too early in their training and being frightened of the sound for the rest of their lives.

The key to introducing your English Setter to gun noises is to gradually desensitize the puppy. Expose your English Setter to as many different noises as possible, such as having the radio on in the background and slowly increasing the volume. Or play gunfire noises in the background while your pooch is eating and gradually increase the volume.

Once your dog seems totally oblivious to the background sounds, then clay shoots and country fairs are in order, but at a distance. If you take your time, you should eventually have a much bolder gundog who is not afraid of anything.

How to Prevent Common Issues with Gundogs

> Be consistent with your training. If you have worked your dog on backing or honoring and he blinks (refuses) to back while hunting, make sure he is corrected at that moment. A lot of dogs get away with a lot of mistakes while hunting because the handler is concentrating on killing birds.
>
> BOB BARKER
> *Open Range Kennels*

If you are a veteran gun dog owner, you know it is rare to make it through hunting season without encountering one or two badly behaved gundogs. Here are some of the most common issues with gundogs and how to avoid them.

Whining and making noise

Whining dogs can be distracting and frustrating for both the handler and other fellow hunters while hunting. The same goes for dogs that whine or bark while inside their crates in the car or at the camp. Dogs normally whine because they are impatient and desperately want to get or do something.

 **SOLUTION** – *If you notice your dog whining or making noise on shoot day, do not simply ignore it and hope it will get better. Go back to the basics and avoid taking your pooch out shooting again until he has proven himself to stay calm even when he is excited. Return to a controlled environment and practice with food, dummies, and game, only progressing to the next stage when your dog stays quiet throughout each stage.*

Hunting on their own accord

It is common for dogs to think they are better hunters than their owners.

SOLUTION: *Never allow your young English Setter to stray far away from you. Always teach hunting as a controlled exercise. For example, you may drop a dummy near your feet when your pooch is not looking.*

Running in

Running in is when your English Setter decides to run in and flush game without a direct command. Many hunters refer to these dogs as spoiled brats, as they do not obey their parents. The key to avoiding this happening is to lay a solid foundation before you take your English Setter shooting.

SOLUTION: *If your dog runs in without you giving the recall command, run after him. Trust me; he will be surprised to see you there. Put him on the lead, give him the recall command again, and walk with him to where you recalled it. If your dog runs in, do not start whistling or calling his name, as this will just teach him to ignore your commands, and he will only return to you when he has had his fun.*

Bad behavior around other dogs

Not only can this be embarrassing, but it can even be dangerous. On shoot day, a wide range of dogs of all breeds and temperaments will be present. It is vital that they all get along and concentrate on the job at hand instead of on one another.

> SOLUTION: *Be sure to start socializing your English Setter with a wide range of dogs and other animals as soon as he is fully vaccinated. I recommend introducing young dogs to other dogs in a calm, controlled environment. If your dog is aggressive or overly excitable, then maybe you should consider visiting a professional dog trainer.*

How to choose a Professional Hunting Dog Trainer

Finding a gundog trainer is not an easy task, as you will need to send your beloved pooch away for training. Often, the breeder where you purchased your English Setter will have a list of professional gundog trainers that specialize in training English Setters. In case they do not have any suggestions, here are some helpful recommendations to help you choose a professional gundog trainer.

When visiting a gundog trainer and their kennel, there are several things to take into consideration. Be sure to take your time to observe all aspects of the kennel, the trainer's philosophies, and do not be shy about asking questions.

Are the property and kennel in good condition?

Some gun-dog owners argue that if the trainer has a good reputation, the condition of the property or kennel does not matter. While reputation is important, it is even more important that your dog is cared for during the training. A clean kennel shows you that your English Setter is valued and respected. Property in good condition means the trainer takes his job seriously and wants to provide the best environment for your dog.

Are the kennels safe, clean, and protected?

When your English Setter is placed inside a kennel with other dogs, there is always a risk of disease or infection. Be sure to ask the trainer how often the kennels are cleaned and sanitized. Rule of thumb: they should be cleaned and sanitized at least once a day.

In addition, the kennels should be made from good quality steel and have a bed, access to clean water, and a roof over the top. The roof is especially important if your English Setter is not neutered or spayed, as some dogs can climb chain-link fences to get at a female in heat.

Not all trainers have a kennel for their canine students. Some prefer keeping the dogs in crates inside their house; others keep them outside in crates. Be sure to get the exact details on where your pooch will be housed, and how much time he will be spending in the crate.

Is the kennel heated or air conditioned?

The requirements for this will depend on where your trainer is located. Just make sure the temperature control is appropriate for where your dog will stay while being trained to be a hunter.

Does the trainer live on-site with the dogs?

Naturally, we would assume the answer would be yes. But there are some trainers that live somewhere else, often miles away from the kennel. If the trainer does not live on-site where the dogs are housed, proceed with caution. You want your English Setter to be safe and protected while training. Having your dog left unattended for long periods of time puts him at risk.

How are the dogs transported?

For hunting and competition training, often the dogs are transported in dog trucks or trailers. Make sure the equipment is in good shape and looks safe. I have also heard too many horror stories about dogs getting pregnant while in the trainer's control. Make sure the trainer takes measures to train boys with boys and girls with girls.

How long are the training programs?

Every trainer varies in how long the training programs are. Training a gundog takes time and does not happen overnight. Avoid trainers that claim they can transform your dog into a hunting or a competition dog in a few weeks. Remember the saying, "If it sounds too good to be true, it probably is not." For effective training, the program should be a minimum of 10 weeks or longer.

What does an average day look like for my dog while being trained?

Often, the trainer will tell you what time training begins each morning and what different training sessions are composed of. Also, the trainer should let you know what time the dogs will return to the kennel each night. Also, be sure to ask how your English Setter will spend his free time on his day off from training.

How frequently will your dog be trained?

You want your English Setter to be trained at least once a day, but preferably twice a day. A reputable gundog trainer will often have a morning and an afternoon training session. Sessions may vary from 15 minutes to an hour. A good trainer will keep the number of their canine students low so that they can take their time to work with each individual dog, reinforcing concepts. Trainers who have more canine students do not have the luxury of working through concepts until they are mastered. A general rule of thumb: the larger the kennel, the less time the trainer is spending with your dog.

Who will be training my dog?

In larger kennels, the chance of your English Setter being trained by the main trainer or owner is almost impossible. While this is not a big issue, you should definitely try to personally meet the trainer who will be training your dog. You want to get a feeling for the person who will be working hands-on with your English Setter.

Can you evaluate the dogs already in training?

Professional dog trainers are used to potential clients coming to watch training sessions. If the trainer is reluctant to let you watch, consider that a huge red flag. Most trainers will encourage their clients to come and observe their dogs in training sessions. Often, as the dog advances in the lessons, the trainer will encourage the dog owner to take part in the training sessions to learn the cues.

How do the dogs look during the training sessions?

If you notice that the dogs back away or cower when the trainer comes near them, this is a red flag. The dogs should be healthy, happy, and energetic not cowering or acting aggressively.

How responsive is your trainer to your calls or messages?

Trainers are generally very busy, but you want a trainer who treats you as a valued client. After all, how he treats you is a reflection of how he will treat your dog. The trainer should give you bi-weekly updates on your dog's progress, often including pictures. In the past, this was not a common practice, but due to technology, more and more trainers offer at least weekly updates.

Reviews and references

In today's world, it is easy to read reviews on Google or Facebook. You can always ask the trainer for personal references to call and inquire about their opinion. It is important to see what actual clients have to say about their experience with the trainer.

> **"**
>
> *Do not try and teach a command in the field while hunting or in the presence of game. Bad habits develop. Teach Setters the command or skill long before you get in the field. The hunt is the application and polishing time for skills. Trying to handle a dog on live game with a loaded gun in your hand and other people around is a recipe for disaster. You cannot concentrate on all the variables. Hunting is hunting and training is training. Combine the two and you will be very disappointed in the results of both, I promise you.*
>
> MARK D. DENEKA
> *Twilight Setter Kennels*
>
> **"**

Photo Courtesy of Amber Vick

Field Trials and Tests

The majority of gun-dog owners, especially newbies, do not know the difference between field trials and hunt tests. Both activities are a fantastic way to keep you and your English Setter in shape and practice training skills during off-season; however, it can be confusing to know which activity is best suited for you and your dog.

Field trials

Field trials are competitive events. In a typical field trial, only one dog will win, or depending on the event, one dog from each division will win.

Hunt tests

Hunt tests are non-competitive, and each dog is judged individually and awarded a score based on its performance. The dogs are not compared against each other as in a field trial. At the end of the hunt test, there may be several dogs with close-to-perfect scores and other dogs who did not pass the test. The objective of a hunt test is to evaluate each dog independently.

Field trials and hunt tests provide breeders with an opportunity to assess their dogs. Both activities serve the purpose of producing a better hunting dog by fine-tuning the dog's inherent abilities and training. Field trials and hunt tests have annual events at a the local, state, and national level for both puppies and adult dogs.

Whether your dog is an amateur or an expert, you can find a program to participate in. Field trials and hunt tests provide the perfect opportunity to hook up with fellow gundog owners. Often, they will gladly share suggestions on how to improve your dog's training program.

There are quite a few different organizations regularly running field trials. However, the format and style may vary. Some field trials use

Photo Courtesy of David Weaver

pen-raised birds, and others may observe the dog flushing out wild birds. The American Kennel Club, American Field Sporting Dog Association, and the National Bird Hunters Association sponsor the majority of national field trials.

As for hunt tests, the North American Versatile Hunting Dogs Association, United Kennel Club and the North American Hunting Retriever Association are leaders in noncompetitive events such as hunt tests. One of the advantages of these programs is that they provide an excellent opportunity to train yourself and your dog for field trials without the pressure.

Field trials have the dog perform once a day. On the other hand, with the hunt tests, the dog can be performing several times each day. For example, in the utility test, each dog is required to perform a 30-minute hunt, plus a 10-minute duck search in a large body of water, a heeling sequence, a tracked field retrieve, and a combination of retrieving tasks. Both the field trials and hunt tests have complex scoring criteria to ensure the judges' evaluations are as objective as possible.

Depending on the field trial or hunt test, the dog will be required to demonstrate his ability to search for game, hold point, flush, shot and drop, and retrieve downed game. English Setters are versatile hunting dogs, so they will be expected to search the water for game and mark and retrieve downed game, as well as flush out wildfowl on land.

If you are unsure what type of event is best suited for your English Setter, attend a couple of field trials and hunt tests. Talk to your dog's breeder for recommendations and research what activities are available in your area. Then grab your English Setter and have some fun together.

CHAPTER 9

Living with Your English Setter

"he journey of life is sweeter when traveled with a dog." – Unknown Your English Setter is special! He is your best friend, companion, and a source of unconditional love. Chances are you chose an English Setter because they have certain traits that mesh with your lifestyle, such as their energetic, active, and affectionate personalities. Sharing your life with your Setter involves happy moments, funny moments, sad moments, and everything in between.

Your English Setter will not only fill your heart with love, but he will make it stronger. Recent studies have shown that having a canine companion can lower your blood pressure, cholesterol, and triglyceride

Photo Courtesy of David Weaver

levels. Also, your English Setter can have a positive effect on your mental health and well-being.

Your dog will be an essential part of your life and family, so you will want to give him the best life possible in every aspect. In this chapter, we will discuss some fundamental day-to-day activities you can do with your English Setter.

Physical Exercise

> "
>
> *Setters love to open up the throttle and run. They need a physical outlet several times a week. Exercise sessions don't need to be hours in duration, but they should be varied. Games that involve their nose are wonderful. Hide treats, give them a search command, and stand back! Swimming in lakes is great exercise, and rivers with moderate currents are even better. Setters introduced to water when young usually learn to love to swim. It's healthy, gives them a free bath, is easy on their joints, and builds muscle.*
>
> MARK D. DENEKA
> *Twilight Setter Kennels*
>
> "

Your English Setter's love for life makes him a bundle of energy, and you love him for it! This country boy prefers to stay away from the city. Although Setters are affectionate and docile, they have high exercise requirements.

Being a good puppy parent means providing your pup with daily physical activity. The benefits of regularly exercising your English Setter are endless. Regular physical activity helps your English Setter to sleep better at night. Just a slight case of sleep deprivation for your dog can cause all sorts of behavioral issues. You will notice your pup's overall mood will improve with daily exercise.

Another reason to regularly exercise your English Setter is that it helps keep his weight down. In the United States, more than 50 percent of dogs are considered to be overweight or obese. Excess weight leads to a long list of health problems. Exercise also improves blood circulation, which decreases the risk of cardiovascular diseases.

A few health benefits for dogs derived from regular physical activity

- Maintains and builds muscle mass, which can reduce risk of injury
- Helps to prevent canine diabetes and certain cancers
- Decreases the risk of urinary tract infections, as exercise stimulates frequent urination
- Helps to reduce the risk of arthritis
- May increase your dog's life span

There are other benefits to providing your English Setter with a regular exercise regime. For example, just sticking to a walking schedule can combat many common behavioral problems, such as barking, aggression, and chewing.

Exercise Requirements for Your English Setter

> *A tired Setter is a happy Setter. Retrieving and scent work will engage the dog's mind and is good for developing hunting skills later. Keep in mind that an adult Setter can easily run 20 to 25 miles per day.*
>
> KAREN STROHMEYER
> *Bristle Ridge Llewellins*

As mentioned above, exercise plays a vital role in your English Setter's overall health and may even extend his life span. However, providing your pooch with adequate exercise goes beyond taking him out for an occasional walk or two.

All English Setters are considered to be high-energy dogs and require at least 60 minutes of exercise each day to keep them healthy and to keep boredom at bay.

Photo Courtesy of
Jan Darnell

Puppies – Puppies need several bouts of short exercise sessions throughout the day, but excessive exercise for puppies may be detrimental to their growth. Over-exercise refers to repetitive actions, such as walking briskly or running for an extended period of time, not typical playing in the yard or romping around the house.

Adults – An adult English Setter is considered to be in his prime from one year old to seven years old, and requires, on average, 60 minutes of exercise per day or more. There will be days when the weather is bad, so you will need to offer other indoor alternatives.

Seniors – Do not make the mistake of assuming your elderly English Setter does not need exercise. Unless your pooch has serious health conditions that prevent him from exercising, you will want to continue with his daily walks. Regular exercise can relieve joint pain and maintain muscle mass. Plus, being out in the fresh air will put a little pep in your old pup's step.

Health exceptions – Some health conditions, such as patellar luxation (trick knee), may require strict bed rest while recovering to reduce swelling and manage pain. However, after that, a veterinarian will suggest doing strengthening exercises, such as walking uphill to build muscles around the dog's knee.

Pregnancy – In general, pregnant English Setters should be taken for daily walks and exercised as normal, except for the last week of pregnancy. Regular exercise will help the pregnant dog stay in shape, which will help in her labor and delivery. Exercise can gradually resume two to three weeks after the dog gives birth.

Mental Enrichment

How can you outwork a working dog or high-energy dog like an English Setter?

One common myth is that you can tire out your dog by taking him for multiple walks and runs a day. However, typically what happens is the same as with humans; if we keep walking and running, we turn into athletes, which means your puppy or dog is going to require even more physical exercise. Physical exercise is important, but do not underestimate the power of mental exercise, such as obedience, agility, and tracking training.

English Setters are extremely intelligent animals, and it is crucial that we provide them with plenty of mental stimulation to exercise their brains. If they do not use their brains, they can quickly become bored, and bored dogs may begin to develop a wide range of behavioral issues.

What is meant by mental enrichment for canines? Enrichment stimulates your dog's mental state by using a variety of activities designed to challenge and exercise the brain. These activities are designed to encourage your dog to solve problems, learn new skills, and be more confident. These activities are even more important during the colder, shorter days in the winter months, as your English Setter may spend more time indoors than during the summer.

Here are some of my favorite ideas. As you will notice, they do not need to cost a fortune, nor do you need to be creative to create something fun for your dog to do. I recommend you enjoy the opportunity to play with your dog and keep him under close supervision.

FAMOUS ENGLISH SETTER

English Setter in the White House

Franklin D. Roosevelt, the 32nd president of the United States, had a number of dogs during his life. One of these beloved canines was an English Setter, Winks, who supposedly earned his name from the black ring around his left eye. The Roosevelt family brought Winks home from Georgia in late 1933, but unfortunately, the Setter met an untimely end in 1934.

Tug-of-war

This is every dog's all-time favorite game. Your English Setter should grab the rope or toy when you tell him, then he should start pulling the rope. The dog should be the one doing most of the pulling, tugging, and head shaking. Some puppies may need a little encouragement or guidance from you to understand the rules of the game.

Kongs

Kongs make mealtimes and snack times more interesting for your pup. You can pack a portion of your dog's meal into the Kong for him to figure out how to get the food out, and during the summer months, you can even freeze the Kong to make it more of a fun struggle. You can also put treats, peanut butter, or liver paste into the Kong. Just a word of caution: make sure you purchase the appropriate size for your English Setter and never leave him unsupervised with a Kong.

Follow the scent

Place some homemade beef broth in a squirt bottle and squirt a path around your backyard, leading to a handful of your dog's favorite treats. English Setters love to hunt and forage for their food and follow the scent. Setters were originally bred to track scents, so any game that requires your dog to follow the scent of something delicious will stimulate your pup.

Hide-and-seek

Your dog will love it if you play a game of hide-and-seek with him. The game consists of you telling your dog to sit and stay or have someone physically hold on to your dog while you go and hide, and then your pooch needs to find you. However, you can always make the game more of a challenge by scattering a few treats along the way to distract your dog or lead him to your hiding spot.

Running Partner

> "
>
> *English Setters under two years of age should have low-impact exercise while their bones and joints are growing. After they are two years old, Setters make great running and jogging partners and can be exercised off-leash if taught proper recall.*
>
> JULIA CRAWFORD
> *Crown Setters*
> "

Running with your English Setter will help keep his weight in check, which is particularly important, as veterinarians report an increasing number of overweight dogs. Plus, running can do wonders for your Setter's mental health. The sights, smells, and sounds your dog will encounter on a run, and the change of scenery, will provide him with more than enough mental stimulation to reduce anxiety and boredom.

Running is a positive outlet for dogs who exhibit destructive behaviors. Instead of tearing through your favorite pillow, he can burn off his excess energy tearing through the countryside. But before hitting the running trail with your English Setter, there are a few things you need to consider.

Consider your Setter's age

Take into consideration your Setter's age and health condition. It is not advisable to start running with your puppy until he has finished growing, as he is more prone to injury as a puppy. Wait until your English Setter is at least one year old before taking him on vigorous runs. Similarly, this would apply to running with a dog who suffers from joint problems or has weight issues. If you want to help your dog to lose weight, talk first to your vet for some suggestions for an activity that is less painful on his joints.

Remember, it is not a race

There is no denying the truth; English Setters love to run and run. But if you are trying to break a new sprinting record, it probably is best not to take your dog with you. Remember that you will still need to stop and clean up after your dog, and all dogs can easily get distracted by sniffing their surroundings. Running with your dog needs to be a fun occasion for both of you, and your pooch should feel free to stop if he needs to. Instead of breaking records, try to see running as a healthy activity you can do leisurely with your pooch.

Start off slowly

If you want to start running with your English Setter, take things slowly. Can you imagine how you would feel if someone took you on a 5-mile run and you had not been running in some time? Your English Setter may be full of energy, but he still needs to build up tolerance. Start with a mile and slowly work up to a longer distance. Find a running area that both of you enjoy. Remember, never let your pooch off the lead unless he has mastered basic commands and you can trust him to stay close to you at all times.

Do not push your English Setter too hard

Do not be fooled by your pup's energy. Dogs do not sweat through their skin; instead, they cool their body temperature down by panting. Pushing your dog too hard for too long can lead to hyperventilation and breathing difficulties. Stop frequently to give your English Setter a break; trust me, he will appreciate it. Remember, you and your Setter are a team, and you need to be aware of his body language, as he cannot tell you when he has had enough.

Hiking Partner

Your English Setter is a great companion for adventures in the great outdoors, as he is always ready, willing, and eager to hit the trail. Hiking is one of the best activities you can do with your English Setter, as it will deepen your bond of friendship through shared experiences.

Before you hit the trails with your English Setter, consider the following guidelines

Make sure dogs are allowed on the hiking trails you will be hiking, and obey any restrictions concerning off-limit areas.

Keep your English Setter on a leash at all times. Most national parks allow dogs on the hiking trails if they are always on their leash. Keeping your dog on the leash will prevent him from chasing after wildlife or tearing up the delicate forest undergrowth. Many parks have hefty fines if they find you hiking with your dog off leash.

Another factor to consider is that your dog can leave behind his predator scent, which may disrupt the local wildlife and hinder feeding and nesting activities. Unleashed dogs can also quickly catch the scent of something and may disappear from your view instantly.

Never assume that other hikers will love your English Setter as much as you. Always keep your dog on a leash so other hikers do not feel frightened or threatened. This is especially important if you are hiking through bear country. Many unleashed dogs have been mistaken for wild animals and accidentally sprayed with bear spray. Also, never assume other dogs you encounter on a hiking trail will be happy to meet your Setter.

Photo Courtesy of Amber Vick

Always clean up after your dog. Carry along a small spade and bury his waste in the ground or carry it out with you in a plastic bag. Dog waste contains fecal coliform bacteria, salmonella, and giardia, which can cause other animals to become sick.

Make sure your dog has mastered all of the basic commands and is completely vaccinated before hitting the trails. The following is a list of gear for hiking with your English Setter.

Collar or a harness – Never use a choke collar, as it could get caught on a twig or branch and strangle your dog. Make sure you can slip two fingers under the collar or harness to prevent your dog from hyperventilating on the trail.

Leash – Make sure you use a heavy-duty leash that can withstand the rigors of hiking. If you plan to use an extendable leash, keep the leash short enough to maintain control over your dog.

Water – Carry at least eight ounces of water per hour of hiking. If you are hiking in hot weather, freeze your dog's water bottles the night before; the ice will melt as you hike, providing your dog with a cool drink. Water found in ponds, streams, and creeks may contain harmful bacteria and parasites that cause your English Setter to become sick.

Food – Be sure to bring along enough food for your English Setter for the duration of the trip. I recommend feeding your pooch smaller quantities but more frequently to prevent the discomfort of exercising on a full tummy.

Collapsible bowl – A collapsible bowl does not weigh much and will make it easy to give your English Setter water or food along the hike. Most collapsible bowls for dogs can be attached to the outside of your bag for convenience.

Plastic bags or a small spade – Bring a small spade if you decide to bury your dog's fecal matter in the ground, or bring plastic bags if you plan to carry out his waste.

Canine first aid kit – Just as you would bring along a first aid kit for yourself, be sure to bring along extra items for your dog. Be sure your first aid kit has the following items: hydrogen peroxide to disinfect cuts,

Photo Courtesy of Angela Cloke

scissors with a rounded tip to cut back any fur around a wound, bandages and gauze, and a small sock to protect a sore or wounded paw.

Reflective lights – Reflective lights can be attached to your English Setter's harness, leash, or collar to protect him when crossing the road at night.

Specialized clothing – For adverse weather conditions or special activities, have on hand booties, bandanas, canine flotation devices, or insulating jackets. Before heading out into the great outdoors, check the weather conditions and determine what type of clothing your English Setter may require.

Fun Sport – Agility and Flyball

Canine sports are becoming more popular with pet owners around the world. Maybe you have heard of agility, fly ball, or nose work but are unsure what they are. Or maybe you are interested in trying them out but do not know which sport is best suited for your English Setter. Here is a quick rundown of each sport.

Agility

Agility requires your English Setter to go through an obstacle course, such as jumping through hoops or over poles, crawling through tunnels, and more, as quickly as possible. Your dog will be faulted if he misses an obstacle in the course or disobeys the instructions. Agility is a fantastic way to challenge your pup's mind and body.

Fly-ball

Flyball requires your Setter to reach the ball dispenser at the end of the relay race. But before reaching the dispenser, your dog will have to pass through several obstacles, grab the dispensed ball, and run back through the obstacles before the next dog is released to do the same thing. Often the dogs will work in teams of four, and the fastest team will win the race. Fly ball is exhilarating not only for your dog but also for spectators.

Nose or scent work

Nose or scent work involves your English Setter's exceptional sniffer. A course will be set up with hidden scent markers, and your dog's task is to find all of the different scent markers in order to get a reward. The course is quite similar to how dogs are trained for search and rescue work or police work. This option is great for a shy dog, as the course is performed by one dog at a time. Nose work may not provide as much physical exercise as the above two options, but it is great mental stimulation for your English Setter.

Which sport is the best choice for your English Setter? It will depend on your preferences and your dog's personality. For example, if your dog thrives on being active, then give agility a try. If your dog is very social and enjoys being around other dogs, then maybe flyball. If your pooch is less social and enjoys seeking out objects, then nose work may be best suited for him. No matter what you choose, agility, flyball, and nose work are all mentally stimulating sports.

Show Life

A show dog is not born a show dog. Preparing your dog to become a show dog requires a lot of time, energy, money, care, and determination. Here are some things you should know about show dogs.

Show dogs are not easy to find – Show dogs are not easy to come by, so do not expect to phone a breeder and request a show dog, especially if the breeder has never met you. Show dogs are the cream of the crop, and not every litter produces a show-dog quality pup. Often, you will have to wait one year or more for a show dog. Some people wait years for a dog out of a specific litter.

Show dogs have to remain intact – Show dogs cannot be neutered or spayed. Often you do not have a say in the gender of your show dog. Show dogs originally were designed to show off the breeding stock of the dog's bloodline. The dog's appearance and structure are judged according to the dog's ability to produce quality pedigree puppies.

Be prepared for co-ownership

The majority of breeders who agree to sell you a show dog will retain partial ownership of the dog. Perhaps the breeder will want to maintain the breeding rights to the dog or protect the bloodline and prevent the dog from being bred irresponsibly. Be sure to read the fine print on the contract before you sign.

Be determined to work – Show dogs do not get in the ring and automatically strut their stuff. Your English Setter will need conformation classes to learn how to have a proper gait, be properly socialized, and travel well.

Do not expect to get rich – Dog shows are not money makers; instead, they are quite expensive. However, if your dog places first, you will get bragging rights.

How dog shows work

Each dog registered at the dog show will be presented to a judge by its owner or breeder. However, some pet owners prefer to hire a professional handler or exhibitor.

The sole purpose of a dog show is to evaluate the dog's breeding stock. Your English Setter will start off in classes competing for points toward his AKC championship. Your dog will win points according to the number of dogs he defeats in the dog show. The more dogs of the same breed who enter a competition, the more points a dog will win. Your dog will need 15 points that have been awarded by three different judges to become an AKC champion.

Dog shows are a process of elimination, and only the Best of Breed winners will be able to compete. There are seven different groups: Sporting, Hunting, Working, Terrier, Toy, Non-Sporting, and Herding. Setters are allowed to participate in the Sporting and Hunting Group. The judges will select the Best in Show winner.

The judges will judge each dog against a written standard describing the ideal dog of the specified breed. The standards for English Setters are established by the AKC. Each judge will give his or her own opinion as to which dog represents the breed's standard appropriately.

CHAPTER 10

Traveling

> "
> *Don't expect that because your Setter is the perfect child at home it will be the same when a new place and new people are presented. There's a chance that the dog's anxiety will be a bit elevated until it adjusts to the new surroundings. Again, patience and gentleness will go a long way.*
>
> JEFFREY GILLASPIE
> *Tinker Kennels, LLC*
> "

A recent survey discovered that more than 95 percent of dog owners plan at least one overnight trip each year with their dogs. Most English Setters love to travel, but it can be stressful on your dog and you if you are not well-prepared.

Before hitting the road with your pooch, take the time to choose the safest and most comfortable option for your English Setter. Ask yourself how much time you will be spending with your dog on your vacation. If he will be spending the majority of time alone, then he will most likely be happier left at home than tagging along with you on your journey.

By planning ahead, you can have a safe, stress-free trip.

Preparing to Travel with Your English Setter

> *Crate train every dog so you can easily travel, as you don't know when you may not be allowed to bring your dog into a place of business. Take the dog for car rides early and often. Don't feed it before traveling, as this helps with having to stop too often. And, if possible, bring water from home or use bottled water. Water change can be hard on a dog.*
>
> GREG AND CARLA FRYAR
> *High Fly'n Kennels*

Whether you are planning to travel with your English Setter for necessity or pleasure, you will need to take some definite steps to prepare for your dog's needs along the way. Car travel and air travel, especially longer trips, require some forethought. Never assume you will be able to find everything you need for your pooch during the journey.

Food – Be sure to pack enough dog food for the duration of the entire trip, as switching your dog's food may cause him to have an upset tummy. If you are planning on traveling for a longer period of time, research ahead of time whether your Setter's regular dog food will be available at your final destination.

Water – Throw in a bottle or two of clean drinking water to keep your dog hydrated throughout the journey. Never allow your dog to drink water from an unfamiliar source, such as a creek, puddle, or pond.

Food and water dishes – Do not forget to bring your pup's food and water dishes along. Be sure to place them in an area where you can easily reach them throughout the trip. If you are tight on space, look for a set of pop-off food dishes.

Crate or carrier – Depending on your method of travel, you might need either a hard-cover crate or a soft-cover carrier. Make sure to choose a comfortable traveling case, as it will most likely be used as your dog's personal bedroom when you reach the final destination. How to choose an appropriate crate is discussed on the following pages.

Toys – Be sure to bring along a few of your English Setter's favorite toys for the journey, as this will keep him distracted during long-haul trips and help to relieve stress.

Blankets and doggy beds – A nice fluffy blanket will keep your English Setter warm during the journey, plus the familiar scent will keep him calm. If you have space in your luggage, bring along a doggy bed so your dog can use it at the final destination.

Collar, leash, and ID tags – Be sure to place your dog's collar and ID tags on him before leaving the house, and do not remove them until you return home. If your English Setter is an adventure seeker, he may suddenly escape to explore his new surroundings, so you may also want to invest in a GPS dog tracker tag.

Cleaning supplies – Traveling with dogs can get messy. Be prepared by bringing along potty pads, baby wipes, paper towels, disposable garbage bags, and of course, a pet-friendly stain remover.

Medications – If your English Setter is taking any type of medicine or supplements, make sure you have enough for the duration of your trip.

Health and vaccination certificates – Do not forget to bring along your English Setter's medical information when traveling, in case of an emergency.

Traveling by Car

66

I come from a medical background, so safety is my first priority. My own dogs ride in crates in the car, starting at a very young age. There are safe harnesses for adult dogs. When I travel with a young dog, I take along a 'clean-up kit.' This contains poop bags, paper towels, wet wipes, and large garbage bags in the event I need to change out the entire crate pad. Having extra crate bedding is wise. It's helpful for puppies to ride in the car at least once a week so they don't develop motion sickness.

LIN SELL, MD
Linwood English Setters

99

Photo Courtesy of Dawn Gode

Whether you are taking your English Setter on a short trip or a long journey, you will want to ensure your pup is comfortable and safe.

Avoid the temptation to let your English Setter sit in the front seat or roam freely about the vehicle while it is in motion. If you have a car accident due to being distracted by your dog, you could be held accountable. Even worse, you or your pooch or other parties could be seriously injured.

 DO

- Secure your Setter inside a hard-cover crate that has been anchored to the vehicle by using a seat belt or other secure means or placed on the floor.
- Bring along plenty of clean drinking water to keep your pooch hydrated, especially during summer months.
- Give your dog plenty of rest stops, not only for your English Setter to relieve himself, but also so he can stretch his legs and drink some water.

- If you have the air conditioner on or a window open, make sure it is not directly blowing on your English Setter. If the window is open, make sure your dog cannot stick his head out or accidentally jump out.
- If your pooch suffers from motion sickness, ask your vet to prescribe a mild medication and follow the vet's instructions for administering it.
- Make sure your English Setter feels at home inside his crate by bringing along some familiar items, such as his blanket, chew toys, etc.
- Bring along a human buddy. Whenever possible, share the driving and dog caretaking duties with a friend or family member. You will be able to use the facilities or grab a quick bite to eat, knowing someone you trust is keeping a watchful eye on your English Setter.

 DON'T

- Never transport your English Setter in the back of an open pickup truck.
- Do not allow your dog to sit in the front seat and hang his head out of the vehicle while it is in motion. He could be injured by particles of debris or get sick from breathing cold air forced into his lungs.
- Never leave your English Setter alone inside a hot car. It only takes a few minutes for your dog to become overheated. This may cause irreversible organ damage or even death.
- Do not feed your Setter at least two hours prior to traveling in order to prevent motion sickness.

A year-round hazard is leaving your English Setter unattended in your car. In addition to the dangers of heat and cold, anytime you leave a dog alone inside the car, you are making an unspoken invitation to pet thieves.

Choosing the Right Crate for Long-distance Car Travel

Whether your English Setter loves long road trips or quivers at the very thought of getting into the car, you will want to make the journey as comfortable and pleasant for him as possible. Dog travel crates are designed to provide a safe, enclosed place for your pooch to travel in comfort. These crates differ from your English Setter's home crate, as they come with extra security features, such as fasteners, to keep the crate secure while traveling.

Here are the factors to consider when choosing a travel crate for your English Setter

Size – The crate should be big enough for your Setter to sit, stand, lie down, and turn around in, but small enough to keep him secure. A general rule of thumb is that travel crates should be no more than six inches longer than your pooch. A bigger crate may give your dog more space to move about, but this also means he may involuntarily slide around inside the crate while the vehicle is in motion.

Photo Courtesy of David Weaver

Soft vs. hard cover – A soft carrier may be more comfortable for your English Setter. However, for car travel, a hard crate provides your dog with more protection if you get into an accident. Another advantage of hard cover crates is that they are easier to clean up if your dog has an accident or gets carsick.

Harness – Due to new state laws, many car crates come with a built-in harness, which allows the crate to be securely fastened to the seat belt for extra stability. By fastening the crate to the seat belt, you are creating a more secure ride for your English Setter, as the crate will not slide around on sharp corners or fly forward if you come to a sudden stop.

Visibility – English Setters are very curious by nature and love to observe their surroundings. Choose a crate that will give your dog an unhindered view and lots of fresh air. If your dog is nervous about car travel, then the more visibility, the better.

Traveling by Plane

Traveling by plane with your English Setter can be complicated and more expensive than flying solo, but it is possible with a little extra research ahead of time.

Generally, veterinarians and breeders do not recommend flying with your pet unless absolutely necessary. Ideally, dogs should not fly unless their owner is permanently moving to a new location or taking a long trip of two to three weeks minimum. This is because flying can be extremely stressful for your English Setter.

Air travel removes your pooch from his comfortable home and familiar surroundings, forcing him into a strange environment with loud noises, bright lights, changes in air pressures and cabin temperature, and to make matters worse, few opportunities to use the bathroom.

Cargo or carry-on?

If you must fly with your English Setter, ideally, the best place for him would be in the cabin under the seat in front of you. However, each airline has different rules and regulations as to where your pooch will be allowed to spend his time during the flight, depending on his size.

Typically, your dog will be allowed to fly in the cabin as a carry-on if he is small enough to fit in a carrier under the seat in front of you. Most airlines have a weight limit of 20 pounds for dogs flying in the cabin, though there are some exceptions, such support animals. So, unless your English Setter is still a puppy, most likely, your dog will have to travel in the cargo hold, along with the luggage and freight.

Every year, hundreds of thousands of dogs fly in the cargo without incident, but there are many unknown variables that you have no control over once you hand your English Setter over to airline personnel.

Airlines do their best to make your dog comfortable in the cargo hold. However, baggage handlers are often just trying to get the plane loaded or unloaded on time. They are not paid to give your dog extra attention inside of his kennel. Unfortunately, many pet owners have horror stories of their pets being injured, becoming seriously ill, getting lost, or even dying after flying in the cargo hold.

Unfortunately, a full-grown English Setter is too big to fit under the seat in most airplane cabins, so the only option will be to place him in the cargo hold.

Familiarize your English Setter with his carrier or crate well in advance of the actual flight. If possible, take your dog to the airport's departure area several times so he becomes more comfortable with this noisy, strange place.

How much does it cost?

Prices may vary from airline to airline, but the average price for your English Setter to travel in the cargo hold is approximately $75 each way. Of course, the price will vary depending on the traveling distance, as well as the combined weight of your dog and his crate. The majority of airlines will provide you with access to an online calculator to estimate the cost.

Research

As mentioned above, each airline company has different rules and regulations, and these are constantly changing. It is important to read through these rules thoroughly before traveling so that your English Setter is not turned away before boarding the plane. To avoid this, a few days before flying, phone the airline company to double-check that

FUN FACT

Gentlemen of the Dog World

English Setters are affectionately referred to as the gentlemen of the dog world because of their stately appearance and devoted loyalty. These graceful companions have joined the families of notable people such as Clark Gable, Annie Oakley, and Glenn Gould. One English Setter, Count Noble, was so well known and beloved that upon his death, the *New York Times* ran an obituary for the dog.

you have all the required documents for traveling with your English Setter.

Look for nonstop flights with no transfers. Avoid traveling with your English Setter during the holiday season when airports are busy and flights are packed. This is to minimize the risks of any unexpected changes or cancelations.

Consider the weather at your final destination. If you are traveling somewhere cooler, choose flights in the middle of the day when the temperature is not as cold. If you are traveling somewhere warmer, choose flights later in the evening or early mornings before the temperature rises. Keep in mind, most airlines will not let your pet travel in the cargo hold if the temperatures are too extreme at the final destination.

The majority of airlines allow only a certain number of dogs on each flight, so always call the airline and make sure they have space for both you and your English Setter. Always make reservations for you and your dog at the same time to avoid unwanted last-minute surprises at the airport.

Consider your destination

If you are planning on traveling internationally or even to some U.S. states such as Hawaii or Puerto Rico, be sure to check local animal transportation regulations before purchasing your ticket. Many international destinations have a complicated process and/or lengthy quarantine periods, which may mean you will be separated from your Setter for part or most of your trip.

The CDC has recently suspended dogs coming in from high-risk countries for dog rabies. American citizens and lawful citizens can request an import permit, but these permits will be issued on an extremely limited basis. If you are planning to travel to one of these countries, be aware that your dog may not be permitted to reenter the United States.

Before traveling, research the departing and destination airport so you know exactly where any pet-relief areas are located inside the airport. If you have flight transfers, your English Setter will thank you for letting him relieve himself and stretch his legs. Consult the terminal, so once your flight lands, you will know where to head with your dog.

Consult with your vet

Before planning any flight with your English Setter, be sure to consult with your veterinarian about food, water, and medication. The American Veterinary Medical Association does not recommend sedating dogs prior to flying. There are health risks with sedating dogs, and certain airlines prohibit sedating pets without a certified note from the dog's veterinarian.

If your English Setter is slightly overweight, your vet can formulate a weight loss plan to help the dog lose those extra pounds before the big journey. This is important, as obese dogs are at a higher risk of having their airways collapse while traveling.

Many airlines require that your Setter have a clean bill of health before flying. Your veterinarian can issue a health certificate stating that your dog is healthy enough to fly and is up to date on his vaccinations. If the duration of your trip is longer than the certificate's validity, then you will need to get another certificate from a veterinarian while on vacation in order to meet the requirements of your English Setter's return flight.

At the airport

Make sure to arrive at the airport with plenty of extra time to avoid being stressed.

If your dog is traveling in the cargo hold

Most airlines require you to arrive at least three hours before domestic flights and at least five hours before international flights. You may have to take your English Setter to a separate cargo drop-off section in the terminal, so review your departure and arrival airport maps ahead of time to avoid confusion.

Be sure to paste a current picture of your dog on the crate along with his name. Also, you can tape a bag of food to the outside of the crate in case of a long delay. Be sure to have a current picture of your English Setter on your phone and a picture of his crate in case the airline accidentally misplaces your dog, which is not likely to happen, but it is better to be prepared than sorry.

If your dog is traveling in the cabin

Go directly to the passenger check-in desk, where the agent will request to see your dog's health certification and proof of immunizations.

Once you pay the pet carry-on fee, head directly to security. Deal with your personal items, such as computers, jackets, shoes, etc., before tending to your dog. Remove your English Setter from his carrier case and walk him through security while his carrier goes through the X-ray machine. To speed things up, do not forget to remove your dog's harness or collar so it does not set off the metal detector.

On the plane

Unfortunately, due to the size of an English Setter, your dog will only be allowed to travel in the plane cabin if he has special certification, such as an emotional-support dog or guide dog, etc.

Keep your English Setter well hydrated throughout the flight by using an attachable water dispenser. Your dog's ears can pop due to the pressurization upon take-off and landing. To avoid this, give your English Setter a few pieces of chewy jerky to munch on during this portion of the flight, but be careful not to give him too much, as he could get airsick.

In the cargo hold

Make sure you invest in a good quality hard-cover crate with adequate ventilation, waterproof bottom, spring-locked door, and no handles. Your English Setter should be able to completely turn around and stand up in the crate without hunching over. Do not compromise on your pooch's comfort; make sure he has enough room to stretch out.

Go the extra mile to cable-tie the crate's doors shut. Spring locks are hard to get open, but go the extra step to ensure no accidents happen.

Attach a latch water bottle with an easy-to-use water dispenser inside of the crate. Do not place it on the outside, as it could easily get knocked off as the baggage handlers transport your dog. Fill and freeze the water bottle the night before for dripless, refreshing hydration.

If your dog is hesitant to drink from the water bottle, then entice him by filling the bottle with lukewarm chicken broth. Water dispensers have a ball inside of the cap that rolls around when touched, releasing water. You might have to encourage your English Setter by rolling the ball around and releasing the irresistible scent of chicken broth. Reward him when he drinks from the bottle and slowly wean him off the chicken broth by replacing it with water.

Place visible identification and documentation on your dog's crate. Make sure the following information is attached to the crate: your full name, flight information, name of your pet, picture of your pet, your home and cell phone number, any medical considerations, dog temperament issues (if any), and veterinary information.

Make sure your dog has his collar on with his ID tag. Inside the crate, make sure your English Setter is comfortable with a soft blanket. Place some super-absorbent potty pads under the blanket just in case your dog has an accident or two.

Upon arrival

If your English Setter traveled in the cargo hold, pick up your checked luggage upon arrival and go straight to your airline's specified location for cargo. Airlines often state that dogs will be available 30 minutes after the flight's arrival. If your dog is not picked up within four hours of arrival, the airline will hand the dog over to a veterinarian or boarding facility at your expense.

Whether your English Setter flew in the cabin or the cargo hold, take him immediately for a walk, so he can stretch his legs and relieve himself in a designated relief area for pets, either inside or outside the terminal. Even though the journey may seem complicated, you both will breathe a sigh of relief when you arrive at your final destination together.

Lodging Away from Home

Have dog, will travel.

If your vacation or trip away from home is not complete without your English Setter by your side, you'll be happy to know there are many dog-friendly options to bring your pooch along.

Hotel stays

Many hotel chains are not only dog-friendly nowadays but also give their canine guests the royal treatment. A recent survey by the American Hotel & Lodging Association discovered that almost 80 percent of luxury, mid-scale, and economy hotels in the United States now allow pets. Below are some tips to ensure your English Setter will be welcome at a hotel.

Talk directly with the hotel

Book directly with the hotel over the phone. This way, you will be able to ask any specific questions regarding the hotel's policies and fees for overnight pet guests. Ask the following questions:

- If there is a pet fee, is the fee per night or a flat rate for the entire stay?
- Does the hotel require a damage deposit?
- Is the entire hotel pet-friendly or only a designated floor? If the latter, ask whether the restaurants or lobby area are pet-friendly.
- Can you leave your dog in the hotel room alone, or does he need to be supervised? If so, how long does the hotel's policy allow your dog to be left unattended?
- Does the hotel offer dog sitters or dog walkers? If so, what are the costs and availability for your stay?
- Are there any charges associated with damages from your pet?

The majority of hotels charge a nominal fee for dogs; $25 to $50 is a standard price per night. Many major hotel chains or boutique hotels offer discounts for pets during the off-season.

Take your English Setter's behavior into consideration

You will never really know how your dog will act when traveling until you try it, but taking into consideration his behavior at home will help you determine how he will act at a hotel. For example, if your pooch tends to bark at people walking past the window, then request a hotel room on a higher floor. Or if your English Setter gets nervous on elevator rides, request a room on the lower floor so you can just walk up the stairs.

If you have to leave your pup alone in the room, turn the television on so that he will not get nervous or excited by hearing people walking and talking in the hallways. If you are unsure how your pup will act, you can always plan a short one-night stay at a local pet-friendly hotel. Or if your Setter loves the sound of his own voice, maybe consider staying at a pet-friendly rental property.

Have a backup plan if you cannot leave your dog alone

If the hotel policy is that you cannot leave your dog alone in the room, make sure you have a backup plan. Many hotels offer additional services, such as a dog sitter or a dog walker for hire. Another option is to take your English Setter to a day spa or groomer for the day.

If the hotel lets you leave your pooch alone in the hotel room, always give the front desk staff a heads-up and leave them your cell phone number in case of any noise complaints or other issues. Also, do not forget to place a DO NOT DISTURB sign on the door to prevent your pup from unexpectedly surprising the housekeeper.

Choose the right pet-friendly hotel

Just because a hotel lets your dog stay as a guest does not necessarily mean it is pet-friendly. Many boutique hotels provide amenities to cater to their four-pawed guests, such as a dog bed, a piddle pad, yummy treats, and food dishes at no extra charge. A few chain hotels even have a special dining menu for their canine guests, along with grooming and walking services for an additional fee.

Research pet-friendly restaurants and activities

If you cannot leave your pooch alone in the hotel room, you are going to want to find restaurants or activities that are pet-friendly. The majority of hotels will provide you with a list of nearby restaurants that allow pets. Often, if a hotel is pet-friendly, at least a part of the lobby or on-site restaurant will accommodate your pooch.

Look for fun activities to do with your English Setter that are dog-friendly, such as a walking tour of the city or spending the day exploring a dog beach or park. Many galleries, zoos, and wineries are pet-friendly if your dog is leashed at all times and under your supervision.

Tips for a quiet hotel stay

Trust me, you do not want to be that person whose dog barks inside the hotel room. Nothing can be more embarrassing than being informed that your dog is disturbing the peace of other hotel guests. Plus, it can be an expensive inconvenience if the hotel requests you evacuate the property immediately.

If you must leave your furry friend alone in a hotel room, even if it is a short period of time, these steps will help you and your dog avoid any problems:

- Do not leave your English Setter alone until he has become acclimated to the new space. Take the time to establish in your dog's mind that this room is his "new home."
- Try doing a few practices by leaving the room for a few minutes, then coming back inside. This will help your dog understand that if you leave, you will be returning promptly.
- Keep your time away as short as possible.
- If available, upgrade your room to a suite. By having two separate living spaces, you can place your dog's crate in the furthermost corner from the hallway. This will act as a buffer, giving your pooch some space from those strange noises outside of his door.
- Tired dogs make less ruckus. Be sure to take your English Setter for a long walk with plenty of opportunities to relieve himself outside.

- Pack something extra special to keep your dog distracted while you are out and about, such as a toy stuffed with a delicious treat. If your pup's mouth is busy, he will be less likely to bark.
- Help your English Setter relax by playing classical music, and leave it playing when you go out to cover any hallway noises that may trigger barking.

Staying with friends and family

Today's society has become quite tolerant of dogs, but not everyone wants a dog at their next family gathering. No matter where you are planning on staying, your pup needs to learn to be a gracious house guest. The sooner you can start teaching your dog proper pet etiquette, the better.

Training is a critical aspect of whether your English Setter will make a gracious house guest. The better trained your pooch is, the more welcome both of you will be as guests. Ask yourself if your pooch has mastered the basic commands, such as sit, stay, and come. It may seem like a long list, but they are key elements for your dog to be a charming guest.

You are taking your dog into someone else's house. Ask where your dog will be allowed to go and what areas are off-limits. Also, if your dog accidentally goes to the bathroom on the lawn, clean up after him promptly.

If things do not work out as planned, have a contingency plan, such as a pet-friendly hotel nearby or a reputable boarding kennel. No matter how things go, send a thank-you card to express your gratitude and, if necessary, to apologize.

No matter where you are planning on staying, these are some helpful suggestions on how to minimize friction.

Ask first. Never just show up to stay at someone's house with your dog in tow. Always ask permission to bring along your furry friend. Not everyone wants a dog as a house guest. Even dog lovers appreciate an advance warning, as it allows them to puppy-proof their home, such as putting away those collectible porcelain figurines on display.

The strain of an unwelcome dog can permanently damage relationships. So, even if your English Setter was welcome somewhere in the past, never assume he is welcome again – ask first!

Talk it over. Another factor to take into consideration is if the host or other house guests may be allergic to dogs, or maybe there are small children present who are uncomfortable around rambunctious pups, such as your English Setter. Take into consideration those who may be at high risk of injury around a dog, such as your great aunt, who has already broken her hip twice.

Be considerate. If your English Setter is prone to bad behavior, such as destructive chewing, nonstop barking, or house-soiling, it is unfair to expect your host to welcome your dog into their house.

Camping with your English Setter

Camping with your English Setter will enhance the adventure of being outside in the great outdoors. Your Setter's joie de vie will remind you to drink in the moment. However, since camping is done on public land, there are a wide variety of rules and regulations that can vary, depending on the destination.

The majority of developed campsites welcome dogs, allowing a specified number of pets per site. For instance, while your furry companion is not allowed on trails in Rocky Mountain National Park, Acadia National Park offers hundreds of miles of dog-friendly trekking and camping. Be sure to do your research before you grab your sleeping bag and tent.

Many states and counties throughout the United States provide an extensive list of dog-related information to help you pick an ideal camping destination for you and your English Setter. This is handy, as some parks and campsites have definite rules for dogs year-round, while others have seasonal rules. For example, in the Sawtooth Wilderness near Sun Valley, Idaho, dogs are required to be on a leash on trails from July 1 through Labor Day.

Rules for camping at regulated campsites or in the backcountry are quite similar. Here are some of the basics.

Co-sleeping – As there may be wildlife roaming near your campsite at night, the rules often will require your dog to sleep with you either inside of your car or inside of the tent. The last thing you want is your English Setter running into a skunk or a coyote. The best place for your pooch is right by your side at night. You can keep him safe and out of trouble and prevent barking.

Leave no trace – Depending on the rules of the campsite you are staying at, you may have to pick up your dog's waste and dispose of it later or bury it with dirt. Some parks require you to carry out your dog's waste to prevent the spread of noxious weeds, bacteria, and parasites.

Keep your pooch on a leash while at the camp – If you are staying at a public campsite, there are endless temptations for your pooch to explore, such as your neighbors' sizzling steaks or scurrying squirrels. Most campsites, whether regulated or in the backcountry, require all dogs to be on a leash no longer than six feet long.

Constant supervision – Never assume you can leave your dog alone at the campsite while you run down to the marina to buy a bag of potato chips. Leaving your English Setter alone, whether tied up or kept inside the car or tent, can be a disruptive disturbance to other campers. It can also put your furry companion in danger, as weather can change quickly, wildlife may wander into your campsite, or there could be other unforeseen circumstances.

Kenneling vs. Dog Sitters

You and your English Setter do everything together — from long walks in the woods to sitting in front of the fire on a cold winter day. You are two peas in a pod, which is why the very idea of leaving your tail-wagging best friend behind is so painful. Unfortunately, there will be occasions when you cannot take your English Setter with you, meaning you will have to choose between boarding your dog in a kennel or hiring a dog sitter to watch over him while you are out of town.

Who will care for him? Will his caregiver give him plenty of cuddles and ear scratches? Is your dog better off at home with a professional dog sitter, at a friend's house, or boarded at a local kennel? There is no ideal solution, but taking into consideration your English Setter's age, temperament, and needs will make the decision a little less worrisome.

Boarding Kennels

The best way to describe a boarding kennel is as a pet hotel for your English Setter.

Boarding kennels pride themselves on providing your dog with a safe environment. But just to be on the safe side, be sure to do your research beforehand to determine which kennel is right for your fur baby. Here are some things to consider.

How much space will your English Setter have?

Where will your dog stay? How big are the sleeping areas and the outside run? Will he have enough space to stretch out, exercise, and play? English Setters are high-energy dogs and do not do well locked in a small, enclosed space.

Will your English Setter have social time?

Some kennels have a common area for the dogs to exercise and socialize with other dogs at a specific time each day. It is important your Setter gets at least three to four playtimes a day; otherwise, he will feel cooped up. If your pooch is antisocial or aggressive, ask the kennel if they can provide a separate area for your dog to play.

How many caregivers will be around during the day and at night?

You are paying for the kennel to care for all of your dog's needs, so it is important your dog receives the proper amount of attention. Ask how many people work at the kennel throughout the day and how they interact with the dogs. Also, check into their experience and certification.

What are the fees, requirements, and inclusions?

Check out the kennel's fees and understand exactly what is included in the price per night. For example: Does the fee cover food and additional services, or do you have to provide the food and pay extra for grooming? Depending on the kennel's regulations, you might have to take your dog to a health screening to make sure he is up to date on his vaccinations before a kennel will accept him.

What is the kennel's reputation?

Look at the kennel website and social media pages for customer reviews or testimonials. If you know any friends who have boarded their dogs at a certain kennel before, ask them for an honest opinion.

Your English Setter's stay at the boarding kennel includes grooming, attention, and daily exercise. Depending on the kennel you choose, they will offer a variety of packages and prices to cater to your pup's individual requirements. If you are considering this option, here are a few advantages and disadvantages:

Advantages to boarding kennels

ADVANTAGES

- Boarding kennels provide a secure environment with experienced, dog-loving employees who will constantly monitor your English Setter to prevent any incidents.
- Often a kennel will host other friendly canines, giving your English Setter plenty of fun opportunities to socialize with other dogs.
- Your pup will follow a strict schedule during his stay, which will reduce his stress levels. From your Setter's first day there, he will be fed and exercised according to a schedule.
- Often there is a veterinarian on-site or on-call if there are any emergencies. This option is especially helpful if your English Setter has chronic health problems, as he will receive constant monitoring.

Disadvantages to boarding kennels

DISADVANTAGES

- With all the different dogs staying at the kennel, things can get quite chaotic and noisy at times, which can be stressful for sensitive dogs. If your English Setter tends to get nervous in a new environment or around other dogs, maybe boarding your dog might not be the best option.
- Although the kennel staff will do their best to keep everything in check, certain situations can get out of control. There is a small risk factor if your pooch accidentally gets into a scuffle with another dog.
- Depending on the size of the boarding facility, staff could mix up food, toys, or blankets between different dogs. Often, this does not cause too many problems, except perhaps an upset tummy.
- Keep in mind, if you leave your English Setter at a boarding kennel, he will spend the majority of his time inside his kennel.

All boarding kennels require that their doggy guests' vaccinations and immunizations be up to date. No matter the age of your dog, he is

required to have received his rabies and Bordetella (kennel cough) vaccine at least seven days prior to your dog's planned arrival date.

Bordetella is an airborne upper respiratory infection. There are almost 60 different strains, and the current vaccine only protects against 14. There is no way to fully protect your English Setter from kennel cough, as it is highly contagious. For this reason, it is of utmost importance to search for a boarding kennel that prides itself on regularly sanitizing everything your pup might come into contact with, such as playground areas, daycare areas, toys, food and water dishes, etc.

Boarding kennels have the right to refuse admittance to any dog if the pet owner lacks adequate proof of a dog's vaccinations, if the dog has serious health conditions, or if he displays aggressive behavior.

Dog Sitters

A dog sitter is someone who cares for your dog in your home while you are temporarily absent. Typically, the dog sitter will stay in your house or drop by several times a day while you are away, allowing your English Setter to feel safe and secure in his own territory. Having a dog sitter stay overnight is the ideal solution if your pooch suffers from separation anxiety or if you prefer not to leave him alone at night.

Advantages to a dog sitter

ADVANTAGES

- While you are away, your English Setter is in the comfort of his own home. There is no need to worry about your pooch being exposed to a new environment, people, or other animals.
- The risk of accidents or injury is reduced because a single person is devoted to caring for your English Setter.
- Your dog sitter will carefully follow all of your care instructions for your dog and perhaps even water your plants if you ask them to. If you have a younger pup, you can teach the dog sitter how to work on your dog's obedience training and basic commands.
- A dog sitter will directly communicate with you if there are any problems, etc. The direct line of communication will give you peace of mind, so you can focus on your travels.

Disadvantages to a dog sitter

DISADVANTAGES

- A dog sitter needs to come into your house, and it is imperative you and your English Setter trust her or him. If your pooch is protective of his home or does not react well to new people, perhaps a dog sitter is not the best option.
- Having a dog sitter stay in your home requires extra preparation, such as readying the guest bedroom.
- During the holiday season, it can be almost impossible to find a reliable dog sitter. Be sure to book ahead of time.

- If you hired a dog sitter to drop by a few times a day, and there's bad weather, the person might not be able to get to your house regularly.

Choosing the right sitter – Try to choose someone whose energy level and personality match that of your dog. For example, leaving your rambunctious puppy with an elderly relative is a recipe for disaster. Make sure you feel comfortable with the dog sitter and that he or she understands your English Setter's individual needs.

Finding a professional and responsible dog sitter should not be taken lightly; after all, the dog sitter will be responsible for your pup's welfare, and you are entrusting him or her with the keys to your house. Here are a few suggestions to help you find a reputable dog sitter for your dog:

- **Ask your veterinarian** – If your English Setter is elderly or has health issues, finding a dog sitter with a good recommendation from your vet will give you peace of mind, especially if there is a medical emergency.
- **Word of mouth** – Anyone can look good on paper, but a qualified, reputable dog sitter will come recommended by a close friend or a relative.
- **Ask for references** – Any reputable dog sitter will be able to provide you with a list of regular clients who would be more than willing to verify the person's professionalism.
- **Look for a certified dog sitter** – There are two nationwide agencies that train and certify dog sitters: Pet Sitters International (PSI) and the National Association of Professional Pet Sitters (NAPPS). Be sure to check out their webpages to locate a certified dog sitter in your locality; plus, you can check out reviews from previous clients.

Location – Ideally, you want someone who can stay at your house to maintain your English Setter's regular routine and schedule. This involves keeping your dog on the same walking, feeding, and sleeping routine as when you are at home. If you must change your dog's routine, get him used to the changes a few weeks ahead of time to prevent separation anxiety or other issues.

If you plan on leaving your dog at a friend's house while you are away, you might want to get him familiar with the new location a few times before actually leaving your dog there for an extended stay.

Details – Just as parents leave a checklist for a babysitter, you can make a checklist for your dog sitter. Include important information such as the vet's phone number and address, any medications your dog needs to take while you are away, allergies, feeding schedule, the closest 24-hour emergency veterinary clinic, and any behavioral problems.

Share with the dog sitter any house rules for your English Setter, such as whether he is allowed on the furniture and how often he gets a treat — basically, any information you feel will keep your pup feeling happy, and secure while you are away.

Do not drag out goodbyes – Your Setter is used to seeing you leave the house without him, so do not make a big production of your departure this time. If you do, you might make your pooch anxious. Be confident and casual when you say goodbye; both of you will be more relaxed.

Keep watch – If you are still uncomfortable about leaving your fur baby with a stranger, you could invest in a dog camera. Many smart dog cameras are designed to let you interact with your dog.

Relax – Now, take a deep breath and relax! You have taken all of the necessary steps to ensure that your English Setter has a pleasant experience while you are away, so enjoy your trip.

Carefully consider the advantages and disadvantages of each dog-care option. If you cannot decide which is the best choice for your canine friend, you can always try a short stay at a boarding kennel and another with a dog sitter before planned trip to see how your dog reacts.

CHAPTER 11

Nutrition

> *Take your veterinarian's advice on proper feeding. Most dogs do fine on a chicken-, lamb-, or beef-based diet. Grain-free diets are not necessary unless your dog has a specific allergy to grain. Dogs can process the protein from corn and wheat but may have larger stools. Soy is best avoided, as it can interfere with hormone function. Find the best quality that fits within your budget. Skip the table scraps, as they lead to an unbalanced diet and a dog that learns to beg.*
>
> KAREN STROHMEYER
> *Bristle Ridge Llewellins*

A balanced and nutritious diet is essential to keep your English Setter healthy, but providing him with the right amount of nourishment can be tricky.

Obesity is one of the most common dog problems observed by veterinarians and often is due to an unbalanced diet of too many treats and not enough wholesome ingredients. In this chapter, you will learn everything you need to know about feeding your dog at every stage of his life.

Importance of a Wholesome Diet

> *Puppies should never have a diet too high in calcium, to prevent growth concerns. Allergies are not too common in the breed, so we have always had luck with a chicken-and-rice food that is between 25 and 30% protein and 15 and 20% fat. Be especially careful with grain-free foods because of their recent association with dilated cardiomyopathy (DCM).*
>
> KAYLA KOZAK
> *Kei-Rin Kennel*

Every English Setter is different. Some Setters love to eat, while others are picky eaters or have sensitive stomachs, and there are also dogs with dietary sensitivities. Deciding what to feed your dog is a very personal choice; however, his diet will have a direct impact on his health and happiness.

Just like humans, dogs require essential nutrients to develop properly and stay healthy. The wrong diet can lead to a life of health issues and obesity; on the other hand, the right diet can keep your dog slim, healthy, and in tip-top shape.

The old saying "you are what you eat" applies to your English Setter as much as yourself. Dog food made with high-quality ingredients equals a better quality of life, resulting in fewer infections, digestive issues, skin conditions, and so on. The impact of a wholesome diet does not end there, as it can also directly impact your dog's personality and behavior.

Your dog's behavior is a direct result of activity in his central nervous center. If he is not receiving the necessary nutrients, he will be lethargic, moody, and inactive. Here are a few examples of how the food you give and the frequency by which you feed your English Setter will impact his mood and behavior.

Unbalanced diet – Many health and behavioral issues in dogs are caused by a poorly balanced diet. For example, a diet deficient in nutrients may cause your English Setter to suffer from frequent urinary tract infections that cause him to become irritable due to discomfort and pain. Make sure your Setter only eats a well-balanced, high-quality dog food to maintain good mental and physical health.

Inadequate food – If your English Setter is not consuming enough calories throughout the day, he will be hungry and may engage in disruptive behaviors such as scavenging through your neighbor's garbage or eating feces. Dogs who are not receiving sufficient nutrients in their diet may develop a condition called pica, which causes them to eat non-food items such as soil and plants.

Pet food ingredients – The ingredients in your pup's pet food may also affect his behavior. For instance, research has found that senior dogs who receive a diet rich in antioxidants are able to learn complicated tasks faster than dogs who do not. Studies have shown that senior dogs who have always received a high-quality dog food suffer from fewer behavioral changes common to cognitive decline.

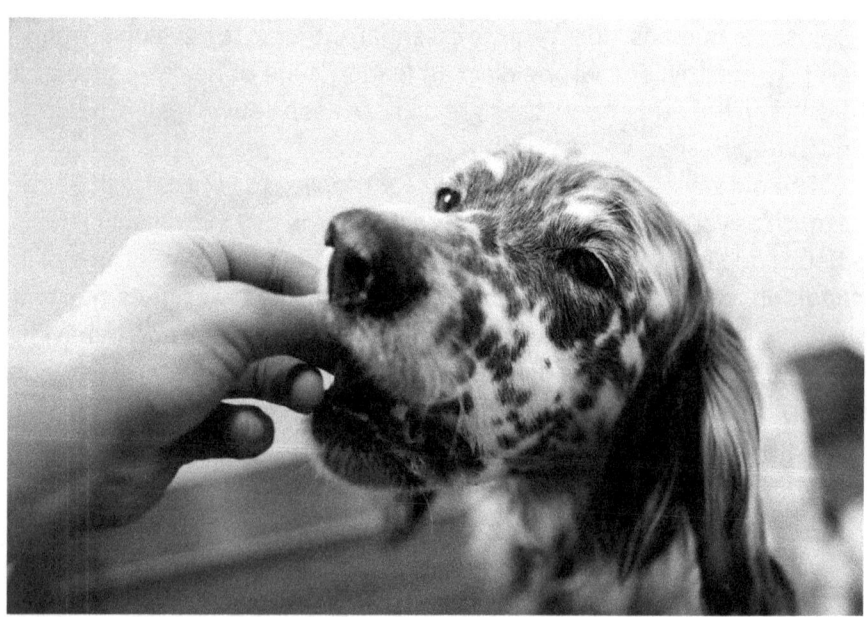

A well-balanced diet will promote stable blood sugar levels through-out the day, which will directly affect your English Setter's serotonin levels. Serotonin not only improves your dog's mood but also his concentration, behavior, and training response. Another advantage to a wholesome diet is your dog's immune system will be in excellent condition.

Talk to your veterinarian before changing your English Setter's diet. Your vet will recommend a brand of food that is suitable for your dog's age, size, weight, medical history, and lifestyle. Nutrition has an exten-sive impact on your dog's overall health, so make sure you feed him a wholesome diet.

Here are some common health issues related to your English Setter's diet

Heart disease – Dogs often have issues with heart disease, especially if their diet is not well-balanced. Increased levels of sodium are one of the main factors of heart disease in dogs. Since high-quality commercial dog foods are low in sodium, the main source of sodium is probably coming from those table scraps you are slipping your dog under the table.

Diabetes – Overweight dogs tend to develop diabetes as they age. There is no known cure for diabetes. A dog with diabetes will require daily insulin shots, a special diet, and extra medical attention. The best and only prevention is to keep your English Setter on a healthy diet and give him an active lifestyle. Avoid dog food that contains starchy fillers and sugar, which offer little to no nutritional value and will spike your dog's blood sugar level.

Obesity – Obese dogs are prone to arthritis, diabetes, breathing issues, high-blood pressure, and cancer. Decreased life expectancy is linked to obesity in dogs. Your English Setter does not need excessive calories each day. Be sure to follow the instructions on the food bag for his weight, size, and age.

Pancreatitis – Pancreatitis is caused by a diet high in fats. Consult with your vet to see if your dog's current dietary fat intake may be increas-ing his risk of pancreatitis.

Food allergies and sensitivities

Food allergies and sensitivities are not the same thing. It is important to take into consideration how a particular food affects your English Setter. If your dog's energy level is normal for his age, if his coat and skin are healthy, if his stools are brown and well-formed, and if he appears to be healthy, then his food is doing its job.

However, if your English Setter has diarrhea, skin issues, or an extremely itchy coat, your dog may have a food sensitivity. In this case, discuss the issue with your veterinarian. He will be able to help you create a feeding plan that works best for your dog's health. Often, your veterinarian will place your dog on an elimination diet and slowly reintroduce foods to determine what foods are causing the allergic reaction.

A food allergy involves the immune system and is often caused by a protein molecule. Food allergies present an immediate immunological response, such as anaphylactic shock, which may mean your dog is having difficulty breathing. In this case, you should take your pooch to the nearest veterinarian clinic immediately. A less severe reaction may present with facial swelling, hives, or itchiness. If you suspect your Setter has a food allergy, it is vital that you talk to your vet to identify the cause.

A food sensitivity is an abnormal response to a certain ingredient. Food sensitivities can easily be managed and often will disappear over time. If you suspect your dog has a food intolerance, talk to your vet; look for a hypoallergenic food that avoids common allergens, such as beef or wheat, and choose a dog food with a single protein source.

Human Foods to Avoid

> **"**
>
> *People food is for people. Feeding dogs from the table creates bad habits and can cause health issues.*
>
> JOHN MCILTROT
> *Seranoa Kennels*
> **"**

Slipping your English Setter a morsel or two under the table may be tempting, but it can cause your dog some serious health issues or even be fatal. You might be surprised at some of the foods your furry friend needs to avoid at all costs!

Alcohol – Even the tiniest amount of any type of alcohol can be fatal for your English Setter. Alcohol causes dogs to have coordination problems, vomiting, diarrhea, breathing issues, and even death.

Avocado – All dogs are allergic to persin, which is found in high quantities in avocados. Persin is not only found in the flesh of the avocado but also in the leaves, peel, bark of the tree, seed, etc. If you have an avocado tree in your backyard, be sure to keep your dog away from it at all times.

Bones or fat trimmings – It might seem like second nature to give your pooch a bone to chew on, but dogs can easily choke on them, or the bone may splinter and become lodged in his throat or cut up his digestive system. Furthermore, pieces of grease or fat can cause your English Setter to develop pancreatitis.

Caffeine – All types of caffeine are fatal for your dog, including cocoa, energy drinks, Guarana, tea, caffeinated carbonated beverages, and soda. If your dog accidentally consumes a product with caffeine, go immediately to the nearest veterinarian office.

Chocolate – Dark, white, and milk chocolate are deadly for dogs. Even the smallest morsel can cause diarrhea, vomiting, cardiac failure, seizures, and even death.

Dairy products – Dairy products such as milk, whipped cream, and ice cream can cause your dog to experience digestive discomfort and diarrhea. Many dogs who are lactose intolerant have extremely itchy skin. That said, the majority of dogs can tolerate cheese and yogurt due to the natural digestive enzymes and probiotics.

Garlic and onions – Keep all types of garlic and onions far away from your pooch, including fresh, dry, powdered, dehydrated, or cooked. Even the smallest pinch can cause your English Setter's blood count to drop, causing him to become anemic.

Grapes or raisins – Grapes and raisins seem the perfect bite-sized treat for your dog, but a few can cause kidney failure. If you think your English Setter may have consumed some grapes or raisins, call your veterinarian if you notice any sluggish behavior or severe vomiting.

Macadamia nuts – Eating just three macadamia nuts can cause your English Setter to become seriously ill. Eating chocolate-covered macadamia nuts will intensify the symptoms, which will eventually lead to death. Macadamia nuts cause vomiting, muscle tremors, fever, and loss of muscle control.

Pitted fruits – Fruits such as peaches, persimmons, cherries, and plums have pits or seeds that can get lodged in your dog's intestines, causing a blockage. Some pits, such as from a plum or a peach, contain cyanide, which is fatal if consumed.

Raw eggs – Raw eggs are a source of bacteria, such as salmonella or E. coli. Avoid feeding your English Setter raw or undercooked eggs or any type of raw animal products, such as fish, beef, pork, or chicken.

Raw yeast dough – Before baking, yeast dough needs to rise. If your English Setter eats some raw dough, it will continue to rise inside his stomach, stretching out your dog's abdomen, and causing extreme pain. The yeast can also cause alcohol poisoning.

Salt – A word of caution: do not share your salted popcorn or pretzels with your furry friend.

Too much salt can cause sodium ion poisoning, vomiting, diarrhea, fever, or seizures and may be fatal if left untreated.

Xylitol – Xylitol is a common sweetener used in baked goods, toothpaste, and diet products. It causes your dog's blood sugar levels to drop, which leads to liver failure.

If your English Setter got into the pantry and ate something he shouldn't have, call your local vet immediately or call the Animal Poison Control Center at (888) 426-4435.

It is not advisable to make a practice out of giving your English Setter leftovers, bits of meat, or other scraps, as he may begin to refuse to eat his normal food. Also, it can unbalance your dog's regular diet, causing him to gain weight. Human foods can cause gas, which may not be a problem for your dog, but it could be for you!

After all that talk about harmful human foods for your pooch, you are probably wondering: "Is all human food bad for my dog?" Although you may use great self-control to keep your Setter on his canine diet, sometimes you may not be able to resist the urge to slip him a piece of cheese.

Before giving your dog any foods that are not on this list, do some research to make sure they are safe. If your pup experiences any sort of reaction or allergy, immediately consult a veterinarian.

Here are some of the best human food choices for your four-pawed furry friend

Peanut butter – Peanut butter is a favorite treat for English Setter. Also, it is an excellent source of protein, healthy fats, vitamin B, and niacin. Be sure to only use unsalted peanut butter. Make sure you are not using sugar-free or light peanut butter, as it may contain artificial sweeteners such as xylitol.

Cooked chicken or turkey – Cooked chicken is a healthy source of protein and makes a great alternative to high-calorie treats used in obedience training. Plus, if you accidentally run out of dog food, it makes a healthy meal replacement.

Cheese – Cheese is an excellent snack for your pooch if he is not lactose intolerant. Choose low-fat varieties and do not overfeed, as most cheeses are high in fat and may cause constipation. Cottage cheese is typically a good option for Setters.

Carrots – Carrots are a yummy low-calorie snack for your dog and are great for your dog's teeth. They are also high in fiber, beta-carotene, and vitamins. You can feed your dog raw or cooked carrots; just be sure to cut them into small pieces to prevent him from accidentally choking on them.

Yogurt – Yogurt is high in calcium and protein. Also, its active probiotics can aid your dog's digestive system and improve his breath.

Salmon – Salmon is an excellent source of omega-3 fatty acids, which will help keep your English Setter's coat healthy and shiny and support his immune system. Try adding cooked salmon to your dog's kibble, or slip him some unwanted fish skins.

Pumpkin – Pumpkins are part of the squash family, all of which are excellent sources of fiber, beta-carotene, and vitamin A. Plus, pumpkin can keep your dog's GI tract moving and aid with digestive issues.

Eggs – A scrambled egg will give your English Setter's diet a protein boost. Eggs are remarkably high in protein and a source of digestible riboflavin and selenium. Always thoroughly cook the eggs to avoid any risk of salmonella.

Green beans – Green beans are another healthy snack for your English Setter, as they are a source of protein, calcium, vitamin K, and iron. Raw and cooked green beans are filling and low in calories. Just remember to only serve them without salt or other seasonings.

Apple slices – Sliced apples are high in fiber and vitamins and are a healthy treat for your pooch. Additionally, apple slices are known for cleaning teeth and freshening breath. Before giving your dog a few apple slices, make sure to remove the seeds and the core, as they can be a choking hazard.

Oatmeal – Cooked oatmeal is an excellent source of soluble fiber, which is especially beneficial to senior dogs with bowel irregularity issues. It is a fantastic grain option for dogs allergic to wheat. Always cook oatmeal before serving it to your pup, and only use oatmeal that has no added sugar or additives.

If you decide to give your pooch a treat or two from your table, make sure it is not seasoned, fatty, salty, or raw. Certain fruits, such as thin slices of apples, bananas, or watermelon, all make yummy treats for your English Setter. Be sure to remove any seeds, peels, or stems that could get stuck in your dog's digestive tract.

Cooked, plain white rice or noodles with a piece of boiled chicken might be the best solution if your pooch has an upset tummy.

Commercial Dog Food

"

We find a brand we like and rotate every other bag to a new recipe within that brand: a bag of salmon, then lamb and rice, etc. Food rotation will help avoid creating a finicky eater. Be sure to mix the last five to 10 servings of the old bag into the first servings of the new bag. Most dogs won't have an issue with a food change, but it's best to err on the side of caution and introduce the new food over the course of a few meals, just to be sure.

MARK D. DENEKA
Twilight Setter Kennels

"

In the last few years, commercial dog food has improved enormously. A few decades ago, there were only a few generic brands of dog food on the shelves, whereas today, you can find countless brands, catering to different breeds, ages, and dietary restrictions. However, with so many choices out there, it can be overwhelming to narrow down what type of dog food is best suited for your English Setter.

Learning about how commercial dog food is made will help you understand the nutritional value of the food you are feeding your English Setter. There are two main types of commercially prepared dog food: canned food and dry kibble. Commercially produced fresh dog food is a newcomer to the dog food aisle and is quickly gaining popularity but is not yet widely available.

Wet dog food

Wet dog food may be sold in cans, boxes, or single-serving pouches, often consisting of 35–75 percent water, depending on the quality. Be sure to look for the moisture content on the label. Wet foods contain a variety of meats, such as beef, chicken, lamb, salmon, or venison.

Once the can or package is opened, it must be refrigerated to maintain its freshness, and most dogs will not eat cold food. To solve this problem, you can warm up the meal portion before serving. Note that wet foods have the highest cost per serving, and cheaper brands of wet food are high in fillers, sugar, and fat.

Wet dog food is made using fresh and frozen meat. Many commercial brands use animal parts such as organs or fatty tissue. One of the advantages of these parts is they have a higher nutritional value than meats typically consumed by humans. The meat is then ground and mixed in large machines to ensure even distribution of the calories and nutrients.

The packaging method used for wet food uses a high heat sterilization method to kill off any bacteria, but an unwanted side effect is that it also destroys the nutrients and vitamins. The sterilization and vacuum-sealing process ensures a longer shelf life without the need to use harmful chemicals.

However, due to the processing method, wet foods are notorious for being void of nutrients. If you want your dog to get his daily nutritional requirements, you will need to give him a huge portion at each meal, which will eventually result in weight gain.

Dry food

The vast majority of dogs throughout the United States are fed dry kibble.

Dry dog food contains similar ingredients to wet dog food, but instead of adding gravy and canning the product, the meat mixture is pulverized and mixed together to create a consistent mass of dough that can then be cooked. The dough can be manufactured by one of the following methods.

Baked – The dough is extruded through specially shaped holes and then baked at a low temperature. Once baked, the kibble is left out to dry and then sprayed with fats, oils, minerals, and vitamins; often, baked kibble contains wheat gluten to aid in binding the ingredients together.

Cold-pressed – This is a newbie in the dog food aisle that is quickly gaining popularity with both pet owners and dogs alike. Cold-pressed dog food often prides itself on only using the freshest of ingredients. The manufacturer will grind the ingredients together, forming a thick, coarse paste, which is then left to dry before being pressed out to remove the excess moisture. It is then baked at a very low temperature to prevent any nutrient loss.

Extrusion – This method is similar to baking, except before extruding the dough through specially shaped holes, the mixture is first cooked in huge steam and pressure cookers to kill off any bacteria, etc. Then, when the mixture cools, it is pressed through an extruding machine, shaping the kibble. After this, the kibble is placed into a high-heat convection oven to remove any excess moisture.

It is worth mentioning that this type of kibble's double exposure to extreme heat removes the majority of the nutrients and vitamins.

Freeze-dried – The fresh food is mixed together, then ground into a coarse paste, formed into small pieces of kibble, and placed inside a type of vacuum oven that removes all excess moisture. The process preserves the majority of the nutrients, making it one of the healthiest food choices for your English Setter.

Freeze-dried foods have a long shelf life without the need for harmful preservatives. Some freeze-dried foods may need to be rehydrated with water before serving. This is one of the most expensive dry dog food options.

Fresh food

Fresh dog food is quickly gaining popularity in the dog food aisle, as it is a convenient alternative to homemade dog food. Fresh dog food manufacturers pride themselves on using only fresh, organic ingredients and human-grade proteins. Many companies provide the option of using recyclable, reusable serving trays.

One of the main advantages of fresh dog food is the high nutritional value due to the low level of processing required. On the other hand, since it does contain preservatives, fresh food has a maximum life span of seven to 14 days and will need to be stored in the refrigerator. It is not recommended to freeze fresh dog food, as many of the nutrients will be lost.

Wet dog food vs. dry dog food

As you can see above, both wet dog food and dry can be good choices, depending on the quality of ingredients and the process used to manufacture the dog food. However, they each offer different benefits and drawbacks, depending on your English Setter's nutritional needs.

Benefits of wet dog food compared to dry dog food

- **Higher moisture content** – Your veterinarian may recommend a wet dog food diet if your dog frequently suffers from urinary tract infections or dislikes drinking water.

- **Palatability** – Wet dog food is preferred by dogs who are finicky eaters. Also, wet dog food is ideal for concealing medications. It is ideal for elderly or sick dogs whose appetite has decreased.
- **Easier to chew** – Dogs who have dental issues or other oral abnormalities may find eating wet food easier than dry food.
- **Satiety** – Wet dog food tends to cause a longer-lasting feeling of being full. Increased satiety is especially useful in managing your dog's weight.

Benefits of dry dog food compared to wet dog food
- **Dental health** – One of the main advantages to dry food is it acts like a toothbrush, helping to remove and prevent the buildup of plaque and tartar on your dog's teeth.
- **Convenience and cost-effectiveness** – Kibble's popularity is due to the convenience for feeding and cost (as with most things, the larger the bag, the better the savings). In addition, it stays fresh longer than wet foods once the package has been opened.
- **Food enrichment** – Kibble is easy to use with food puzzles that help to keep your dog mentally stimulated and improve the quality of his life.

As you can see, there are quite a few factors to take into consideration when choosing the best dog food for your English Setter. Ultimately, choosing the right dog food is a very personal decision and depends on your budget and personal preferences. The right dog food for your English Setter will meet his nutritional requirements and keep him happy and healthy.

How to Read Dog Food Labels

The dog food nutrition label is similar to the nutrition facts on packaged food for humans. The label is designed to help you compare products and learn more about what you are considering purchasing and feeding your dog.

QUICK TIP: *Look past the attractive packaging and marketing; instead, learn to read the ingredients.*

 GENERAL RULE OF THUMB: *If humans are not allowed to eat it, then you should not feed it to your dog either.*

Just as with packaged food for humans, dog food must list the ingredients according to weight, starting with the heaviest. But a word of caution: if the first ingredient is a protein, keep in mind that proteins are typically about 75 percent water.

Dog food labels are required to contain:
- Product brand name
- Quantity displayed in terms of weight, liquid measure, or count, depending on the formulation of the dog food
- Ingredients listed in descending order by weight
- Feeding instructions for your dog's age, activity level, and weight
- Nutritional statement backed up by research and testing to prove the food provides the required daily nutritional requirements
- Manufacturer's name and address
- Calorie statement and the life stages the food is appropriate for

Continue reading to learn which ingredients to avoid and why they can harm your English Setter's health.

Artificial preservatives – Avoid dog foods that contain ethoxyquin, BHA, and BHT on the ingredient list. The National Institute of Health has deemed BHA and BHT to be carcinogenic and unfit for human consumption. Ethoxyquin is linked to cancer, chronic immune diseases, and kidney failure in both humans and animals.

Corn and rice fillers – Corn and rice fillers are commonly used for fattening up animals, and the last thing your English Setter needs is a carbohydrate-rich diet. A low-protein diet is one of the main causes of obesity in smaller breeds, such as your English Setter. A diet high in corn and rice can cause chronic digestive issues, such as bloating, gas, and diarrhea.

Food coloring – Many dog food manufacturers add food coloring to their kibble and/or treats to make them look more appealing and appetizing. But your English Setter is not concerned about the appearance or color of his food; he just cares whether it is tasty. Avoid dog foods that contain food dyes such as Blue 2, Red 40, or Yellow 5 because they are linked to allergies, hyperactivity, and cancer.

MSG – Monosodium glutamate (MSG) is a well-known flavor enhancer for Chinese food and dog food. MSG overstimulates your dog's brain, causing him to produce a hormone called dopamine, making him become addicted to his food. Recent studies have shown when dogs regularly consume food with MSG over time, they can develop brain damage, obesity, and behavioral issues.

Nondescript fats – Fat is essential for your English Setter's overall health. Most dog food manufacturers list generic animal fat as one of the ingredients, which often is fat derived from sick or rancid animals. Choose a dog food that specifies the type of fat used, such as salmon fat instead of fish fat or coconut oil instead of vegetable oil, etc.

Propylene glycol – Propylene glycol is a common ingredient in antifreeze and is extremely toxic for dogs. However, many dog food manufacturers add it to their products to reduce moisture from building up inside of the packaging, to prevent bacterial growth, and to lengthen the product's life span.

Rendered foods – Rendered meat is often listed on the ingredient list as animal by-product meal, which is a mix of animal parts, such as blood, brains, spleens, entrails, and internal organs. Often, it includes discarded animal parts that were considered to be unfit for human consumption. The nutritional value of rendered meat is extremely low, and it can be a source of salmonella and toxins.

Sugar – Many dog foods contain sugar to mask a bitter flavor and to improve texture. Once your English Setter is addicted to sugar, it is extremely difficult to switch him to a healthier, sugar-free alternative. Sugar additives to watch out for are cane sugar, beet pulp, corn syrup, sucrose, fructose-glucose, xylitol, molasses, and sorbitol.

Some dog owners shy away from buying food that contains synthetic preservatives such as BHA (butylated hydroxyanisole), BHT (butylated hydroxytoluene), or ethoxyquin. These synthetic preservatives prevent fat from turning rancid and can keep dry dog food fresh for at least a year. The FDA has approved these preservatives as safe for animals in small amounts.

Ethoxyquin came under scrutiny because a long list of complaints, such as skin allergies, reproductive problems, cancer, and organ failure in some dogs who were given food with this preservative. The FDA requested dog food manufacturers reduce the amount of ethoxyquin to half of the previously approved amount.

But just because the FDA approves a certain chemical or preservative does not make it healthy and safe for your dog. Use discretion and investigate before using dog food with this chemical added.

Some dog food manufacturers have opted to use natural preservatives such as vitamin E (mixed tocopherols), vitamin C (ascorbic acid), and plant extracts such as rosemary. These natural preservatives help to keep dry food fresh, but for a shortened life span. Be sure to check your dog food bag for the "best by" date on the label before buying or feeding it to your English Setter.

Deciphering terms

Recently there are so many new trends in the dog food market that it can be challenging to decipher the terms. Here are some terms that can be difficult to understand:

Organic – As of the moment this book went to print, the US Department of Agriculture (USDA) was still developing official regulations regarding the labeling of organic foods for pets. In the meantime, dog foods that claim to be organic must meet the requirements established by the USDA's National Organic Program, which means organic dog food has to meet the same standards as organic human food.

Organic dog food must contain no artificial sweeteners, preservatives, flavorings, or food colorings. Plus, meat and meat by-products must be sourced from animals with no antibiotics or growth hormones. Generally speaking, dogs with sensitive tummies do better on an organic diet.

NOTE: *"Natural" dog food is not the same as "organic." The term "natural dog food" refers to the lack of artificial ingredients used in the product.*

Grain-free – Recent studies by the FDA have discovered grain-free dog foods are linked to canine dilated cardiomyopathy (CDC), which causes the dog's heart to enlarge and prevents the blood from circulating freely throughout the body. The FDA recommends pet owners avoid feeding their dogs grain-free foods. Dogs need a diet based on high-quality proteins, natural fats, vegetables, and whole grains to meet their dietary needs.

New proteins – The term "new proteins" refers to new meats in the dog food market, such as bison, kangaroo, rabbit, lamb, and other exotic animals. At the moment, it is difficult to rate the benefits of this food due to a lack of research on the different nutrient profiles when compared with common proteins, such as beef, chicken, or fish.

Human-grade dog food – This is defined as legally edible and safe for human consumption. Human-grade dog food is tightly regulated by the FDA and the USDA. Also, the Association of American Feed Control Officials (AAFCO) requires that human-grade dog food be manufactured, packaged, and held in accordance with federal regulations for manufacturing, packaging, and holding human food.

Light, low-calorie, and low-fat – If labeled with one of these terms, dog food must have a significant reduction in fat or calories when compared to the brand's standard dog food. The AAFCO requires that any dog food label claiming to be light, low-calorie, or low-fat must show the reduction on the label and name the product in comparison.

Good foods to watch out for

Finding a wholesome, healthy, and delicious food for your English Setter may seem like a challenge, but it is not impossible. When choosing a dog food for your pooch, look for a variety of ingredients such as meat, veggies, grains, and fruits. Look for some of the following ingredients on the nutrition label:

Meat – Your English Setter is a high-energy dog who needs plenty of healthy proteins to maintain his body, muscle, and immune system. Look for commercial dog foods made from human-grade proteins, such as beef, chicken, salmon, rabbit, etc.

Whole-meat meal – Often, meat meal is from by-products such as rendered meats, whereas whole-meat meal is a high source of protein and is simply a fancier way of saying ground beef. However, the ingredient list should specify the type of whole-meat meal used, such as chicken, beef, etc. Meat meal contains more protein, as it is ground up, then dried to a 10 percent moisture level, making the protein level at least 65 percent and at least 12 percent fat.

Carbohydrates and grains – Whole grains are an exceptional source of energy for your English Setter, and they improve his digestion. Avoid dog foods made from corn, soy, or white rice; instead, look for higher-quality ingredients, such as brown rice, whole oats, barley, and peas. Carbohydrates and grains should never be one of the first ingredients on the list.

Vegetables and fruits – Both provide essential nutrients, minerals, vitamins, fiber, and antioxidants. For example, sweet potatoes are an excellent source of potassium, vitamin B, and antioxidants. Unsweetened cranberries provide vitamin C, prevent urinary tract infections, and protect your pup's teeth from harmful bacteria.

Fats – Fats are necessary for your English Setter's overall health, proper cell function, and digestion. Fats help your English Setter to absorb minerals and vitamins and keep his coat and teeth in tip-top shape. Look for dog foods that contain wholesome fats like omega-3 and omega-6 fatty acids, canola oil, salmon fat, olive, and coconut oils.

Word of caution

Pay attention to the product name, as it will give you a clue about the ingredients in the dog food you are considering. Most dog owners base their decision on a specific ingredient. Many brands will highlight that ingredient on the product's label.

Stay away from commercial dog foods that use the term "with," such as "with chicken" or "with beef." Manufacturers are only required to use 3 percent of protein in the dog food. Avoid dog food whose labels include the wording "flavor," such as beef or chicken flavor, as this indicates it was made with an exceedingly small percentage of the actual product and mostly contains artificial flavoring.

Just because a dog food manufacturer claims to provide everything your English Setter needs for his optimum health does not necessarily mean the food is really healthy. Take the time to carefully read the ingredient list and make a decision based on the ingredients, not based on the attractive packaging.

B.A.R.F. Diet

The B.A.R.F. diet stands for two common phrases: Biologically Appropriate Raw Food and Bones and Raw Food. B.A.R.F. was developed by nutritionist and veterinarian Dr. Ian Billinghurst, and the main principle behind the diet is feeding canines a diet similar to what they would eat in the wild. The raw diet is composed of proteins, vegetables, and fruits that are all uncooked.

The B.A.R.F. diet basically consists of a hearty portion of protein, such as muscle meat, raw meaty bones, organ meat, and a moderate quantity of vegetables and fruits. Some pet owners also add supplements to their dog's diet under the guidance of their veterinarian.

According to recent studies, there are quite a few health benefits to feeding your English Setter a raw food diet:

- **Healthy weight** – Your English Setter will have a leaner, more muscular build and will maintain a healthy weight.
- **Improved appearance** – Most pet owners who feed their dogs a raw food diet have noticed an overall improvement in the appearance of their skin and hair. Plus, their dogs have cleaner teeth and fresher breath.
- **Increased energy** – Many pet owners who feed a raw diet to their canines state their dogs have increased energy levels.

- **Improved bowel movements** – Dogs who suffer from diarrhea with a regular diet often have firmer and smaller stools on a raw food diet.

However, there are also many disadvantages to giving your English Setter a raw diet, such as:

- **An unbalanced diet** – An unbalanced diet can cause nutrient deficiencies and future health problems.
- **Bacteria and other pathogens** – Raw dog food, if not stored correctly or consumed immediately, becomes an ideal breeding ground for potentially dangerous bacteria or pathogens that can make your dog very sick.
- **Cross-contamination** – The risk of contamination with raw meat can make humans extremely ill.
- **High cost and time investment** – Providing your dog with human-grade proteins each day can be very expensive, not to mention time-consuming to prepare.

If you decide to give your English Setter a raw food diet, be sure to consult with your vet beforehand to decide whether it is suitable for your dog's health and lifestyle. Your veterinarian will need to closely monitor your dog's overall health for the first few months to ensure he has no allergies or other health issues.

If you decide that a raw food diet is something you are interested in but do not feel comfortable in preparing your Setter's meals every day, ask your veterinarian to recommend a company that makes raw dog food in your locality.

Even though what you decide to feed your dog is a very personal decision, you should be aware that a raw diet is not appropriate for every dog. For example, a raw food diet is not recommended for dogs with health issues such as kidney and liver failure. Dogs with cancer, on chemotherapy, or with other immunosuppressive diseases also should not be on a raw diet. Due to the lack of calcium and the potential for harmful bacteria, raw food is not recommended for puppies.

Making Homemade Dog Food

Is homemade dog food healthier than commercial dog food? Many pet owners assume it must be better because eating a home-cooked meal is better than chowing down on fast food, but does this stand true for your English Setter?

Many dog food recipes fall short of the nutrients needed to keep your English Setter strong and healthy, such as iron, copper, calcium, and zinc. A recent study by the University of California School of Veterinary Medicine tested more than 200 online recipes written by respected veterinarians. Unfortunately, the researchers discovered more than 90 percent of the recipes lacked essential nutrients for canine health.

One of the main advantages of preparing your own dog food is you know exactly what you are feeding your dog. Commercially made dog food is convenient and is a fantastic way to ensure your dog is receiving all of the necessary nutrients he needs. However, making your pooch homemade meals involves more than just throwing a bunch of ingredients into the slow cooker and hoping for the best. It involves careful planning to prepare a well-balanced and complete meal that meets all of your dog's nutritional needs.

If you decide to make your dog's meals yourself, be sure to consult with your vet before switching the dog over to the new diet. A homemade diet is not recommended for puppies or expecting mothers.

As I mentioned before, English Setters are high-energy dogs and need a well-balanced diet to maintain lean muscle and support their immune system. Your dog's daily diet requires protein (animal meat, seafood, dairy, eggs, and so on), fat (from animal organs or oil), and carbohydrates (grains and vegetables). Your English Setter will also need calcium from dairy products or egg shells and essential fatty acids (oils, egg yolks, oatmeal, etc.).

The following guidelines will help you create your own balanced, homemade dog food recipe:

Meat products – Protein should make up 50 to 65 percent of your Setter's diet. As it is the main component of your dog's meal, choose organic lean meats without skin and fat. Include in your dog's diet boneless chicken, beef, and fish. Make sure the meat is cut into small pieces as it will facilitate chewing and digestion. Including up to 5 percent beef liver in your preparation is a nutritious and tasty addition.

Eggs – Eggs are an excellent source of protein; however, medium-sized dogs such as your English Setter should only eat one whole egg per day.

Dairy – The majority of dogs can tolerate plain yogurt, cottage cheese, and ricotta. If your pooch suffers from lactose intolerance, try substituting dairy products with goat milk. Avoid using other types of cheese as they tend to be high in cholesterol, fats, and calories.

Starchy vegetables – Beans, peas, potatoes, squash, and sweet potatoes are all great sources of fiber for your English Setter. If your pooch is overweight, you will need to reduce the percentage of starchy vegetables in his dog food. Cook all grains, beans, and starchy vegetables to make them easier to digest.

Other vegetables – Leafy veggies are high in fiber and low in calories, plus they are full of wholesome nutrients for your pooch. Avoid using raw, cruciferous vegetables, such as broccoli and cauliflower, as they can cause digestive issues for your dog. Chop and blend the vegetables together before adding them to the meat mixture when cooking.

Fruit – Fruit supports your English Setter's digestive health and provides a long list of vitamins, nutrients, and antioxidants. Apples, bananas, berries, and papaya are all excellent options. Avoid grapes and raisins as they cause kidney failure.

Grains – Whole grains such as quinoa, barley, brown rice, oatmeal, and pasta are all excellent sources of fiber. All grains need to be well-cooked so they can be properly digested by your English Setter. Note: white rice has low nutritional value and should only be used to settle an upset tummy.

Supplements – Even the best homemade dog food recipe, using the highest quality organic ingredients, will still lack certain nutrients such as calcium. Another reason to add supplements to your dog's homemade food is if you are freezing the food into daily portions; many nutrients are lost when food is frozen and then thawed. Closely follow the instructions on the supplement packaging for your dog's weight, size, and age. If you have doubts, talk to a pet nutritionist.

Make sure the homemade diet is working

After your English Setter has been enjoying his homemade meals for one to two months, take him to the vet to make sure he is not gaining or losing too much weight. If your dog's weight has changed slightly, check it again in a few weeks. Your vet will regularly check your dog's coat, skin, teeth, and body condition for any issues that might be related to his homemade diet.

Are meatless diets safe for my English Setter?

Due to climate change and ethical considerations, many people have decided to become vegetarians or vegans, and they often wonder if their dogs can be vegetarian or vegan too. Can dogs be healthy on a meatless diet?

Dogs are not considered to be obligate carnivores. Obligate carnivores, such as cats, have to eat animal proteins, as their body needs the amino acids found in animal proteins. This means, theoretically, dogs can eat a plant-based diet and get amino acids from plants or produce the amino acids themselves in their own liver. There have been a few pilot studies that have shown dogs, even sport dogs such as Setters, thrive on a meat-free diet.

One of the main side effects of meatless diets is they tend to make the dog's urine more alkaline, causing painful kidney and gallbladder stones that often need to be surgically removed. Veterinarians do not recommend feeding your dog a meatless homemade diet. Getting the right nutrients is difficult in a normal homemade dog food and almost impossible for a meatless diet.

The good news is there are quite a few meatless dog foods on the market, and more are being launched all the time. There are some great meatless diets out there that are complete and balanced. If you do not want to purchase a meatless dog food, ask a veterinary nutritionist to help you plan a balanced recipe for your dog's lifestyle and age.

A meatless diet is not recommended for young dogs still in the growth stage (under the age of 18 months).

Remember, if your dog has any medical conditions or is prone to an upset stomach, it is best to discuss your options first with your veterinarian.

A Basic Recipe for Homemade Dog Food

The following recipe is a healthy alternative to canned dog food, as it is loaded with iron from fresh protein and veggies. It can be stored in the fridge for up to a week or be frozen and reheated later. The recipe below is a basic guideline, which you can adapt to your English Setter's personal preferences.

Doggy Style Stew

Ingredients

Total: Makes four cups (32 fluid ounces)
- 1 pound chicken or beef, without fat, skin, or bones (cut into small pieces)
- 4 oz. of beef liver, chopped
- 1 medium, steamed sweet potato, chopped
- 1/2 cup steamed green beans, chopped
- 1 cup cooked quinoa or oatmeal
- 1 cup spinach, blended with a cup of water
- 1 tbsp fish oil or coconut oil

Directions

1. Sauté the meat and liver together with the oil in a large pot until thoroughly cooked.
2. Add the rest of the ingredients and leave to simmer on low heat for 10 to 15 minutes.
3. Let cool and serve.
4. Store the leftovers in the fridge for a maximum of five days.

As mentioned before, be sure to cook all animal products thoroughly to kill any harmful bacteria, and cook all grains, starchy vegetables, and beans to make them easier for your English Setter to digest. Before switching your dog to a homemade diet, be sure to discuss your dog's specific nutritional needs with your veterinarian. Remember that switching your dog's food to homemade from kibble is a slow process, so patience is essential.

Weight Monitoring

> *Don't overfeed; you should be able to see the dog's ribs. Think about how your knuckle feels and looks when you make a fist— that is how the ribs of the dog should look. Get your hands on the dog to help you to know when something isn't right.*
>
> GREG AND CARLA FRYAR
> *High Fly'n Kennels*

More than 60 percent of all dogs in the United States are considered to be overweight, and nearly all of their owners are in denial! Obesity is one of the greatest threats to your dog's long-term health.

Dogs, like people, have a harder time getting around if they are overweight. Losing weight can be a challenge for dogs at any age, but even more so as they get older. Despite the challenges, weight loss for dogs of any age is worth the effort. Slender pups enjoy longer lives, show fewer visible signs of aging, and have fewer chances of developing canine arthritis.

Health problems that are more common in overweight dogs include pancreatitis, diabetes, heart disease, joint pain, ruptured ligaments, hip dysplasia, compromised immune system, and different types of cancer. If you cannot feel your English Setter's ribs and shoulder blades, if his waist is not discernible (a tuck behind his ribs), or if there is a roll of fat at the base of his tail, then it is time to face reality and put your pooch on a diet.

If in doubt, ask your vet for his professional opinion about your dog's weight.

Weight loss tips for your English Setter:

Feed your dog more protein and fewer carbohydrates

When it comes to weight loss, the ratio of carbohydrates to fats and proteins matters more than calorie counting. English Setters thrive on a high-protein diet, as it builds lean muscle and improves mood and mental agility. If your English Setter is overweight, look for a dog food that is high in protein, low in carbs, and moderate in healthy fats.

Avoid feeding your English Setter a high-fiber diet

Fiber will not satisfy your dog and can interfere with nutrient absorption. Instead, look for dog foods that contain whole grains such as quinoa, whole oats, and brown rice, as they are an excellent source of fiber and protein yet are low in carbohydrates.

Reduce your English Setter's portion size

Instead of making drastic changes, start slowly by cutting back your dog's meal portion size by 5 percent. Reduce this by 5 percent every three weeks until you are giving your pooch the amount of food specified for him on the dog food package. This strategy prevents your English Setter from losing weight too fast, then gaining it back. Slow, steady weight loss means long-term success.

Measure everything your English Setter eats

One of the reasons your English Setter is overweight is probably because you have been eyeballing his dog food. The only way to accurately measure your dog's food is either by using measuring cups or, even better, by using an electronic scale to weigh every meal. This takes a lot of discipline on your part, but you will be surprised to find that you were often feeding your dog twice as much as required. You can find a small scale at an office or kitchen supply store or online.

Make your dog's weight loss a family project

Feeding your furry companion a smaller portion will not help him lose weight if he is getting breakfast leftovers, an afternoon snack, and/ or a treat or two throughout the day. Discuss your dog's diet plan with the entire family and be sure they cooperate. Allot each family member a certain number of training treats to give your English Setter each day, and encourage everyone to focus on calorie-free treats and rewards, such as playing fetch, games, or praise.

Rethink the treats you give your dog

Treats and rewards often have three to five calories, and they can quickly add up in a training session. Instead of store-bought treats, try using pieces of cut-up skinless chicken breast. Most dogs are more concerned about the number of treats they are receiving and do not notice the size of the actual treat, so cut up chewy treats into smaller pieces. Use raw baby carrots, zucchini slices, or small slices of apple, banana, or melon for a healthier treat.

Why is Your English Setter Not Eating?

Whether you have had your English Setter for years or just adopted your first puppy, it can be distressing when your pooch refuses to eat. There are a variety of reasons for your English Setter's loss of appetite.

Often, a loss of appetite in dogs can be an indication of illness. For this reason, it is important to seek veterinary care if you notice any changes to your dog's eating habits. Just like humans, there are several reasons why your dog refuses to eat.

Illness – A decreased appetite often is a sign of illness, especially if your dog is exhibiting other symptoms. Loss of appetite is not always an indication of a serious illness, but prompt veterinary attention will rule out any serious health conditions, such as cancer, infections, pain, liver problems, and kidney failure.

Dental disease – Your dog may be wary about gobbling up his dinner because it is causing pain in his mouth. Have your veterinarian check your dog's mouth for loose teeth, oral tumors, or even gingivitis.

Recent vaccination – Although vaccinations protect your dog from various contagious canine diseases, they do have some adverse side effects. The majority of these side effects are only temporary and minor, such as a brief loss of appetite.

Travel and other unfamiliar surroundings – If your English Setter's appetite was normal prior to your trip with him or before you moved to a new home, most likely, this is the cause of your dog's lack of appetite. Some Setters get motion sickness when traveling or are nervous in new surroundings.

Pickiness – Some English Setters are just picky eaters. However, never assume your dog's lack of interest in mealtime is caused by being a picky eater without ruling out other possibilities first.

What to do when your English Setter refuses to eat

If your English Setter's loss of appetite is caused by an illness, your vet may recommend a prescription diet to meet your dog's nutritional needs while the underlying illness is being treated. In more severe cases, your vet may prescribe an appetite-stimulating medication.

If your dog's lack of appetite is caused by something not related to a medical condition, there are a number of things you can do to encourage your dog to eat. Here are some suggestions to stimulate your dog's appetite:

- Cut back on treats and feed your dog on a regular schedule, usually twice a day.
- Take your dog for a walk before mealtime.
- Change your dog's feeding situation. If you normally feed your English Setter with other pets, try feeding him alone. Or try putting a few pieces of food on the floor next to the dish.
- Try using a different kind of food, such as wet canned food.
- Add a bit of warm bone broth to your dog's kibble to make it more appetizing.

CHAPTER 12

Grooming Your English Setter

> **"**
>
> *English Setters can grow long coats. They require frequent bathing and will need their long feathering brushed out and their nails trimmed weekly. The coat can be de-shedded by using an Andis fine-tooth de-shedding tool. The feathering can be kept tangle free by using a pin brush and a comb. The hair on the feet should be trimmed short for the dog's health and to prevent dirt and debris from being brought into your home. Besides home bathing and combing out the feathering weekly at home, an English Setter should be groomed every six to eight weeks by a professional groomer.*
>
> JULIA CRAWFORD
> *Crown Setters*
>
> **"**

Good grooming helps your English Setter feel and look his best. Routine grooming sessions give you an opportunity to examine your pup's coat, eyes, teeth, ears, and nails for any health problems.

Brushing

> *The look of beautiful feathers on the legs, tail, and ears is something we all adore on our Setters. Daily brushing keeps them in top shape. After a romp in the field, Setters will have every imaginable stick or cocklebur stuck to or tangled in their coat. Many Setters will self-groom much of the debris out, but for those that don't, nonstick cooking spray, lightly sprayed onto the fur, will help with combing out the debris.*
>
> KAREN STROHMEYER
> *Bristle Ridge Llewellins*

Adult English Setters have beautiful, long, feathered ears and silky hair under their chest, legs, and underbelly. This must be regularly brushed to keep it clean and free of knots. Regularly brushing your dog for a few minutes at a time can accomplish a lot in terms of keeping him clean, as it removes dirt, burrs, and grass.

Get your dog accustomed to being brushed while he is standing, as a groomer would, instead of lying down. If you have a hard time remembering to brush your English Setter daily, place his brushes in a place where you will see them, such as beside the television remote.

All dogs shed, and your English Setter is no exception. Excessive shedding can easily be prevented by providing your dog with a healthy diet, plenty of exercise, and fresh air. If, while brushing your dog, you notice, that he is losing more hair than normal, the cause may be one of the following factors:

- Hot spots
- Sarcoptic mange
- Food-related allergies
- Parasites, such as fleas, lice, or mites
- An immune disorder, such as adrenal or thyroid diseases
- Cancer
- Anxiety or stress

- Pregnancy or lactation
- A bacterial or fungal infection, such as ringworm

Your English Setter will love running outdoors year-round, which means you will need to check him daily for ticks. In the following chapter, we will discuss how to remove a tick.

As you brush your pooch, look for sores, rashes, or signs of infection, such as redness, swelling, skin inflammation, and tenderness. The same is true if you notice any patches of dry, brittle skin.

If you notice any foreign objects lodged in your dog's eyes, ears, skin, mouth, or paw pads, do not attempt to remove them yourself; always consult with your veterinarian beforehand.

If matted hair is an issue, leave your household scissors in the drawer where they belong. One wrong move by a nervous pooch could result in an injury to you or your dog. The best way to remove a knot or mat is by using your fingers, some pet-friendly conditioner, a comb, and a whole lot of patience.

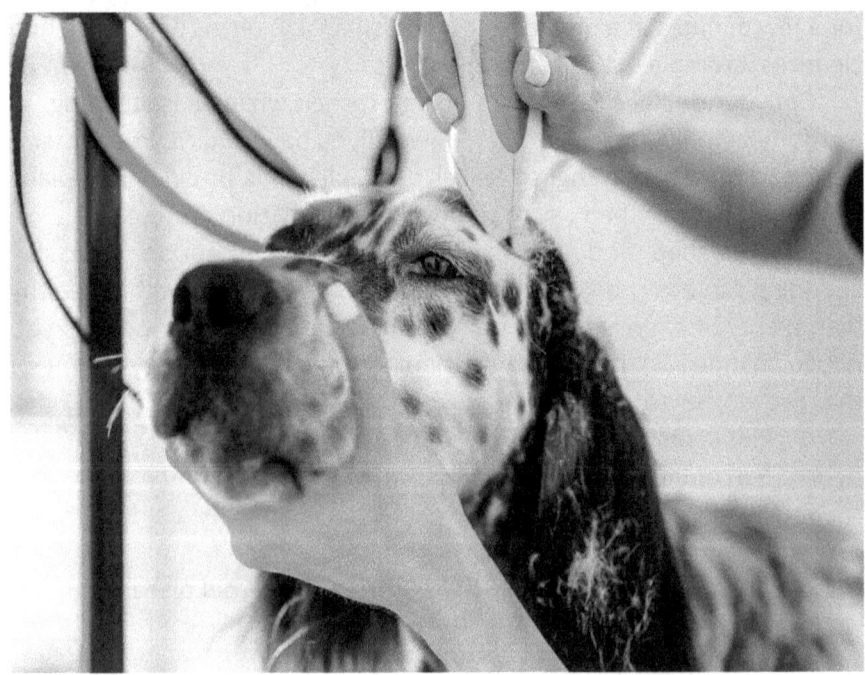

Bathing

> "
> *Use cotton in the ears when bathing to prevent water from getting in. Water is the main cause of ear infections. Brush the long furnishings (longer hair around the eyebrows and face) at least twice a week. Shampoo your Setter often. A clean coat is much easier to keep tangle free.*
>
> SHEILA FLYNN
> *Plaisance*
> "

Your English Setter is an active dog and will need to be bathed at least every six weeks, sometimes more often. Regularly bathing your dog will help to keep his coat clean and tangle-free.

Never spray your pooch with scents or perfumes. Dogs are very sensitive to fragrances, and most fragrances contain harmful ingredients that can make your dog very sick if he ingests them while cleaning himself. Fragrances can result in respiratory problems. The best way to keep your English Setter smelling his best is by regularly bathing him.

How to give your English Setter a bath:
1. Before your English Setter's bath, take extra time to brush out any extra hair, debris, or heavy dirt. Place your pup in a large basin or tub filled with approximately four to six inches of lukewarm water.
2. Thoroughly wet your dog down using a large pitcher or spray hose. If using a spray nozzle, make sure the water is neither too hot nor too cold.
3. Avoid getting water or soap in your English Setter's eyes, nose, and ears. Use a damp washcloth to remove any dirt or debris around your pup's face.
4. Once your English Setter is completely wet, gently massage pet-friendly shampoo into his coat. Start from the top of his head, working your way down to his tail. Pay close attention to under his legs, as English Setters tend to sweat under these

areas. Dilute the dog-formulated shampoo in water so it is easier to rinse out.

5. Rinse and repeat if needed. Hold your dog still to prevent him from shaking the excess water out.

6. Take your English Setter out of the tub or basin and dry him off using a large, fluffy towel.

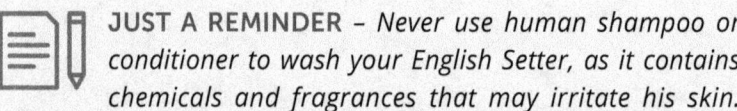 **JUST A REMINDER** – *Never use human shampoo or conditioner to wash your English Setter, as it contains chemicals and fragrances that may irritate his skin. Instead, choose a high-quality shampoo specifically formulated for dogs. Avoid using inexpensive dog shampoos, as they often are made with harsh ingredients.*

Since your English Setter is a water dog, he can easily confuse bath time with playtime. If your dog has a hard time standing still, ask a family member to help you.

What to do when a skunk sprays your dog

Skunks live all over the place, even in big cities, and if your English Setter decides to get close to one, he will end up with a face full of stinky skunk spray. If your pooch gets sprayed, there are a few ways you can quickly get rid of the unpleasant scent without having to buy hundreds of cans of tomato juice.

Step 1: Keep your dog outside

Keep your dog outside while you get organized so he does not carry the smell indoors. Check your pup's eyes; if they are irritated, flush with cold water.

Step 2: Mix the ingredients

Mix together the following ingredients:

- 1 quart of three percent hydrogen peroxide (available at any pharmacy)
- 1/4 cup baking soda
- 1 tablespoon liquid dishwashing soap

 **WORD OF CAUTION:** *Do not make this solution ahead of time, as it will explode if left in a bottle.*

Wearing rubber gloves, wash your dog with the solution immediately after he has been sprayed by a skunk. Do not get the liquid in your dog's eyes. (If you do not have hydrogen peroxide, baking soda, and liquid soap on hand, you can use vinegar diluted in water). There are also shampoos designed to de-skunk your dog after being sprayed.

Step 3: Clean and rinse

Massage the solution through your dog's fur, but avoid leaving it on too long, as peroxide can bleach fur. Rinse your dog thoroughly.

Step 4: Shampoo

After rinsing away all of the peroxide solution, shampoo your dog with a shampoo designed for pets. By now, your English Setter should be de-skunked and smelling clean. Rinse away the shampoo, thoroughly towel dry him and place him in a warm, sunny spot to dry off.

Step 5: Owner clean-up

Most likely, some of the scent rubbed off onto you, you can wash your clothes in a solution of regular laundry detergent and half a cup of baking soda.

Nail Clipping

Most Setters are squeamish about having their nails trimmed, so do not expect it to be your favorite shared activity, no matter how many treats your pooch gets afterward.

Chances are your English Setter's nails will need to be trimmed every four to six weeks or so, unless he is running around on hard surfaces, such as cement that keep his nails short. A general rule of thumb: if you can hear your pup's nails clicking against the floor or his nails get snagged on the carpet, then it is time for a trim.

> *Keep their toenails trimmed weekly as well. I prefer grinding nails with a Dremel drill. Just keep the drill on low speed at first and reward your dog frequently. I don't think it sets the right example to have someone else hold the dog and fight over doing nails. Shape this behavior by handling feet and ears and tails when you pet your dog. My dogs learn to lie on their side on a grooming table for nail trims and treats.*
>
> LIN SELL, MD
> *Linwood English Setters*

If possible, get your English Setter used to having his nails clipped at a young age by rubbing your hands up and down his legs and gently pressing down between his toes each time. Never forget to give your pooch a yummy treat, followed by a big, boisterous "Good boy!" After about two weeks of massaging your Setter's feet, you can attempt clipping his nails. This method works especially well if your older dog is ticklish or wary about having his feet touched.

If you are unsure about how to cut your English Setter's nails, ask your veterinarian or groomer; they will gladly give you a short demonstration on how to trim your dog's nails to the right length.

There are two different types of nail clippers — scissor-type and guillotine. Both styles come highly recommended, so choose the style you feel most comfortable with. Another option is a nail grinder, which sands the nails down; however, it makes a loud grinding noise, and the vibration can frighten you and your dog.

Be sure to give your English Setter a vigorous workout to burn off excess energy before clipping his nails. If your dog is skittish, ask a family member to help you. There is no need to clip all of your dog's nails at once; you can clip one paw at a time, with breaks in between.

How to clip your English Setter's nails

1. Hold your English Setter's foot steadily but gently as you spread out each toe. Hold the nail clipper at a slight angle, snipping

from the top to the bottom. Cut off the tip of the nail. Avoid giving the nail a blunt edge; instead, follow the natural curvature of the nail.

2. Snip off the tip of the nail, avoiding the quick. The quick is the darker-colored circle inside of the nail, which is the blood vein. If you accidentally cut the quick, you will have one very unhappy dog.

3. If you accidentally cut your English Setter's nail quick, use a nail cauterizer, such as cornstarch or styptic powder, which you can apply with a Q-Tip. Be sure to have a moist washcloth on hand to clean up the mess. Cutting your dog's nail quick hurts, and trust me — he will remember this unpleasant experience for a long time.

4. Once you have finished clipping your dog's nails, do not forget to generously praise your English Setter with yummy treats and a healthy scratch behind his ears.

If you are using a nail grinder to trim your English Setter's nails, follow the method above; simply hold your pup's foot and grind a little off each nail. Do not forget to trim your English Setter's dewclaws. Since they do not touch the ground, they tend to grow longer and will eventually grow back into your dog's paw, which can be very painful and may cause health complications.

If your English Setter has darker nails, you will need to be extra careful because it is almost impossible to notice the nail quick. If you have a hard time keeping your hands steady or your pooch shows aggressive behavior while getting his nails clipped, feel free to ask the groomer to clip his nails for you.

Importance of Good Dental Care

You have probably heard the expression that a dog's mouth is cleaner than a human's mouth. The truth is a dog's mouth is no cleaner than a human's mouth; it just is home to an entirely different group of bacteria.

Your Setter can develop dental issues such as tartar, plaque, and gingivitis. As if bad breath was not enough, these canine dental problems can lead to life-threatening infections, not to mention dental extractions, which can be very costly. The only way to prevent this is by practicing good oral care.

Since your English Setter cannot brush his teeth on his own, you will need to brush his teeth regularly. Older dogs can learn to be comfortable with getting their teeth brushed, but you can make things easier for yourself by starting early with your dog when he is still a puppy.

Get your pooch used to having his teeth cleaned by gently massaging his gums for about 20 to 30 seconds daily for about two weeks. Once he is comfortable with you touching his gumline, do the same procedure daily but including his teeth for another two weeks.

How to brush your English Setter's teeth

1. Place a pea-sized amount of canine toothpaste on the tip of your finger, then let your dog smell it and taste it.
2. Gently massage the toothpaste onto his gums. This will allow him to get used to the texture and the flavor.
3. Use a double-headed canine toothbrush held at a 45-degree angle to clean below the gumline.
4. Work on one spot at a time until your English Setter gets used to the feel of the toothbrush inside of his mouth.

Your pup may not be keen on getting his teeth brushed at first, but over time he will get used to it. Choose a time when he is more likely to sit still for the entire procedure, such as after a vigorous walk or a game of fetch outside.

Make sure you speak softly and soothingly throughout the entire process, and do not forget to reward your dog with a yummy treat afterward. Be cautious not to overdo it the first few times or if your pooch becomes agitated. Take your time and increase the length of each session slowly.

If brushing your pup's teeth ends with tears, hurt feelings, or blood, there are still a few other choices you can make to improve his oral health. Dry kibble is better for your English Setter's teeth than soft or wet food, as soft food can become stuck between his teeth, causing tooth decay. There are also synthetic bones and chew toys that have been specifically designed to strengthen your dog's gums and teeth.

Never use human toothpaste or mouthwash for your English Setter, as it contains fluoride, which is toxic for dogs. Look for a specially formulated toothpaste at your local pet store; often, they come in a variety of flavors such as beef, chicken, or salmon. There is also dog mouthwash that is diluted in water to kill bacteria and prevent plaque buildup.

Routine dental cleanings

No matter how disciplined you are about cleaning your English Setter's teeth, you will never really be able to give him a deep, thorough cleaning with just a toothbrush. Even if your dog has healthy teeth, it is wise to have your veterinarian give him an annual cleaning to remove any plaque and tartar buildup, clean the gum line, and polish his teeth.

Common Dental Issues in English Setters

No matter how often you brush your English Setter's teeth, you should inspect the inside of his mouth at least once a week. If you notice any of the following signs, take your dog to the vet as soon as possible:

- Bad breath
- Constantly pawing at his face or mouth.
- A change of eating or chewing habits.
- Depression
- Excessive drooling
- Red, swollen, painful, or bleeding gums
- Bumps or growths inside of the gum line
- Yellowish tartar buildup along the gum line
- Discolored, missing, or misaligned teeth

Canine dental care may be a hassle, but regular maintenance is a money saver in the long run and may even be a lifesaver. Letting your dog's teeth deteriorate leads to expensive and painful vet visits down the road. Many dogs will need to be given anesthesia to have their teeth and gums cleaned.

Gingivitis – Gingivitis is caused by an accumulation of plaque, bacteria, and tartar around the gum. Signs are swollen, bleeding gums, and extremely bad breath. Fortunately, it can easily be cleared up with regular brushing.

Mouth tumors – Mouth tumors look like small bumps or lumps on your dog's gums. They can be extremely painful and irritating for your dog while eating or drinking water. Mouth tumors will need to be surgically removed by a vet.

Periodontal disease – This gum infection results in tooth loss and a high risk of the infection spreading throughout the body, causing all sorts of maladies. Watch out for bad breath, nasal discharge, mouth pain, lack of appetite, and loose teeth.

Proliferating gum disease – This occurs when your dog's gumline is over his teeth, causing a gum infection. It can easily be treated with antibiotics.

Salivary cysts – These are fluid-filled blisters located under your dog's tongue or along the corners of his mouth. They will need to be professionally drained and cauterized. Often the salivary gland will need to be surgically removed.

 MORAL OF THE STORY: *Keep your English Setter's teeth sparkling white, and you will both be smiling.*

Paws

> 66
>
> *Longer hairs grow frequently between the toes; for a finished look, keep these trimmed. This will also help minimize sloppy, wet, or muddy feet tracking through your house.*
>
> KAREN STROHMEYER
> *Bristle Ridge Llewellins*
> 99

Your English Setter's paws are made for stomping. Your pooch uses his paws for just about everything. You need to keep your dog's paws in tip-top shape by regularly checking them for pebbles, splinters, or any other type of debris that may get stuck in there. If you find a splinter, use a pair of tweezers to gently pull it out. Regularly trim the fur between your English Setter's toes as it could become matted, making it painful for your dog to walk.

Paw pads can crack and bleed if they get too dry. Never use lotions or moisturizers designed for humans on your English Setter as they will soften the pads, leading to further injury. Instead, use a high-quality, dog-formulated paw moisturizer on his feet. Give your pooch a paw massage by rubbing the moisturizer between the pads on his feet.

Winter paws – Winter is not only harsh on you but also on your English Setter's paws. You need to worry about frostbite or hidden debris in the snow that could cut your dog's paws.

The salt used to melt the ice can burn your pup's paw pads, causing them to become chapped or cracked. Rock salt or other ice-melting chemicals are made from toxic chemicals that could be ingested by your pooch if he licks his paws. After coming in the house from a walk, wash your dog's paws in warm water to remove excess chemicals. Using doggy booties and limiting outdoor exposure are the best options.

Summer paws – Asphalt and pavement can get hot enough to scorch your pup's paw pads. Check the ground temperature with the palm of your hand; if you cannot rest it there comfortably for 30 seconds, then the ground is definitely too hot for your dog. Paw pads can easily become burned and blistered. If the ground is too hot, stick to grass or shady places when walking your pooch.

Ears

Your English Setter's long, drooping ears allow him to catch a scent while hunting. But those adorable floppy ears can also trap water and bacteria, leading to painful ear infections. Routine preventative care will reduce your pup's chances of infection and improve the overall health of his ears.

Plucking the ear hair is the best method as it removes both the strand and the root. However, since you have not removed the hair follicle, be aware that the hair strand will grow back. It is not recommended to trim the hair strands, as the shortened hairs create a trap for bacteria, yeast, and debris.

Dog ear powder – This powder is designed for plucking hairs out of your pup's ears. The powder lets you grip the strands and makes for easier removal.

Hemostat – A hemostat is an essential tool designed to grip your English Setter's ear hairs; it is similar to a pair of tweezers but sturdier. It is not recommended to extract the hair strand using your fingers as it will not extract the hair root; plus, pulling the hair out with your fingers will be more painful for your dog.

How to pluck hairs from your English Setter's ears

1. Choose a moment when both you and your English Setter are relaxed, such as when your dog has burned off some of his excess energy with a vigorous walk or a game of fetch.

2. Position your dog so you have a clear view inside of his ear. Gently bend back the ear leather, sprinkle a light dusting of dog ear powder in the ear, and using a disinfected hemostat tool, grip a few hairs, lock, and quickly pull up.
3. Only pluck hairs you can see, as digging around in your dog's ear can cause more damage than good. Therefore, only pull out what you can easily see and grab.
4. Throughout the entire process, use a soft, calming voice, and be sure to reward your English Setter afterward with a nice, yummy treat.

Never insert a Q-Tip in your Setter's ears, as it could easily slip deeper into the ear canal, causing injury. Another word of caution: do not clean your pup's ears too often, as they could become irritated or infected.

How to clean your English Setter's ears
1. If your English Setter's ears appear to be dirty or waxy, use a small piece of gauze, a cotton ball dampened in mineral oil, or a liquid ear cleaner formulated for dogs.
2. Gently fold back your pup's ear and carefully wipe away any ear wax or debris you can see.
3. Instead of rubbing the ear to remove the debris or ear wax, gently wipe it away.

Most English Setters need to have this type of ear cleaning every two to three weeks to keep bacteria and ear infections at bay.

Regularly check your English Setter's ears if you notice any of the following symptoms:
- Brownish or yellowish discharge
- Red and swollen inner ear canal
- Hearing loss
- Excessive shaking of the head or tilting to the side
- Scabby skin around the ear flap
- Strong odor emanating from the ear
- Loss of balance

- Ear scratching or wiping ears on the floor or rubbing ears against the furniture

If you notice a brownish or black buildup of earwax (that looks like coffee grounds) in your English Setter's ear, he could have microscopic ear mites. Be sure to make an appointment with your vet as soon as possible.

> "
>
> *Setters' ears can get waxy and smelly if not cleaned, especially when they are hunting or training hard. Every other week or so, check the ears for brown, waxy buildup. Use a few cotton swabs to clean up the ear canal and the little folds in the ears. You can also buy ear wipes or cleaning solutions that can be put on a heavy-duty towelette to wipe the ear using a fingertip. Keeping the ears clean and free from buildup really reduces the chance of infections or ear mites.*
>
> MARK D. DENEKA
> *Twilight Setter Kennels*
>
> "

Eyes

Regularly check your English Setter's eyes. Have your dog sit in a well-lit part of the house, preferably with natural light. Your dog's eyes should appear bright and clear, and the area surrounding the pupil should be white and not yellow. There should be no crusty discharge at the corner of his eyes. Using your thumb, gently pull down the lower part of your dog's eyelid to observe the inner lining; it should be a pale pink color and not red or white.

On a daily basis, use a clean, damp cotton ball or dog-formulated eye wipe to wipe any gunk away from your dog's eyes. Be careful not to touch your dog's eyeballs. If recommended by your vet, you can use canine eye drops to get rid of tearstains on your English Setter's face.

The following symptoms are clear indications your English Setter may have an eye infection

- Crusty gunk and discharge around the corners of his eyes
- Cloudiness
- Swollen eyelid
- Unequal pupil size
- No desire to open his eyes
- Teary eyes and tear stains

Keep the hair around your English Setter's eyes trimmed. Use a small pair of scissors, like cuticle scissors, to minimize the risk of injuring your dog. Long hair around the eyes can accidentally poke or scratch the pupils. Air conditioners will dry out your dog's eyes, causing irritation and possibly infection.

> *After running in the field, always check the dog for battle damage. Start by checking in between toes and pads for burrs and sticks. Then check the legs and undercarriage for cuts or abrasions. Finally, check the head, ears, and, lastly, the eyes. I pull down each eyelid and check for seeds and leaf debris. More likely than not, you will find pieces of debris in the corners or trapped in the bottom lid. Remove the debris using a cotton swab.*
>
> MARK D. DENEKA
> *Twilight Setter Kennels*

Anal Glands

Setters are prone to anal gland problems; unfortunately, this condition can cause painful sores around the anus. Both female and male English Setters have a pair of anal glands found under the skin that surrounds your dog's anal muscles. Often, they are referred to as scent glands, odor glands, or stinky glands.

Photo Courtesy of
Yvonne Wale

These glands hold an oily substance that is released in minute amounts when one dog meets another, which explains why dogs sniff each other's rear ends. The anal scent tells the other dog the unfamiliar dog's gender, health, and general mood. Also, the oily substance is released every time your dog has a bowel movement.

Often, when a dog is scooting his rear end on the ground after having a bowel movement, the anal sacs are engorged (swollen). Your English Setter will need your help to express his anal glands; otherwise, they could become infected or even break open, which will need to be treated by your veterinarian.

How to tell if your English Setter needs his anal glands expressed

- Scooting his rear end on the ground
- Excessively licking or biting his butt
- Red, swollen skin around his anus
- Bleeding or discharge from around the anus

Most English Setter owners prefer to ask their groomer or vet to express their dog's anal glands. If your dog's anal glands have not been expressed in quite some time, and the oily substance has become solid (impacted), then your veterinarian will need to sedate your dog for the extraction as it is very painful.

Anal glands are expressed in a similar fashion as you would pop a pimple, but due to the location and the discomfort your dog is experiencing, it can be a challenge.

How to express your English Setter's anal glands at home

To begin, you will need a pair of disposable latex gloves, Vaseline or a similar lubricant, paper towels, a warm, soapy washcloth, and someone to help you restrain your English Setter. The smell is not for the faint of heart.

1. Place your dog on the table with his rear end facing you. Your dog should be standing on all fours. Have your helper gently restrain the dog by placing one arm underneath and around your dog's neck and the other arm hugging your dog's body.
2. Put on your latex gloves and lubricate your index finger.
3. Lift your English Setter's tail and insert your index finger about one inch into his rectum.
4. Place your thumb on the outside of your dog's anus. Using your thumb and index finger, feel for a firm, pea-sized object. The anal glands should be located at the four o'clock position and the seven o'clock position.
5. Once you have located the anal glands, using your other hand, place a paper towel in front of your dog's anus, as the glands tend to squirt outward. Using light pressure, gently milk the anal glands. When you can barely feel the gland, it is completely expressed.

6. Follow the same procedure with the other gland.
7. Once you are finished draining both anal sacs, use the warm, soapy wash-cloth to clean the area.
8. Reward your dog with some treats and lots of praise.

> **"**
> *The key is finding a groomer that knows the breed cut. Provide diagrams and very specific instructions at drop-off.*
>
> SHANNON TORBORG
> *SenterStone English Setters*
> **"**

Professional Grooming

Grooming your English Setter may seem like an easy way to save money and bond with your pooch. But the grooming process is not for everyone, as it takes time, patience, and it is a whole lot trickier than it sounds. Thankfully, there is a stress-free option! Professional groomers have the skills and expertise to make sure your dog gets a trim and bath. After all, your furry friend deserves to be pampered.

There are pros and cons associated with taking your dog to a professional groomer. Here is the nitty-gritty:

Advantages
- Professional groomers have years of experience and can groom your dog in less time than you.
- Groomers use professional equipment and tools, ensuring a top-notch job.
- Groomers provide specialized care, such as de-shedding and ringworm treatments.
- They provide a quick medical exam, and upon request, they will pluck and clean your English Setter's ears and express his anal glands.
- Most groomers include nail trimming.

Disadvantages
- The cost can add up, especially if your English Setter gets groomed every six to eight weeks.
- Some Setters suffer from anxiety and stress from being left alone at the groomer for two to three hours.
- Finding the perfect groomer for your English Setter takes time.
- Transporting your dog to and from the groomer may be troublesome if your pup does not enjoy long car rides.

In the end, the decision to use a professional groomer or not depends on your personal preference and situation. Ask yourself if you have the time and patience to groom your English Setter yourself or if you can financially afford to send him regularly to the groomer.

Many dog owners prefer combining both methods in order to save money, and in the meantime, they can gain experience grooming their dog themselves at home. For example, they may get their dog professionally groomed once every four to five months, and in between, they will do minor grooming touch-ups and baths.

Before you choose a groomer, take the time to research your options. Ask friends and colleagues for recommendations. Once you have narrowed down your options, be sure to ask the groomer the following questions to get a better picture of their operation. Feel free to ask any other questions that concern the well-being of your English Setter.

HEALTH ALERT!
Preventing Hip and Elbow Issues

Aging English Setters may experience issues with their hips and elbows. These joints naturally become stiffer as animals age, but English Setters can also be at higher risk for dysplasia of these joints. Elbow and hip dysplasia is an inherited disease. Therefore, the most effective method for preventing this issue is to stop breeding dogs that develop this condition. Before purchasing an English Setter from a breeder, ask for the parent's elbow and hip scores. Treatment for dogs who develop hip or elbow dysplasia includes physical therapy, supplements, anti-inflammatory medications, and other palliative options.

Can I see your facility?

The grooming facility should be clean, well-ventilated, and modern. The washtubs and tables should be sturdy. Ask yourself as you observe the facility if you feel comfortable leaving your furry companion there. If the groomer is standoffish and refuses to let you into the facility, move on to the next option on your list.

Do they have liability?

Any reputable groomer will have liability insurance, as they will be a registered business. Using a groomer with liability coverage will give you peace of mind if your English Setter has an unfortunate accident while in the groomer's care, as any medical expenses incurred will be covered.

What is the total cost?

Never assume that one groomer will charge the same as another. Always ask what services are included in a basic grooming. Groomers often charge different fees depending on the dog's size, coat, and temperament. Often, groomers offer discounts for regular dog clients.

What type of training have they received?

Many groomers are self-trained. Be sure to look for a groomer who has been professionally trained through an apprenticeship, etc. Ask the groomer how long they have been professionally grooming dogs and if they have experience grooming English Setters.

CHAPTER 13

Preventative Medical Care

> "
>
> *By the nature of their profession, gundogs are always at risk of being injured. Cuts from fences, torn paw pads, and punctures from brush slash are some of the most common injuries that occur in the field. When completing a hunt, we examine the Setters on the tailgate of the truck. This check allows them to be at a height to easily be examined. We look for plant debris in eyes and ears and run fingers under gums. This debris could consist of dangerous grass awns that can migrate to other parts of the Setter's body, resulting in serious infections.*
>
> WADE KISNER
> *Sweet Point Setters, LLC*
>
> "

B y making your English Setter's health a priority, you will avoid a long list of medical issues and increase the overall well-being of your furry friend. Get the facts here about preventative care, vaccines, parasites, and even alternative medical treatments to enhance your dog's quality of life.

Choosing a Veterinarian

Choosing the right veterinarian for your English Setter is something you should carefully consider, as this person needs to keep your dog healthy and may even save his life. Both you and your pooch should agree about this person before making a commitment to work with him or her.

Before you start checking out different veterinary clinics in your region, make a list of your priorities for your Setter. This will help you narrow down your options when choosing a vet and help you ask the right questions. Consider your dog's age, family history (if known), and any health concerns. For example, if your furry friend is getting older, look for a vet who specializes in geriatric dog care.

Here is a basic checklist of essential requirements for veterinarians (requirements may vary depending on your dog's needs).

- Proximity to your house – If there is an emergency, can you get to the veterinary clinic quickly?
- Pricing – Every veterinary clinic has different prices; make sure the clinic you choose fits your budget.
- Do the clinic's hours work with your work schedule, or will you need to take time off to take your English Setter there?
- Does the clinic have up-to-date facilities with cutting-edge medical technologies and care?
- Check for generous appointment times, as you do not want to feel rushed during the visit.
- A smaller practice means you will most likely see the same vet every time you visit, plus your English Setter can develop a rapport with the medical staff.
- Does the staff have knowledge of alternative and holistic treatments?
- Is the staff involved in the local animal welfare community, such as pet rescue organizations?

Once you have narrowed down what you want from a veterinarian, it is time to start your search for potential candidates.

Ask for personal recommendations – The best place to start is by word of mouth. Ask fellow dog owners whose pet-care philosophies are in line with your own, about their vets. Or ask a friend or family member for recommendations. Many veterinarian clinics offer a referral program, which may mean discounts for you and the friend who referred you.

Look for licensed personnel – Be sure to check out the American Animal Hospital Association (AAHA) website. There you will find an extensive list of accredited veterinarians in your region, as well as an evaluation of the facility, staff, patient care, and equipment. This is a great option if you have just moved to a new area and do not know who to ask.

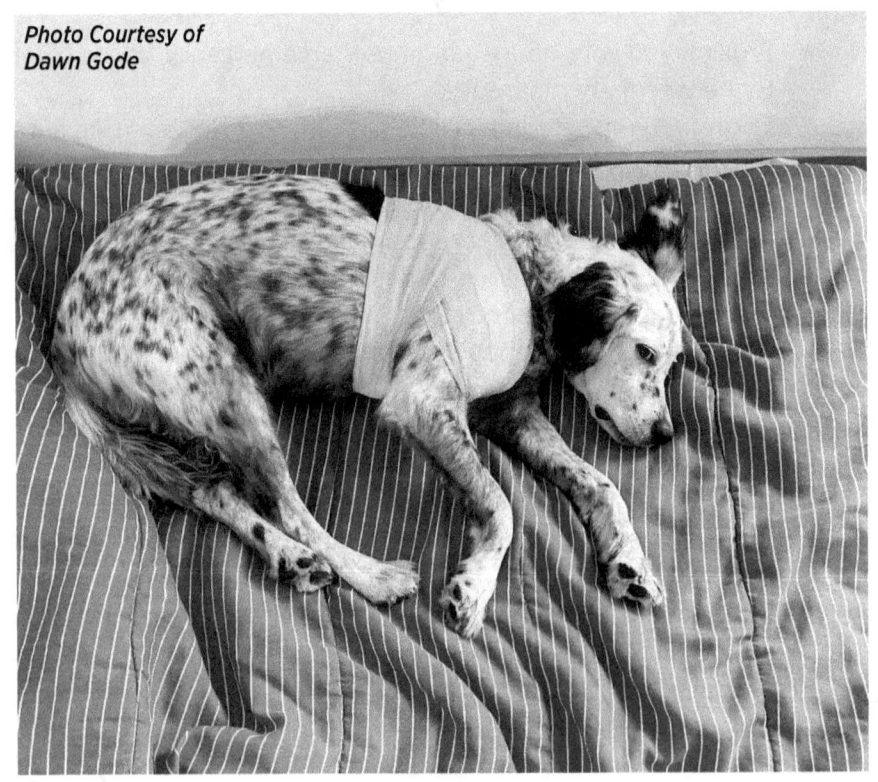

*Photo Courtesy of
Dawn Gode*

Whether you get a referral from a friend or from an online search, you will want to make sure the veterinarian clinic is accredited by the AAHA. The AAHA regularly evaluates veterinary practices throughout the United States on their standards for patient care, pain management, facilities, surgery, medical records, cleanliness, anesthesiology, and more. While veterinary clinics are not required to be accredited by law, accreditation shows you a clinic is committed to maintaining only the highest standard of care or service.

Find a veterinary clinic that specializes in dogs – Not all veterinarians are created equal. Some veterinarians specialize in livestock, such as cows, goats, horses, etc. If you live in a rural area, be sure to verify that the veterinarian has expertise in treating dogs specifically; ask how much experience they have with canines before making an appointment.

Ask for a tour of the veterinary clinic – When you narrow the list down to one or two veterinary practices, ask to take a tour of the facility. Any reputable vet will be more than happy to show you around the clinic and make you feel comfortable. Notice whether the staff is caring, calm, and courteous. Another important aspect to observe is the cleanliness of the lobby, waiting rooms, and exam rooms.

In addition to getting a feel for the facility, ask plenty of questions. Vets appreciate when pet owners are interested in their pets' health and well-being.

Questions you should ask when interviewing the vet
- How are overnight patients monitored?
- Are all diagnostic tests, such as blood work, ultrasounds, X-rays, etc., done on-site or in another referred location?
- Are all of the veterinary technicians employed by the clinic licensed by the state to practice on animals?
- Does the facility refer patients to specialists if needed? (Their answer should be affirmative.)
- What types of payment plans does the practice accept? Are there special payment plans for major surgeries or treatments?

The questions above are simply guidelines. Feel free to ask any other questions that concern you and your English Setter.

Once you have decided on a vet, be a good client. Show up early for appointments to fill out any necessary paperwork. Be patient and understanding if you have to wait longer than expected. Your vet sometimes has to attend to emergencies, which take precedence over routine appointments. Be prepared to be your English Setter's advocate, but know when it is time to step back and let your vet take over.

If you or your dog do not feel comfortable with the vet, do not hesitate to switch facilities. Veterinary clinics expect clients to come and go. However, before your departure, be sure to request a complete copy of your English Setter's medical file. You can ask that your dog's health records be faxed or mailed to either you or the new clinic.

Microchipping

Each year, more than eight million pets end up in a shelter across the country, and fewer than 20 percent are reclaimed.

A microchip is about the size of a grain of rice. It is implanted in the loose skin between your English Setter's shoulder blades, and your dog will not even notice it is there. It is no more invasive than a vaccination. The average cost to get your dog microchipped is around $30 to $50, depending on your vet.

The microchip itself does not have a battery; it is activated by a scanner that is passed over the location where the chip was implanted. The radio waves put out by the scanner activate the chip. The chip sends the scanner an identification number, which appears on the screen. The microchip is not a GPS device and cannot track your dog if he gets lost.

If your English Setter is found and taken to a veterinary clinic or shelter, one of the first things they will do is scan him for a microchip. Once they find the microchip registry information, they will quickly locate you to be reunited with your dog. Make sure to keep your dog's microchip up to date with your personal information.

Another advantage of microchipping is if your dog is ever stolen, the thief will most likely remove your dog's collar and ID tags and toss them in the trash. Often, the thief will resell the dog to an unknown victim. With a microchip, you can prove the dog is yours.

Generally, the entire micro-chipping process takes only a few seconds, or about the time it takes to give your dog an injection. It will take more time for you to fill out all of the paperwork involved than it will to insert the microchip! Microchipping does not necessarily have to be performed by a vet, but it is highly recommended you use a vet's service.

If your dog is squeamish around injections and needles, you might want to consider getting him chipped at the same time he is being neutered. Most pet owners opt to have their pooches chipped

Photo Courtesy of Amber Vick

when they are spayed or neutered for this very reason. The pain is similar to using a needle to draw blood; some dogs flinch, others do not.

Pet doors can be programmed to recognize your dog's microchip, letting him come into the house but keeping other animals outside.

Once your English Setter is microchipped, there are two things you need to do each year. First, ask your veterinarian to scan your pup's microchip at least once a year to make sure it is still working and can be detected. Secondly, keep your online registration information up to date. It only takes a few minutes to check the information, and you can rest easy that you have improved your chances of getting your Setter back if the unexpected should happen.

Neutering and Spaying

There are numerous reasons to spay or neuter your English Setter. Neutering or spaying simplifies pet ownership, as it prevents females from going into heat and, according to some experts, improves dog behavior.

Many English Setter owners get their dogs spayed or neutered to comply with the breeder's contract. However, other dog owners opt to leave their dog's anatomy intact for personal reasons or because they plan on using their English Setter as a show dog. However, be aware that this presents occasional challenges. For example, your intact dog may be barred from some doggy day cares and boarding kennels.

Spaying and neutering have some direct health benefits for your English Setter. Testicular and ovarian cancers are nonexistent in fixed animals, and there is evidence that spaying also reduces the risk of mammary cancer and uterine infections. Another benefit is that fixed dogs live longer than intact dogs.

However, recent research shows that medium to larger-sized dogs fixed before the age of six months have a much higher rate of orthopedic injuries and obesity. For this reason, many breeders request that you wait one year before getting your Setter spayed or neutered.

Spaying is a simple surgical procedure performed by a qualified veterinarian, which involves removing your female dog's ovaries and uterus. Here are a few reasons why you should consider spaying your English Setter.

- Spaying reduces the risk of urinary tract infections and breast cancer. It is highly recommended you spay your English Setter before her first heat to prevent health complications in the future.
- Spaying reduces unwanted pregnancies, which saves you from unplanned expenses.
- A spayed dog will not go into heat. A female dog in heat will urinate all over the house and yowl loudly while trying to attract a mate.

Neutering is a simple procedure performed by a qualified veterinarian, which involves removing your male dog's testicles. Here are a few reasons why you should consider neutering your English Setter.

- Neutering prevents testicular cancer.
- Your neutered Setter will not roam the neighborhood in search of a mate. An unneutered male dog will do everything in his power to find a mate, including digging a hole under the fence or running across a busy highway.
- A neutered dog will be less aggressive and better behaved than an unneutered dog. Also, he will not have the desire to mark his territory by spraying urine everywhere.

Many concerns you may have about getting your English Setter spayed or neutered are just misinformation. Consider the following:

Will your dog feel remorse or loss? No. Dogs do not suffer from emotional insecurities or experience societal pressures to have a family like humans do. They do not need to procreate to feel emotionally fulfilled.

Does spaying or neutering cause obesity? Contrary to popular thought, spaying and neutering will not make your English Setter fat. However, a lack of exercise and overfeeding will.

Are there negative side effects? As with all surgical procedures, there are certain risks, but these are minor and rare and often occur when the procedure is not performed by a reputable veterinarian.

Many states and counties have established low-cost programs for spaying or neutering, which makes these types of surgeries an affordable option for all pet owners. The website for the Humane Society will provide you with a list of local, affordable clinics and funding options to help you cover the cost of the procedure. If you are not planning on professionally breeding your English Setter, then you should definitely consider getting your pooch neutered or spayed.

Internal Parasites

Even though you may do everything possible to protect your pooch, he may be affected by parasites at some point in his life. These microscopic organisms carry disease and can cause serious health issues in your four-legged family member if not treated quickly. Some parasites can be passed to your dog from contaminated soil or other dogs' stool, and certain types of worms may even infect humans.

There are five main types of worms that commonly affect English Setters: hookworms, whipworms, heartworms, roundworms and tapeworms. Most internal parasites in dogs are ingested and affect the dog's gastrointestinal tract.

By familiarizing yourself with these common parasites, you will learn how to keep your dog safe. While each parasite affects dogs differently, there are some general warning signs that your English Setters may have parasites:

- Abdominal pain
- Vomiting
- Diarrhea that lasts longer than 24 hours
- Unexplained weight loss
- Pot-bellied appearance
- Extreme lethargy
- Dehydration
- Poor coat appearance, hair loss, or hot spots
- Coughing

Roundworms – Roundworms are one of the most common types of internal parasites in dogs, and can be transmitted to humans. Many puppies are born with roundworms, as the worms are passed on from the puppies' mother. Roundworms can be diagnosed by your vet with a small fecal sample, and they are treated with deworming medications. If left untreated, roundworms can cause your puppy to become anemic, retard growth, and may be fatal in some cases.

Whipworms – Whipworms live in the large intestine and colon. Dogs can become infected by whipworms by consuming an infested substance, such as fecal matter, soil, food, water, or animal flesh. Eggs can survive in soil for up to five years, which is another reason to clean up after your pooch when he relieves himself. Severe cases of whipworms can cause weight loss, inflammation, diarrhea, and anemia. Often, three-monthly treatments will be required to eliminate whipworms.

Tapeworms – Tapeworms are intestinal parasites that can be transmitted through a flea bite or by consuming dead animals or fleas infested with tapeworms. When a dog consumes a flea infested with tapeworm eggs, the egg will attach itself to the dog's intestines and hatch. Infected dogs may scoot their rear end on the ground.

Often, pieces of the tapeworm may break off and resemble small pieces of rice in the infected dog's stool.

If you suspect your English Setter has tapeworms, take a stool sample to your vet for diagnosis. Treatment involves a combination of oral medicine, injections, and fumigating your houses for fleas.

Hookworms – Hookworms can be fatal in puppies if left untreated. There are several types of hookworms that attach themselves to the dog's intestinal wall to gorge themselves on blood, causing anemia. Your dog can get hookworms from ingesting contaminated fecal matter, or they can be passed on to puppies through their mother's milk. Humans can also become infected with hookworms. Treatment involves a deworming medication, which will need to be administered twice.

Heartworms – Heartworms are transmitted through a mosquito bite but can be easily prevented by giving your dog regular heartworm

HEALTH ALERT!
Malassezia Dermatitis

English Setters are prone to developing skin infections, one of which is caused by yeast: Malassezia Dermatitis. This uncomfortable condition manifests in ears as painful itching, redness, and discharge and can lead to a smelly, greasy, or hairless area on your dog's skin. A veterinarian will swab the affected area and send the sample to a lab to diagnose this condition. Treatment often includes topical antifungals and systemic medical therapy. Malassezia dermatitis can severely impact your English Setter's quality of life if left untreated.

medication. Heartworms grow and multiply at an extraordinary rate inside your dog's heart, causing heart disease, heart failure, organ damage, and ultimately, a painful death. Mosquitoes carrying the heartworm parasite can be found in all 50 states.

The best approach to heartworms is prevention, as treating heartworms is extremely expensive and can have serious side effects. Also, treating heartworms requires keeping your dog confined without exercise for long periods of time in order to prevent heart damage. Even if your dog is regularly taking heartworm preventatives, he will need to be tested regularly for worms.

Diagnosing internal parasites and worms

It is possible to observe some parasites, such as tapeworms, in your dog's fecal matter. However, the majority of internal parasites will need to be diagnosed by your veterinarian via a microscopic examination of your dog's stool. If you notice any of the symptoms mentioned above, your vet will ask you to bring in a small sample of your dog's stool. Even if your dog is not exhibiting any symptoms, it is highly recommended you take a dog stool sample to your English Setter's annual check-up.

Your vet will set up a regular deworming schedule for your English Setter to treat different types of intestinal parasites, as well as prevent heartworms. The bottom line — prevention, flea control, and regular testing are the best actions to prevent consequences caused by internal parasites.

Fleas and Ticks

Your English Setter's soft, warm fur provides the ideal environment for fleas and ticks. These disgusting bugs feed on your dog's blood and may cause a long list of problems, such as allergic reactions and serious illnesses caused by a tick bite. Even though fleas and ticks are more prevalent during the warmer months, you will still need to ward them off during the colder months.

Fleas

These pesky insects not only set up home on your dog but will quickly invade your own home. These blood-sucking insects have the ability to jump almost three feet and can survive in the harshest environments. An average life span for a flea can be 12 days to an entire year. During this time, a single flea can produce millions of baby fleas.

If not controlled, fleas can cause serious health complications for their host. For example, a flea consumes approximately 15 times its body weight in blood each day, causing your English Setter to become anemic. Some dogs have an allergic reaction to flea bites, called allergic dermatitis.

Flea warning signs:

- Hair loss
- Allergic dermatitis
- Flea eggs look like white grains of sand
- Flea droppings look like tiny dirt particles
- Excessive biting, licking, or scratching
- Hot spots or scabs

Flea droppings can be found throughout your English Setter's coat. Use a fine-toothed comb to detect them, especially around your dog's abdomen, ears, mouth, and tail.

Fleas are expert stowaways. They quickly attach themselves to animals while outside or can jump from one dog to another. If not controlled, fleas can invade your house within a day or two.

If your English Setter has fleas, all of your resident pets will need to be treated. In some extreme cases, the inside of your house will need to be fumigated. Your veterinarian will confirm your suspicions and most likely will suggest one or two of the following treatments.

- Oral or topical treatment or dog-formulated shampoo for your English Setter
- Thoroughly cleaning your house, including bedding, rugs, and upholstery. A severe infestation will require professional help, which means you and all your pets will have to temporarily evacuate your home.

- If your English Setter gets reinfested every time he goes into the backyard, you may need to fumigate your lawn.

How to prevent fleas

- Wash your English Setter's bedding at least once a week in hot, soapy water and brush him using a flea brush.
- Rake up any grass clippings or leaves in your backyard, as fleas tend to conceal themselves in dark, moist areas.
- There are preventive flea-control measures available either by prescription or over the counter. Be aware some flea collars can be carcinogenic for animals and humans. Always consult with your vet beforehand.

Ticks

Ticks are considered parasites as they feed on the host's blood. Ticks are experts at concealing themselves by burrowing into their hosts then gorging on their blood. They can transmit serious diseases to both animals and humans. Transmission varies in certain areas and climates. Ask your vet what types of ticks are in your locality.

Your English Setter loves running through the grass, which makes him an easy target for ticks. You will need to be alert year-round, but be extra vigilant during late spring and early summer.

How to check your English Setter for ticks

Ticks are very small, making them very easy to miss until they bite your dog and begin to swell up with all the blood they have sucked. Carefully run your fingers through your English Setter's coat, paying extra attention to warm spots such as the inside of his ears and around his feet and face. Be sure to repeat this every time your pooch comes inside from playing.

Health complications caused by tick bites include

- Blood loss and anemia
- Tick paralysis
- Allergic dermatitis

If you find a tick attached to your English Setter, it is essential you carefully remove it, as the tick's blood may infect you or your dog. Humans may contract Lyme Disease from deer ticks; these ticks are the primary carriers of Lyme Disease. The illness causes depression, fever, loss of appetite, painful joints, and kidney failure. Lyme disease needs to be caught in time to be successfully treated with antibiotics.

Follow these instructions to safely remove a tick
1. Prepare a glass jar with rubbing alcohol inside. This allows you to take a tick in for testing at your veterinary clinic. Put on latex gloves and ask a family member to distract your English Setter while you extract the tick.
2. Using a pair of disinfected tweezers, gently grasp the tick as close as you can to the dog's skin. Pull straight upward, using even pressure, then place the tick into the jar with rubbing alcohol. Do not twist the tick out, as this could leave the head attached inside the dog or cause the tick to regurgitate infected fluids.
3. Disinfect the bitten area and the tweezers; wash your hands with warm, soapy water afterward. Monitor the area for the next few weeks for any signs of an infection. If there is a sign of infection, take your English Setter and the tick to the veterinarian.

Many products used to treat or prevent fleas are also useful in killing ticks. Keep your yard tick-free by keeping the grass cut and removing any large weeds that could be hiding places for ticks.

Holistic Alternatives to Conventional Veterinary Medicine

Holistic veterinary care is often combined with conventional medicine to aid a dog's healing process. For example, if your English Setter has a hip or knee replacement, he will need to take medications such as antibiotics to prevent infection. But some veterinarians recommend combining the treatment with holistic care, such as acupuncture or massages to naturally ease the pain and hasten the healing process.

Below are some of the most popular holistic treatments recommended by veterinarians and used by concerned pet parents. Be aware that few of these treatments have been scientifically proven for treating canines. Before starting any type of holistic treatment, be sure to talk over the risks and details with your veterinarian.

Canine acupuncture

Acupuncture uses needles to stimulate pressure points to release the buildup of certain chemicals in the muscles, spinal cord, and brain, thus promoting better health. There is plenty of anecdotal proof that acupuncture can relieve dogs of joint and muscle pain, encourage healing post-surgery, and even treat cancer or other types of traumas.

Hydrotherapy

Hydrotherapy means physical therapy in water. This type of therapy is highly recommended for dogs in need of low-impact exercise due to joint pain from arthritis or recovery from an injury or surgery. Hydrotherapy is proven to build muscle, improve mobility, decrease stress, and increase circulation.

Chinese herbal medicine

Chinese herbal medicine combines certain herbs to relieve pain, improve and restore organ function, and strengthen the immune system. Many pet owners rave about Chinese herbal medicine's effect on their pets. As with all herbs, ask your vet to make sure they are safe to use alongside your dog's conventional medications, such as blood thinners or diuretics.

Magnetic field therapy

According to the Veterinary Clinics of America, magnet therapy is gaining popularity in the United States to treat illness and injury; however, there is not much evidence that the application of magnets can heal your English Setter. Magnet field therapy is affordable, non-invasive, and has virtually no side effects.

Photo Courtesy of
Stuart Casey

Canine massage

Canine massage encourages healing, improves circulation, stimulates nerves, relieves stress, and relaxes your dog's muscles. One of the biggest advantages of a doggy massage is that it makes your pooch feel good and strengthens the bond between you and your dog. Massage will not cure your English Setter's cancer or injury; it will, however, make him feel relaxed and loved.

Nutritional supplements

Nutritional supplements are required to make up for any nutritional deficiencies if you are feeding your dog a homemade or raw diet. Look for nutritional supplements that include calcium, omega fatty acids, vitamins, and amino acids.

When choosing a holistic treatment or supplement for your dog, be sure to use good judgment and always consult with your veterinarian to see if the treatment will help your dog. Note: just because an herbal substance claims it is healthy and beneficial does not mean that it is harmless. Always thoroughly research a product before giving it to your dog.

Vaccinations

Vaccines are a primary prevention against infections and diseases. Your vet will establish a vaccination regimen for your English Setter by taking into account his age, health, lifestyle, and where you live.

Vaccinations are designed to help your dog fight off organisms that cause diseases. Vaccines are made up of antigens, which the immune system identifies as the same disease-ridden organism, but without actually causing your dog to become sick. When the vaccine is introduced into the body, instructs the immune system how to fight off the real virus in its entirety, building antibodies.

The AAHA recommends all dogs receive core vaccines throughout their lives. Your veterinarian may recommend other noncore vaccines depending on geography, lifestyle, and the current prevalence of the disease. For example, a noncore vaccine for kennel cough is required for dogs who frequent doggy daycare, kennels, grooming facilities, and so on.

Puppies

When puppies are about six to eight weeks of age, they will receive a series of three core vaccinations administered by a veterinarian at three to four-week intervals. The final dose should be administered when your English Setter is 16 weeks of age.

Adult dogs

Your English Setter will require annual vaccines or booster shots every two to three years.

Rabies

In the United States, it is mandatory for all dogs to be vaccinated against rabies. However, each state and county have different laws regarding how often your dog will need to be vaccinated. For example, some states require an annual vaccine while others stipulate doses are required once every three years.

The majority of dogs experience no side effects from being vaccinated. However, there are exceedingly rare cases of severe side effects.

Reactions are often short-lived and rarely require veterinary care. Here is a list of common reactions.

- Lack of appetite
- Sluggishness
- Vomiting
- Swelling, pain, redness, or hair loss around the injection site
- Fever
- Diarrhea

Schedule your English Setter's vaccinations when you will be around to monitor him for a few days. If your dog experiences any severe symptoms, like seizures, difficulty breathing, or lameness, call your vet as soon as possible.

Pet Insurance

No matter how careful you are with your English Setter, unexpected accidents do happen, and often they are not cheap.

Veterinary costs are higher than ever. According to the American Pet Product Association, an average dog owner spends almost $250 for annual check-ups. What happens when the unexpected occurs? Costs can quickly add up! For example, for an active dog such as an English Setter, the cost to repair a cruciate ligament tear in the knee (which often happens when the dog comes to a sudden stop while playing fetch) was about $1,200 five years ago. Today, it can cost a whopping $5,000 for each knee.

Pet insurance can help defray these costs. Pet insurance was once a specialty niche, but in the last few years, it has gone mainstream. Currently, there are more than 15 different insurance companies in the United States that offer pet insurance, but less than 1 percent of dog owners purchase this type of insurance.

Just as you can pick a health plan that matches you and your family's needs, you can also choose an insurance plan that is the best fit for your English Setter. Most insurance companies offer three types of coverage: accident and illness, accident only, and a wellness plan. Wellness plans often cover preventative care, such as annual check-ups and routine vaccinations. You can purchase one type of plan or add on an accident or illness policy.

The final price of pet insurance depends on your English Setter's age and the type of coverage you choose. You can expect to pay a monthly premium of about $20 to $50 a month. The deductible depends on the type of policy you choose.

Here are a few benefits and drawbacks of pet insurance

PROS

- It gives you peace of mind knowing you have the resources for any unforeseen medical costs if your English Setter becomes injured or ill.
- Pet insurance gives vets the opportunity to give your pooch top-notch care without having to worry about incurring too many medical costs for you.
- Pet insurance helps your dog live a longer and healthier life, as you will not hesitate to take your dog in for medical treatment before his condition worsens.

CONS

- Some insurance companies look at factors such as the dog's age, whether he is a purebred or a designer-breed dog, and the dog's living environment. Depending on these factors, the monthly insurance premium could increase.
- Many insurance companies have a 48-hour waiting period before approving accident insurance and a 14-day waiting period before approval for illness insurance.
- Depending on the fine print of the insurance plan, it may exclude pre-existing illnesses, pregnancy and/or birth, routine vaccines, and dental maintenance.
- The majority of pet insurance plans require that you pay for the entire veterinary cost upfront and, afterward, submit a claim for reimbursement.

> **NOTE:** *Your pet insurance will be void if your English Setter is not up to date on his vaccinations and deworming. Also, if your dog gets sick from something that is preventable by being vaccinated, most insurance companies will not cover the expenses.*

Consider Self-insuring

If you decide that pet insurance is too expensive for your monthly budget, then another practical option is to set up a personal savings account for your English Setter. You can always deposit a certain amount of money in the account each month and only withdraw from it for your dog's medical care. This is an excellent option if you are disciplined with money.

The bottom line — veterinary care is not cheap, and it can quickly add up, especially if your English Setter needs expensive diagnostics, care, and treatment. If you do decide to purchase pet insurance, take your time and read the fine print very carefully to make sure you completely understand what you are getting yourself into.

Common questions

Anatomically and physiologically, dogs have a lot in common with other pets, but some of their behaviors leave us scratching our heads, asking ourselves, "Why do dogs do that?" Here are some answers to some of your frequently asked questions about your dog.

Why does my dog sniff other dogs' butts?

With a few sniffs, your pooch can determine if the other dog is an old acquaintance or a new one, if it is male or female, and if it is aggressive or friendly. Next time your dog goes in for a sniff, just allow it to happen, otherwise it can leave both dogs confused and one of them may will get on the defensive side.

Why does my English Setter eat grass?

Vets and researchers believe dogs eat grass when they have a belly ache, to make themselves throw up, or to make up for a deficit in fiber. However, only 10 percent of dogs appear to be unwell prior to eating grass, only 15 percent of dogs vomit after consuming grass, and some dogs on a high-fiber diet still munch on grass. Most likely your English Setter is eating grass due to boredom or simply because he likes the taste of it.

Should you worry about your pup eating grass? Vets say it is normal behavior and there is no need to be concerned, as long as your pup is not eating other types of plants that could make him sick.

Why does my dog eat poop?

Eating poop may seem disgusting to us, but it is a natural instinct for dogs. For example, when a wild female dog has a litter of puppies, she cleans up after her puppies when they defecate. This helps keep the den clean and protects the puppies from hungry predators who may be drawn to the scent. Puppies often learn this behavior from their mothers and also due to their natural curiosity and desire to smell and taste everything. Most pups grow out of this disgusting habit, but some adult English Setters eat poop out of boredom or a lack of nutritional diet.

Compulsive licking, biting, and scratching – Should I worry?

Compulsive licking, biting, and scratching are common behaviors in all dogs, and there are a variety of causes. One reason may be because your dog has a hot spot or acute moist dermatitis; since your dog may constantly lick, bite, or scratch the area, it can quickly become irritated and incredibly sore. Here are some common reasons why your dog may be licking, biting, or scratching himself.

- Allergies
- Boredom or anxiety
- Dry skin
- Hormonal imbalances
- Pain
- Parasites

As you can see there are quite a few reasons why dogs chew or scratch, but be sure to check with your veterinarian as soon as you notice a problem. Your vet will figure out the root cause of the compulsive behavior and determine a treatment plan. Depending on the cause of the behavior, this may include the following.

Eliminating parasites – There are a wide variety of flea and tick products that your vet may recommend. If your dog's compulsive biting, licking, and scratching problems are caused by fleas or ticks, be sure to wash your English Setter's bed and vacuum your carpet and any upholstered furniture on a regular basis to reduce the chances of reinfestation. If you have any other pets in your household, then they will need to be treated too.

Changing foods – If food allergies are making your English Setter itch, eliminating any foods that trigger him will make a huge difference. Most English Setters are not allergic to grains but to animal proteins. Your vet will recommend a special diet and fatty acid supplements to address dry skin issues and keep your dog's coat healthy.

Using medication – Your vet may prescribe medication to treat any underlying health issues that may contribute to your dog's compulsive scratching. If your dog has a hot spot or a skin infection, your vet may recommend the use of topical or oral antibiotics or steroids.

Preventing the behavior – Compulsive behaviors can seriously affect your dog's quality of life, so it is important that you try to stop your dog from chewing, licking, or scratching too much. Try applying a pet-friendly bitter spray designed to discourage licking, have your dog wear a special collar to prevent access to the hot spot, or keep your pooch close to you when inside your house.

Address anxiety and boredom – Often, licking, chewing, and scratching develops in response to boredom, lack of mental stimulation, or fear or stress. To reduce this likelihood, make sure you English Setter receives enough exercise, love and attention, and mental stimulation. When you notice your dog chewing or licking, distract his attention with a toy or a bone.

What is canine acne?

Canine acne is an inflammation of the lips and the skin around the muzzle, which appears as red pimples or bumps on the skin. Canine acne may be caused by ingrown hairs or the hair follicle becoming inflamed or infected under the skin. In both of these cases, there is trauma to tissues, and it can become complicated with a secondary condition — bacterial or fungal infections. This condition is fairly common in English Setters. Your vet will treat the acne with anti-inflammatory creams or antibiotics.

Why does my English Setter have a wet nose?

If you have ever been nuzzled by your English Setter before, then you know that you will need to wipe your face afterward. Dogs have wet noses for several important reasons. One reason is because dogs' noses secrete mucus to help them keep track of smells in the air. Another reason is because dogs do not sweat the same way humans do. Dogs' noses act like a cooling mechanism, and fluid on their nose helps them to regulate their body temperature. Finally, your dog may lick his nose to fully experience the scent he was tracking.

CHAPTER 14

Breed-specific Diseases

A ll dogs, purebred and mixed breed, are prone to diseases and abnormalities, which may be genetic. Your purebred English Setter is no exception.

Many of these health issues can be unapparent to the average person for years and can only be detected by a medical screening performed by a veterinarian.

Understanding some of the health problems your English Setter is predisposed to can help you take precautions to avoid future troubles. For example, if a certain dog breed has an inherent risk for intervertebral disc problems, then precautions can be taken to avoid having the dog run up and down the stairs or jump off the furniture.

Common Hereditary Diseases and Health Conditions for English Setters

By purchasing your English Setter from a reputable breeder, you will be able to verify the health of at least up to three generations of your puppy's family health. However, if your pooch was adopted from a shelter, he most likely will not come with a pedigree ensuring a clean health background, so it will be even more useful to be aware of which breed-related health problems to watch out for.

Many diseases and health conditions are genetic, but that does not mean your English Setter will have these health conditions; it just means that he is more at risk than other dog breeds. I will describe the most common issues related to English Setters to give you an idea of what may occur in the future. Of course, I cannot cover every possibility here, so always check with your veterinarian if you notice any unusual symptoms.

Acral Mutilation Syndrome

Acral mutilation syndrome (AMS) is a serious but very rare hereditary disease. AMS causes progressive degeneration of the sensory neurons of the dog's spinal cord, resulting in a loss of pain sensation in the outer extremities, such as the hind legs. Dogs with AMS will often chew, bite,

Photo Courtesy of
David Weaver

and self-mutilate their outer extremities, resulting in bacterial infections and ulcers.

Puppies with AMS are often much smaller in size when compared to their littermates. Often, by the age of three months, the puppy will begin excessively licking, biting, and chewing on his hind feet. The puppy will have no pain or temperature sensation in his feet.

Unfortunately, there is no known treatment for AMS, but there are ways to prevent the dog from mutilating himself, such as Elizabethan collars or cones, bandages, doggie booties, and muzzles. Topical application of specially formulated ointments that taste bad may deter the dog from licking a certain area. Talk to your vet for additional alternatives. If all attempts to prevent the canine from self-mutilating are unsuccessful, then your vet may suggest euthanasia.

AMS is an autosomal-recessive condition, which means the affected dogs must inherit two copies of an abnormal gene (one from each of the parents). If a dog inherits only one abnormal gene from one of his parents, he will have no symptoms of the disease, but the dog will be a carrier and will pass the abnormal gene on to any future offspring. Reputable breeders will test both parents prior to breeding for AMS. The Kennel Club Breed Register also has a record of DNA results tests carried by different breeders.

Even though this condition is extremely rare, make sure the breeder tests the parent dogs prior to breeding for AMS. Also, make sure there is a clause in the breeder's contract that you will be refunded your money if the dog has a genetic disease such as AMS.

Eye Problems

Nothing is as traumatic to the quality of your dog's life as losing his vision. Unfortunately, English Setters can inherit or develop a number of different eye conditions, and some may cause blindness if not treated in time.

Ectropion is a genetic defect that causes the eyelids to droop, exposing the eyeball to environmental contaminants that cause irritation, drying, and infections. The good news is this condition can easily be surgically corrected.

Progressive retinal atrophy refers to a group of different degenerative diseases that affect a dog's vision. This disease causes the light-sensitive layer of cells inside of the eye, the retina, to slowly deteriorate over time, eventually leading to blindness. Retinal dysplasia is diagnosed in puppies around two to three months of age, and a later-onset form is diagnosed in dogs between the ages of four to nine years.

> **FUN FACT** 😊
>
> **Forever Young Setters**
>
> English Setters have a reputation for remaining "forever young." These dogs often remain active and spry into their older years, sometimes not slowing down until they reach nine years old. The average life expectancy for an English Setter is 12 to 14 years old. Unfortunately, cancer is the leading cause of death for this breed. Regular veterinary visits and cancer screenings can help your English Setter enjoy the longest life possible.

Progressive retinal atrophy is an inherited disease that occurs in a long list of breeds and mixed dogs. Affected dogs should not be used in breeding. If a dog develops progressive retinal atrophy, its parents and all of its siblings from previous litters should be prevented from breeding. Unfortunately, there is no known cure for progressive retinal atrophy.

Cone degeneration is often referred to as day blindness, as affected dogs experience temporary blindness when exposed to daylight. Cone cells are responsible for helping a dog see in high light, and rod photoreceptors are responsible for helping canines see in low light. Affected dogs have normal vision in low light, and light sensitivity begins eight to 12 weeks after birth. By the time an affected dog is an adult, it will have completely lost all cone cells; however, it will be able to see normally in a low-light situation.

As this is a genetic condition, and some dogs may be carriers without showing symptoms, many reputable breeders will test the parent dogs for this mutation. It is recommended dogs with this genetic defect be eliminated from breeding lines. There is no known cure.

Keratoconjunctivitis, also known as dry eye, is common in English Setters. The tear ducts no longer produce enough tears to keep the eyes moist, which results in sore, itchy eyes and infections. Often, symptoms include discharge, squinting, pawing at the eyes, and a dull, dry appearance of the eye. If you notice any of these conditions, please call your vet immediately. There is no cure for this disease, but you will need to apply ointment or prescription eye drops for the rest of your dog's life.

Bone and Joint Problems

Joint dysplasia and musculoskeletal problems have been reported in English Setters.

Joint dysplasia is a deformity of the joint that occurs during growth. Joint dysplasia often occurs in the hip joint. The thigh bone and socket for the pelvis need to grow at the same speed. However, in joint dysplasia, this growth does not occur, resulting in a loose joint, which is followed by osteoarthritis or degenerative joint disease as the body tries to stabilize the loose joint.

Joint dysplasia is a genetic disease, but the extent of damage can be affected by diet, environment, exercise, growth rate, and hormones. Medium-sized and larger dogs are most prone to joint dysplasia. Care should be taken to keep your dog at a healthy weight, especially during his growth cycle by feeding him a healthy, balanced diet. Avoid overfeeding your puppy and do not give him calcium supplements until he is at least two years old.

An English Setters' kneecap (patella) may slip out of place; this is called patellar luxation. When this happens, you may notice your English Setter picking up his back leg and hopping for a few strides. Then your dog will kick his leg out sideways to pop the kneecap back into place, and after that the dog will walk normally again. Most likely, your pooch will only require arthritis medication, but when symptoms are more severe, surgery may be required to realign the kneecap to prevent it from popping out of place.

English Setter pups can suffer from another condition called eosinophilic panosteitis, which is a painful inflammation of the long, slender leg bones. This condition usually begins when the pup is six to 10 months old, and it shifts from leg to leg. Your vet will squeeze or palpate your dog's legs and if he exhibits pain, the vet will take an X-ray to diagnose the condition. Panosteitis is normally treated with pain medication.

Nerve diseases

Neuronal ceroid lipofuscinosis is a progressive neurologic disease found in Setters and Spaniels. Clinical symptoms often appear in younger dogs between one to three years of age. In the early stages, the dog exhibits, rear-leg weakness and imbalance, which generally progresses rapidly to all four legs, some dogs also lose their vision. There currently is no cure for this disease, but there is a genetic test available. Dogs carrying this genetic mutation should not be used for breeding as it will be passed to future generations.

Skin Infections

English Setters are susceptible to many different types of skin infections and diseases. The most common is Malassezia dermatitis. When it affects the skin, it leaves greasy, hairless areas around the face, neck, and throat, with a distinctive unpleasant odor. In the ears, it causes itchy red and brown discharge. This condition can easily be treated, but your dog may have flare-ups for the rest of his life.

Dental Abnormalities

Teeth abnormalities are common in purebred dogs like your English Setter. The most common abnormality is an overbite or an underbite called a malocclusion or a bad bite. Another condition is oligodontia which is a condition where only a few teeth are present. Misaligned teeth may also occur and can cause numerous dental issues, but can easily be corrected with braces or extractions.

Other Common Diseases or Health Conditions

Not all diseases and health conditions are hereditary. Diet, life-style, and just plain bad luck are all factors that can affect your dog's long-term health.

Arthritis

As your English Setter ages, you may notice that he begins to show lameness in his legs or struggles to stand up after laying down on his bed. The sooner your vet can diagnose this condition, the better to minimize discomfort and pain. Most likely, your vet will take an X-ray to see how much damage has been caused to your dog's bones and joints; surgery is a good option in severe and life-limiting cases. Keep in mind that obese or overweight dogs will develop arthritis sooner than dogs with a normal weight.

Aortic Stenosis

Aortic stenosis is a hereditary cardiovascular condition. Affected dogs are born with a narrow aorta, which prevents newly oxygenated blood from being pumped out of the heart into the body. Consequently, the narrowed aorta causes the entire heart to work twice as hard to provide the body with the oxygen-rich blood needed to perform bodily functions.

Symptoms of aortic stenosis often are identified early, including fainting, poor growth, sluggishness, and exercise intolerance. Since the dog's heart is constantly overworking, it grows bigger and bigger overtime. Affected dogs tend to develop a constant cough as the heart takes up more space and pushes against the lungs, causing breathing difficulties and heart rhythm abnormalities. Sadly, sudden death is a likely outcome for affected dogs with aortic stenosis.

Vets often identify this condition within the first year of a dog's life via a simple medical exam. The vet will hear a characteristic murmur known to be caused by aortic stenosis. If your English Setter has aortic

Photo Courtesy of Tom Gibbs

stenosis, your vet will recommend reducing the impact of the heart's work by reducing exercise to a bare minimum, along with beta-blockers to reduce a dog's blood pressure.

Discoid Lupus Erythematosus

Discoid lupus erythematosus is an autoimmune disease that causes the immune system to attack the dog's own skin, causing painful inflammation and tissue damage. Discoid lupus erythematosus is the most common type of lupus in dogs but is extremely rare. Dogs with this autoimmune disorder develop a crusty scab around the nose, as well as skin pigmentation loss.

The underlying cause of discoid lupus erythematosus is unknown. Veterinarians have observed that prolonged exposure to ultraviolet light appears to worsen the condition. Affected dogs respond well to a topical steroid medication or ointment. Apply the cream when your dog is distracted, such as during mealtime, to prevent him from licking it off.

Gastric Dilation Volvulus

Gastric dilation volvulus is a life-threatening condition in dogs, as it causes the dog's stomach to expand to the point that neither food nor gas can be expelled. This condition is believed to be caused when a dog eats a large meal; however, the actual cause is not completely understood. An expanded stomach can rotate inside of the abdomen, which is called volvulus. When a rotation occurs, it can lead to a blockage in the blood supply to the dog's spleen and stomach.

When this condition occurs, your vet will need to quickly stabilize your dog by decompressing the stomach, followed by surgery to return the stomach to its original place. During the surgery, the vet will evaluate any damage to the surrounding organs. If this painful condition is left untreated, it can result in a ruptured stomach wall, and put excess pressure on the lungs, causing decreased breathing, and it can be fatal.

*Photo Courtesy of
Kim Ciaputa*

Hepatitis

There are two types of hepatitis in dogs: infectious canine hepatitis and canine chronic hepatitis. Infectious canine hepatitis is a contagious disease caused by a canine adenovirus, and symptoms can vary from fever to lethargy, thirst, or death. If infectious hepatitis is left untreated, it causes chronic hepatitis, affecting the liver to the point of causing inflammation and cell death (necrosis).

If your dog has a fever for more than one day, take him to see the vet immediately. The sooner your dog starts treatment, the better the outcome. This condition can be prevented by routine vaccinations. However, dog owners must stay vigilant and keep their dogs' vaccines up to date, as the disease can develop quickly.

Myasthenia Gravis

Myasthenia gravis is a condition that causes a miscommunication between the nerve and muscle signals. Affected dogs will exhibit extreme lethargy and muscle weakness. Dogs with congenital myasthenia gravis are usually diagnosed between six to eight weeks of age. Acquired myasthenia gravis is more like an autoimmune disease and is not hereditary. It tends to be diagnosed in dogs between two to four years of age.

Most affected dogs can be treated with medication they will need to take for the rest of their lives. If left untreated, the affected dog will eventually have difficulty swallowing food, and it may accidentally inhale food, liquid, or vomit, which will result in aspiration pneumonia. Aspiration pneumonia is extremely serious and requires costly veterinarian care until the dog's condition can be stabilized.

Cruciate Ligament Disease

Cranial cruciate ligament disease occurs when the tough fibrous tissue attached to the hip and knee bone prevents the knee from moving forward, and at the same time, it does not prevent the knee joint from overextending or rotating. The precise cause of this condition is unknown, as the ligament degenerates slowly over time, similar to a fraying rope. Factors such as obesity, hormonal imbalance, and inflammatory conditions of the joint may play a role in this condition.

One of the most common signs of cruciate ligament disease is a dog limping after exercise or standing up after sitting for a long period of time. In severe cases, affected dogs cannot stand up and may be erroneously suspected of having a neurological issue. Your vet will most likely recommend noninvasive treatment measures, such as anti-inflammatory painkillers, physiotherapy, weight management, and exercise modification. If the condition worsens, your vet may recommend surgery.

What to Watch for

Any abnormal symptom may be an indication of a serious health condition, or it could just be a minor health issue. The important thing is knowing when to seek veterinary help and how urgently help is required. Many diseases that affect English Setters have a characteristic combination of symptoms, which will be a clear indication to take your dog to the vet.

Call the veterinarian clinic if you notice any of the following symptoms:
- Change in appetite or water consumption
- Tartar buildup, foul breath, red gums, or broken teeth
- Itchy skin, hair loss
- Lethargy, mental dullness, or excess sleeping
- Unusual aggression, fearfulness, or any behavioral changes

Seek emergency medical care immediately if you notice any of these signs:
- Lumps or bumps, of any size
- Inability or difficulty to urinate or defecate; discolored urine
- Scratching or shaking the head, tender ears, or ear discharge
- Reluctance to run or play
- Leg stiffness, reluctance to rise, sit, use stairs, run, or jump
- Redness, itching, or any other abnormalities involving the eyes.

Your English Setter counts on you to take good care of him, and give him a long and healthy life. Your goal should be to provide your Setter with the best health care possible: health care based on his breed, lifestyle, and age. Please contact your vet whenever you have a doubt about your dog's health.

CHAPTER 15

Caring for a Senior English Setter

> As we age, we all show the signs. It's very important to continue doing the things that your dog loves, even if it means that you can't do these activities for long periods of time. I always try to make sure that my older dogs still get their time in the field. It's the least I can do after they have given me their entire career working and loving what they do.
>
> JEFFREY GILLASPIE
> *Tinker Kennels, LLC*

According to the American Society for the Prevention of Cruelty to Animals (ASPCA), of the 79 million dogs owned in the United States, more than one-third are senior dogs. Aging varies from dog to dog. Some dogs stay physically and mentally active as they age, while others become lethargic and senile. This is just the natural process of growing older.

Physical and Mental Signs of Aging

> *You may begin to notice a slower, methodical pace in the field has replaced the hard charge that always cleared the field of birds. Seniors Setters show a decreased ability to discern whistle commands and may have difficulty tracking downed birds. Shorter field sessions, less difficult cover, and favorable weather conditions can keep them hunting as long as physically possible. It's what they were born to do. I will hunt the old guy by himself, just him and me, no other dogs, hunters, or distractions, while hoping for him to get one more chance to point his bird.*
>
> WADE KISNER
> *Sweet Point Setters, LLC*

Unfortunately, dogs age faster than their pet owners. Generally, a medium-sized dog like your English Setter will enter his senior years at around age eight or nine in human years. The more aware you are of typical signs of aging, the sooner you can make your dog's golden years more comfortable.

Your English Setter is more than a four-legged companion. He is part of your immediate family. Just as your pooch has cared about you over the years, you want to care for him throughout his life, even more so as he ages. Dogs age quite similarly to humans. They too, may lose control of their physical and mental abilities.

As your English Setter ages, you are going to notice some changes such as slowing down, decreased agility and mobility, and personality changes. Perhaps your pooch will become less enthusiastic about his favorite activities, such as going for walks, eating, or even playing a game of fetch. But, with love and care, you can help your English Setter age gracefully.

Senior Setters experience physical and mental signs of aging, such as bathroom issues, hearing loss, poor mobility due to aches and pains, and so on. Some of these changes may affect your dog's behavior. For

example, your mellow companion might suddenly turn into an old grouch. He may be in pain from arthritis. Or maybe your hyperactive English Setter suddenly wants to sleep all day long. Senior dogs need more rest, so — let your pooch sleep.

Your senior English Setter may also begin to display symptoms of cognitive decline, such as forgetting where his water dish is or barking at nothing. Your dog may seem to be going senile, which is entirely possible as dogs can develop cognitive problems just like humans. Many behavioral changes are caused by canine cognitive dysfunction syndrome (CCDS). CCDS is similar to Alzheimer's disease and affects around half of all dogs over 11 years of age.

At around 14 years of age, almost 70 percent of all dogs begin to experience symptoms associated with CCDS. Some behavioral changes your English Setter might display are:

- House soiling
- Increased anxiety
- Fear of familiar people and objects

- Compulsive behaviors
- Excessive barking and vocalization
- Change in activity level
- Insomnia, sleepwalking, or restlessness

If you observe your English Setter displaying any of these symptoms, consult with your vet. Your vet will make a diagnosis by asking you a few questions during the visit. There is no cure for CCDS; however, there are medications and therapeutic options such as dietary therapy, nutritional supplements, and maintaining a healthy and stimulating environment.

Illness and Injury Prevention

> *Old joints may take a while to limber up, especially after a long nap. They need some extra time to get headed in the right direction. Keep nails and pads groomed if they have to walk on hard floors. They tend to slip and slide more if the hair on their pads is long. Soft bedding helps relieve pressure on joints and reduces pressure points. Raised dog beds made of PVC/wooden frames and soft bedding are great for older dogs to sleep on. Hard flooring puts pressure on tired joints, and jumping up on a couch can be difficult.*
>
> MARK D. DENEKA
> *Twilight Setter Kennels*

Strained muscles, sprains, and pulled ligaments are all common senior canine injuries. As your English Setter ages, he will become more susceptible to injury due to brittle bones and arthritis. Research shows dogs experience a similar pain threshold as that of humans. You can easily reduce injuries by incorporating the following strategies into your dog's daily life:

Avoid extreme temperatures – Elderly Setters are more sensitive to extreme temperature changes. They can suffer more easily from heatstroke, frostbite, and hypothermia than younger dogs. If the weather outside is too hot or too cold, keep your pooch inside.

Daily exercise schedule – Even though your senior English Setter has gotten slower in the last few years, that does not mean he does not need regular exercise. Switch up your dog's exercise routine by taking him for shorter walks. Instead of walking on cement, take your canine for a walk on a dirt or grass path, as it will be softer on his sore joints.

Ramp up – Climbing stairs, jumping up on the couch, or getting into the car may become a challenge for your senior dog. At your local pet supply store, you can find a variety of ramps to help your pooch.

Slip-proof your home – Your English Setter may lack the agility he once had during his younger years. Your hardwood or tile floors may cause him to slip, causing injury. Place rugs in the areas your dog spends the majority of his time to help him feel more secure and sure-footed.

Soft, fluffy bed – Your English Setter will thank you for a soft, fluffy bed that supports his old bones and joints. Invest in a doggy bed with soft sides, so your senior pooch can rest his head on a soft surface while he observes his surroundings.

Take it slow – Your elderly English Setter will need extra time for eating, walking, going to the bathroom, etc. Be patient with him and give him the time he needs. Your furry friend also will appreciate any extra attention, love, and affection from you, like cuddling on the couch.

Weight control – Since your senior English Setter is less active, he is burning fewer calories, meaning unwanted weight gain. Extra weight puts pressure on your old dog's bones, joints, and heart, which can cause additional health problems. Consult with your vet for recommendations to improve your dog's diet.

Signs of illness or pain

Each dog will display pain and suffering differently. Any change in your English Setter's behavior may be an early indication that he is ill or in pain.

When your dog is in pain or is ill, his eating or drinking habits will often change. He might lose interest in food or drink excessive amounts of water. He may become withdrawn, be aggressive when petted, or seem unwilling to go for a walk. Your dog may display one or more of these signs of ill health:

- Runny nose, crusty eyes, or discharge coming from the ears
- Excessive drooling
- Vomiting
- Diarrhea
- Constipation
- Difficulty urinating
- Coughing
- Hot spots, excessive scratching, or skin sores under his coat
- Limping, swelling, and lack of mobility

If you notice that your English Setter is displaying any of these symptoms for more than 48 hours, consult with your veterinarian about any health issues.

Age-related Diseases and Conditions in English Setters

During your dog's golden years, he may begin to experience age-associated illnesses and diseases. Many of these conditions can be treated if identified early, so be sure to consult with your vet immediately. The following health issues are commonly associated with geriatric English Setters.

Arthritis – Just like people, dogs develop arthritis as they age. The most common type of arthritis in aging English Setters is osteoarthritis, also called degenerative joint disease. This condition affects the hips, knees, shoulders, and elbows. The changes in joints result in pain, stiffness, and lack of mobility. Osteoarthritis is progressive, meaning there is no cure, but there are many treatments, such as chiropractic, hydrotherapy, and acupuncture, which are known to slow the disease progression and ease joint pain.

Cancer – Unfortunately, cancer is common in older dogs. Different types of cancer can cause a variety of symptoms. Often, symptoms such as lethargy and lack of appetite may be dismissed as signs of aging. As your English Setter ages, it is vital that he receives routine wellness screenings. Lab work, diagnostic imaging, and other exams can pick up on anything unseen to the naked eye. The sooner the cancer is caught, the better the chances of your dog's survival.

Cataracts – Cataracts cause your English Setter's eyes to lose transparency, causing them to appear cloudy. The cataract prevents light from passing through your dog's lens, blocking his vision. Most elderly dogs who develop cataracts will not go completely blind, and they can adjust to their loss of vision. Your vet will need to diagnose the cause of the cataract before coming up with a treatment plan.

Glaucoma – Your dog's eye is made up of a jelly-like substance called aqueous humor. This liquid is constantly being produced by the eye. Normally, the eye drains itself of the old fluid, but if this does not occur, then glaucoma happens. Glaucoma in dogs can have many causes, so be sure to consult with your vet to find the correct treatment for your dog.
Watch out for the following symptoms of glaucoma in your English Setter.
- Cloudy cornea
- Continual blinking or squinting of the eye
- Pupil does not respond to light
- Pupils are a different size in each eye
- Increased sleeping

Diabetes – Setters are prone to developing canine diabetes. Diabetes occurs when the pancreas stops producing normal amounts of insulin and may be caused by heredity, diet, obesity, and certain medications, such as steroids used for treating allergies. Diabetes can easily be regulated with insulin shots and a change in diet.

Incontinence – Age takes a toll on your dog's organs, muscles, and nerves, making it more challenging for him to hold his bladder and

Photo Courtesy of Linda Lawson

bowels the way he used to. Incontinence may be an indication of other health complications, so you will need your vet to rule out some issues first. If the vet does not find any health problems, you may need to let your English Setter out more often for potty breaks or have him wear a doggy diaper.

Kidney Disease – Kidney disease often develops slowly, starting off as renal insufficiency and progressing to full renal failure. Once this disease starts to progress, there is no cure, but if caught in time, it can be successfully treated to slow the progression. Signs of kidney disease include increased thirst, frequent urination, lack of appetite, vomiting, and lethargy.

Lenticular Sclerosis – This condition is often confused with cataracts as it also causes the dog's eyes to form a white, cloudy reflection. Lenticular sclerosis, however, does not affect your Setter's vision. But to be on the safe side, get your dog's eyes checked out by your vet.

Muscle Atrophy – Muscle atrophy is common in older English Setters as they become less active with age. This condition causes rear-leg weakness, limping, ataxia, paw dragging, flabby muscles, and weight loss. Muscle atrophy can be caused by a number of conditions, such as arthritis, injury, and sore muscles from lack of exercise. Your vet will need to give your dog a check-up to diagnose the cause of your English Setter's muscle atrophy before treating him.

Lifestyle Modifications

> *An older dog will benefit from exercise, but it will no longer be able to run 20-plus miles a day! If your dog is slowing down, your vet may suggest glucosamine supplements. A supportive but comfortable bed is better for old joints than a hard floor. Keep the dog's mind busy with puzzle toys or scent work in smaller parts of the yard or living room.*
>
> KAREN STROHMEYER
> *Bristle Ridge Llewellins*

As your English Setter ages, his mobility is going to decline. However, this does not mean he should not be getting any exercise. Actually, by helping your senior dog maintain an active lifestyle, you are decreasing his risks of geriatric ailments such as arthritis and muscle loss. Although your old pup may not chase the ball as fast as he used to, there are still plenty of safe physical activities for him to engage in.

Here are a few suggestions to keep your senior English Setter active

 DO

- Establish a regular exercise regimen. The more active your English Setter is, the more agile he will feel, even if it is several short walks a day instead of one or two long walks.
- Consider the climate before going for a trot around the block. Elderly dogs are more sensitive to extreme weather conditions. During the warmer months, take your English Setter for a walk at cooler times of the day. During the colder winter months, buy your dog a doggy jacket.

- As your English Setter ages, he may lose his hearing and eyesight, so stick with familiar walking routes. New surroundings may cause your furry friend to become anxious and confused.
- Be sure to consult with your vet about whether your English Setter is receiving enough exercise, especially if he has a medical condition.

 DON'T

- Never stop taking your English Setter for daily walks! Maybe your pooch will not be able to endure longer strolls, but he will still be grateful to go for shorter walks. Walking gives your dog the opportunity to stretch his legs, sniff out his surroundings, and enjoy the fresh air.
- Do not set the pace; instead, let your English Setter set the pace. If your dog needs to sit or lie down for a minute or two, then let him rest.
- Do not forget that indoor playtime is exercise. If the weather outside is too extreme, then keep your pooch active by playing hide-and-seek inside.
- Do not assume your dog can keep up with you or go long distances. Just because you don't feel like you are getting a work-out does not mean it is not difficult for your dog.

Regular exercise helps to keep your English Setter's mind stimulated, helps him maintain a healthy weight, and keeps his body agile. Regardless of your furry friend's physical limitations, there are plenty of appropriate exercises for your senior dog.

Walking – Your English Setter will love going for a walk, despite his age or health limitations. Walking is a low-impact exercise if you take into consideration the footing, so grass and dirt are preferable surfaces. Avoid asphalt or rough surfaces that may damage your dog's paws.

Photo Courtesy of
Karen Lishinski

Swimming – Swimming is the lowest-impact exercise for your elderly English Setter, as it puts zero pressure on his joints while providing him with a total body workout. An added bonus is your English Setter adores water and will be the world's happiest dog while he paddles around in a dog-friendly pool or lake. Swimming is often used as a form of physical therapy for dogs who have undergone major surgery for injuries.

There are plenty of other ideas to keep your senior dog active, such as playing fetch in the backyard or providing sniffing games that lead him to a treat. Give your Setter time to follow his surroundings by sniffing out every shred of grass. However, whatever type of physical activity you choose for your dog — do not overdo it!

How much exercise is too much?

Each dog's physical tolerance levels vary depending on weight, life-style, exercise history, and overall health. Your English Setter may be pushing himself past his comfort zone just to please you. Here are a few tell-tale signs your dog has pushed himself past his physical limitations.

Excessive drooling or panting – It is perfectly normal for your English Setter to pant a little after playing a game of fetch; however, excessive panting and drooling are a clear indication that he is dehydrated or overheated.

Reluctant to play – If your English Setter stops playing and wants to sit down, then he is telling you he is tired and needs to rest.

Limping or muscle atrophy – If your pup starts to favor his hind legs by limping while exercising, stop immediately! Observe your dog for the next 24 hours, and if the limp does not go away, take him to see your vet as soon as possible.

Coughing or hacking – If your English Setter begins to cough or hack while exercising, it may be a sign of his trachea collapsing or other health conditions. Repeated hacking can sound like your dog is honking. If your dog begins to make coughing or hacking sounds while exercising, stop immediately! If you notice the coughing noise returns every time your dog exerts himself, consult with your vet.

It helps to keep an exercise journal of your Setter's daily exercise regimen and adjust his routine as needed. Whenever you notice your dog is experiencing pain or discomfort, slow down his workout. Do not hesitate to check in with your vet if you have any questions or concerns.

Old dog, new tricks

You have most likely heard the saying, "If you don't use it, you lose it!" Elderly people play sudoku, do crosswords, or complete brain teasers to keep their minds sharp and alert. Your faithful old companion also needs to keep learning new activities to keep his mind stimulated. When your dog is asked to focus on something, it tends to slow down cognitive degeneration.

Here are some ideas to keep your canine's mind sharp
- Explore new places, such as parks, beaches, or a ferry boat ride.
- Teach your English Setter new tricks or reinforce old ones.
- Reactivate old instincts with a game of tug-of-war.
- Take your old companion swimming or, even better, to a local natural hot spring.
- Play a short game of fetch or hide-and-seek.
- Introduce new toys or games that involve sniffing out a yummy treat.

Grooming

Should your senior English Setter still get groomed? The answer is unabashedly yes!

Grooming is essential throughout your English Setter's life but even more so as he gets older. Grooming sessions are an excellent opportunity to observe any changes in your dog's overall health, as many underlying health issues are revealed through the health of his skin and coat. Fur can begin to thin, and skin irritation, new growths, or lumps may start to appear.

One of the best gifts you can give your aging English Setter is to groom him daily, as it keeps him looking and feeling his best. Plus, your pooch will drink up the extra attention from you. Your dog is never too old to be pampered!

Elderly dogs who loved getting groomed in their younger years may suddenly start to resist the process due to joint pain. Senior dogs may squirm and bark to vocalize their objections to being groomed. However, at the end of the grooming session, your English Setter will be prancing around like he was still a puppy!

Your older English Setter will thank you for his grooming session. A warm bath will relieve those itchy sections your dog is no longer able to reach. Plus, your English Setter will drink up the extra attention and the treats during the grooming and afterward. Nothing is more satisfying than to see your freshly groomed old companion swagger away, feeling renewed and refreshed.

If you prefer to take your English Setter to a professional groomer, avoid using a discount service that may neglect your dog. Not every groomer has the ability or the patience to deal with your faithful old companion's aches and pains, so choose carefully. Look for a groomer who has experience with grooming geriatric dogs.

If you decide to groom your English Setter at home, carefully review the detailed information found in chapter 11 of this book and take into consideration the following tips to adapt the process to your old friend. These tips can go a long way to ensure your elderly dog will receive the level of care and respect he deserves.

Keep sessions short – Lengthy grooming sessions can cause unnecessary discomfort, pain, and stress for your older dog. Many reputable groomers with experience grooming geriatric dogs will schedule multiple grooming sessions instead of one. For example, the first session may include a bath, and the following week might be a haircut and brushing.

Watch for signs of discomfort – Your older dog will communicate his discomfort through body language or by vocalizing. If you notice your English Setter whimpering, squirming, shivering, or even growling, then you need to stop the grooming session. Let your dog take a short rest or find a more comfortable position. If your English Setter becomes agitated or stressed, then discontinue the session and continue another day.

Understand your dog's limitations – It is more than likely your senior English Setter may not be able to handle the same grooming regimen as when he was younger. Pressure sores and benign fatty tumors could mean your dog's coat cannot be trimmed as short as usual. Or if your English Setter has poor eyesight, clipping too close to his face may cause him anxiety.

Bathing – If you decide to bathe your elderly English Setter at home, there are a few precautions you can take to ensure his well-being and comfort. When bathing your dog, place a nonskid mat in the bottom of the basin or tub to secure his footing. Make sure the water is warm enough that your English Setter is not shivering during the bath. Often, geriatric dogs need a special shampoo to treat dry skin or other conditions.

After thoroughly rinsing out the shampoo, dry your dog with warm, fluffy towels. Before using the blow-dryer, let your English Setter shake himself off. Never use the blow-dryer on the hottest setting. Instead, use the cool setting. Be sure to get your old dog as dry as possible, as water trapped close to the skin may cause hot spots.

Brushing – Before you start brushing your English Setter, inspect the brush to make sure it's in good condition. If the brush's teeth are bent or broken, it is best to discard it and get a new one, as the teeth can scratch an older dog's thin, vulnerable skin or damage his coat.

Arthritis and joint pain may make it difficult for your dog to stand in the same position for long periods of time. Place a blanket on the floor and have your English Setter lie on his side while being brushed. Matted, tangled hair does not provide your dog with extra insulation as much as clean, tangle-free hair will.

While brushing your English Setter, be on the lookout for bare patches and brittle hair. This may be an indication of underlying health conditions. Also use your fingers to feel for any new lumps, warts, or sores on your dog's skin. If you notice anything suspicious, consult with your vet.

Nail trimming – Your elderly English Setter will need his nails trimmed more frequently than when he was younger. If your old dog suffers from arthritis or joint problems, it is even more reason to keep his nails trimmed, as the nail length affects your dog's posture and can force him to torque his spine, causing additional discomfort. In the past, his long walks on the sidewalk naturally kept his nails trimmed, but nowadays, because of his shorter strolls, he needs some extra help.

Sanitary areas – The glands and groin area are normally cleaned by your dog daily, but with old age, he may need some help. Regular trimming of the groin area will prevent any fecal matter or urine from getting trapped. Typically, all dogs express their anal glands when they defecate. But smaller breeds such as the English Setter may need help to express their anal glands as they age.

Nutrition Needs

Your English Setter's nutritional needs will vary throughout his lifetime, and once he reaches his golden years, it can become a challenge to understand his new dietary needs. However, switching your dog's regular brand of dog food for a senior one may not be enough.

Watch those calories. As your dog ages, he begins to slow down, which means he burns off fewer calories, and those unneeded calories are stored as fat. Research shows senior dogs require 20 percent fewer calories than an adult dog in order to maintain a healthy weight. However, if your pooch starts losing too much weight, you may need to give him extra calories to help him stay healthy.

Protein is vital for your English Setter's overall health. As your dog ages, he begins to lose muscle mass, even if he is still leading an active lifestyle. As his muscle mass is depleted, so are his protein reserves, causing his immune system to weaken. As your dog's immune system weakens, so does his ability to fight off infections and illnesses. Your senior dog's diet should be made up of 40 percent protein. Avoid dog foods that contain fillers. Instead, opt for foods rich in lean red meats, fish, chicken, and dairy products.

Your senior English Setter will need a low-sodium diet if he has hypertension or, cardiac or kidney problems. Most commercial dog food is extremely high in sodium, so look for brands that are low in sodium or make your own homemade dog food. For more information on how to make your own dog food, see chapter 10 of this book.

> **"**
>
> *As dogs age, their digestive system is not efficient as it once was. Consider giving supplemental vitamins and minerals. There are several gel-based supplements on the market that our dogs do really well with, and they love the liver flavor the best.*
>
> MARK D. DENEKA
> *Twilight Setter Kennels*
>
> **"**

If your senior English Setter will not eat

It is common for senior dogs to lose interest in food. Try adding one to two tablespoons of bone broth or a small amount of canned food to entice your dog. If your elderly pooch refuses to eat for more than 48 hours, consult with your vet to rule out any underlying health problems.

Bone broth is a delicious, nutrient-dense superfood that will improve your English Setter's health and is guaranteed to get him to gobble up his dinner. Bone broth is a stock made from simmering raw bones for several hours, either in your slow-cooker or on low heat on your stove. Bone broth is jam-packed with nutrients that will improve your dog's overall health; plus, he will devour his food.

How to make bone broth for your English Setter

Ingredients

- 4 pounds of raw bones with marrow (you can use chicken, turkey, rabbit, beef, or oxtail bones)
- 1/3 cup fresh parsley, chopped
- 3 stalks of celery, chopped
- 1/4 cup organic apple cider vinegar (helps to pull the marrow and minerals out of the bones)
- 6 to 7 quarts of water

Directions

1. Place all of the ingredients in a large pot or slow cooker.
2. Cook on low heat for 8 to 12 hours on a low simmer or for 24 hours in the slow cooker on the lowest setting. Stir occasionally and add extra water if necessary.
3. Allow to cool. Remove the bones, celery, parsley, and discard. Note that you should never feed cooked bones to your English Setter.
4. Once the broth is completely cool, place in the refrigerator overnight. It will form a layer of fat on top which can easily be skimmed off and discarded.
5. Freeze in small portions in Zip-lock baggies, then thaw before serving your dog. Give him one to two tablespoons with each meal.

Choosing a Premium Senior Dog Food

> **❝**
>
> *Consider senior dog foods with reduced calories to keep weight in check. Even a few extra pounds can be taxing for an aging dog to tote around.*
>
> MARK D. DENEKA
> *Twilight Setter Kennels*
>
> **❞**

The FDA has not established any official regulations for senior dog foods, which is why you need to educate yourself on how to find a premium-quality dog food for your canine friend.

Beyond the caloric intake and protein content, there are several ingredients that can benefit your English Setter's overall health. Here are a few key ingredients to look for when choosing a premium dog food.

- **Glucosamine and Chondroitin** – These supplements help your senior dog's cartilage and joints so he can move around with less pain.
- **Antioxidants** – Antioxidants provide much-needed support for your elderly pup's immune system, helping him to fight off diseases and illnesses.
- **Decreased levels of sodium and phosphorus** – Lower phosphorus helps to maintain healthy kidney function and lower sodium levels keep your dog's blood pressure normal.
- **L-carnitine** – Recent studies have discovered that foods rich in L-carnitine help elderly dogs to burn off stored fat for energy. L-carnitine is found in lean red meats, chicken, fish, healthy fats, and dairy products.
- **Omega-3 fatty acids** – Healthy fats found in fish, nut, and plant oils help to decrease inflammation caused by arthritis and improve kidney and liver health.
- **Extra fiber** – Many senior Setters suffer from constipation, so extra fiber may help. However, too much fiber can cause other problems, so the best way to control constipation is to make

sure your dog gets enough exercise. Some beneficial soluble fibers for your dog are sweet potatoes, carrots, brown rice, milled flaxseed, wheatgerm, kale, and kelp.

When choosing a senior dog food, it is important to consider your English Setter's individual needs and recognize that these needs can change over time. So, just because one type of senior dog food is suitable for your dog now does not mean it will always be. The right dog food will have a direct impact on your dog's health, so take your time to do your research and talk to your vet to find the best diet for your faithful companion.

Look for a senior dog food made from premium quality ingredients, such as human-grade organic lean red meats, free of artificial

Photo Courtesy of
James Justus

preservatives. No matter how healthy your English Setter is, there is no need to put a strain on his immune system by feeding him poor-quality, generic dog food with little to no nutritional value.

Transition your pooch slowly to a new senior dog food. It is best to start gradually by adding a small amount of the new food to his current food. Each day you can add a little more of the new food. Ideally, it should take seven to 10 days to completely switch your dog to the new food.

Listen to your vet's recommendations, especially if your dog has been diagnosed with a condition such as diabetes; kidney, liver, or heart disease; arthritis, etc. Your vet will most likely recommend a prescription diet. While these diets often do not include the word "senior" in the title, they are formulated to manage disease conditions commonly seen in elderly dogs.

Saying Goodbye

66

I believe that there are three things that every person should be able to say: 'Thank you,' 'I'm sorry,' and 'Goodbye.' If you ever love a dog, you'll learn to say all of them.

JOHN MCILTROT
Seranoa Kennels

99

For every person who loves and shares their life with an English Setter, the dreaded and inevitable day will arrive when you have to ask yourself whether or not to intervene in how and when your best friend's life must come to an end. The very thought of having to say goodbye to your four-pawed companion for the last time is beyond heart-wrenching.

Often, when we begin to observe signs that our dog is suffering and dying, we start to second guess ourselves or even go into denial. This often causes our beloved dogs to suffer far longer than they should. The question is, how do you know? When is the right time to put your best friend into a forever sleep?

Tell-tale signs your English Setter is dying

Prolonged lethargy or disinterest – One of the most common signs of the dying process is finding your dog lying in the same spot (often not where he would normally rest), barely acknowledging you or other family members. Dogs may become lethargic due to other health conditions, but if the veterinarian has ruled this out and the lethargy lasts for more than a few days, then maybe it is time to consider saying goodbye.

Stops eating or drinking – Another classic sign something is wrong with your English Setter is when you offer him the tastiest treat imaginable, and he refuses to even sniff it. Often at this point, the dog will stop drinking water, as his organs are starting to shut down. Try keeping your dog hydrated by giving him water using a dropper or turkey baster, but if he still refuses to swallow, there is not much you can do at this point. Be sure to rule out other health conditions with your vet.

Lack of coordination – The next sign is when your dog begins to lose balance and motor control. When your elderly English Setter tries to stand up, he may be very wobbly or disoriented. Or he could shake or convulse while lying down. In this case, make your dog as comfortable as possible and remove any objects he could knock over if he tries to stand up. Note: saying goodbye to your dog means protecting him, creating a safe area for him, and providing whatever help he needs.

Incontinence – When a dog is dying, often, he will not even move from the spot to relieve himself, even if he has diarrhea. This is an indication that your dog's organs are starting to shut down. During this stage, make sure you keep him and his bed clean and dry.

Labored breathing – As heartbreaking as it sounds, toward the end, many dogs display labored breathing. Your dog's breathing may become difficult, with lengthy gasps between each breath. This is an extremely hard moment; as you know, at this point, your dog is suffering.

Seeking comfort – This is one of the hardest moments, as despite your dog's quickly deteriorating health, he will look for comfort from his people — from you. During these final hours, be with your dog, reassuring him of your love and affection.

Making the decision

The signs above are not always consistent and will vary, as some dogs suddenly pass away in their sleep without any indications of ill health. Part of preparing to say farewell to your English Setter is realizing you may have to make the difficult decision for your dog by intervening. Before making a decision, talk over all of your options with your family and come to a mutual agreement.

Once you have come to the decision to intervene to end your dog's suffering, discuss the options with your vet.

Veterinarians are required to follow a set of guidelines called the "Humane Euthanasia Protocol," whether the euthanasia is performed inside of the clinic or in the tranquility of your own house. The entire process is painless and stress-free for your English Setter. The Humane Euthanasia Protocol is considered the kindest way to put your dog to sleep.

The Humane Euthanasia Protocol

1. The veterinarian will inject your dog with a pain tranquilizer.
2. Once your dog is relaxed and sedated, then your vet will insert an IV to administer the euthanasia solution.
3. The vet will leave you alone with your dog for a few minutes for any final goodbyes, then return to administer the final drug to stop your Setter's heart.

In certain parts of the United States, veterinarians are not required by law to adhere to the Humane Euthanasia Protocol. Instead, they practice a quicker and more affordable method to stop the animal's heart with a single injection of barbiturates. Barbiturates cause the animal's central nervous system to slow down, causing a painful death. This type of euthanasia is not humane, as it is not pain-free, causing the animal short-term distress and anxiety.

Ensure your veterinarian agrees to apply the Humane Euthanasia Protocol to your dog. If not, look for another veterinarian who will.

Most dogs are euthanized inside the veterinary clinic, but many vets will make house calls. If your vet is unable to make house calls, you can find an extensive list of reputable veterinarians throughout the United States and Canada online at the In-Home Pet Euthanasia Directory. (www. inhomepeteuthanasia.com)

Here is a quick overview of the pros and cons of getting your English Setter euthanized at home versus at the clinic.

At-home euthanasia may be the right choice for you if:
- Your English Setter is too sick to be transported comfortably to the veterinary clinic.
- You personally feel more comfortable with grieving at home.
- Car trips or visits to the veterinary clinic cause your dog anxiety and stress.
- Money is not an issue, as at-home procedures cost more.

- Vet clinic euthanasia may be the right choice for you if:
- You want your usual vet to perform the procedure, but they are unable to perform house calls.
- You prefer a more neutral environment for the procedure.
- Your dog is still mobile enough to be comfortably transported in your car.
- Cost is a concern.

Whether you decide on euthanasia at home or at the veterinary clinic is a very personal decision. There is no right or wrong answer.

The cost of clinical euthanasia can be between $80 to $350, depending on where you live. The cost of at-home euthanasia can cost between $300 to $800. The higher cost may include add-ons, such as cremations, funeral services, or getting the vet to take an impression of your dog's paw to cast into a memento.

It is highly recommended you pay for the euthanasia before the procedure as emotions can be running high when the procedure is final, and the last thing you need is to relive the heartbreak by receiving the bill later. When it is all over, you can request the veterinary clinic to dispose of your dog for an extra cost. Some clinics offer cremation or a professional burial service at a nearby pet cemetery.

Take your time grieving your English Setter and coming to terms with your loss. Everybody does it in their own way. Saying goodbye to your dog does not mean forgetting about him. With time, you may start thinking about opening up your heart to another dog.

Dogs' lives are too short. Their only fault, really.

Agnes Sligh Turnbull

www.ingramcontent.com/pod-product-compliance
Lightning Source LLC
Chambersburg PA
CBHW070904120626
46546CB00001B/125